Distance Education

The Complete Guide to
Design, Delivery, and Improvement

Distance Education

The Complete Guide to Design, Delivery, and Improvement

JUDITH L. JOHNSON

Foreword by George Connick

Teachers College, Columbia University
New York and London

For
Jacob
and his
"Opa"

Published by Teachers College Press, 1234 Amsterdam Avenue, New York, NY 10027

Library of Congress Cataloging-in-Publication Data

Johnson, Judith L., 1946–
    Distance education : the complete guide to design, delivery, and improvement / Judith L.
  Johnson ; foreword by George Connick.
       p. cm.
    Includes bibliographical references and index.
    ISBN 0-8077-4373-9 (paper : alk. paper) — ISBN 0-8077-4374-7 (cloth)
     1. Distance education—United States. I. Title.
  LC5805.J64 2003
  371.3'5'0973—dc21   2003044045

ISBN 0-8077-4373-9 (paper)
ISBN 0-8077-4374-7 (cloth)

Printed on acid-free paper
Manufactured in the United States of America

10 09 08 07 06 05 04 03   8 7 6 5 4 3 2 1

Contents

Foreword

Since World War II, public policy makers and higher education leaders have been focused on three major educational issues: access, quality, and productivity. Until the 1990s, these three issues seemed to work at odds with each other. If an institution tried to expand access, it often was criticized for lowering quality. As enrollment increased, so did costs and, it was often argued, quality declined.

It has been educational technology, and specifically distance learning, which has fundamentally changed the way in which these policy issues may be addressed. Distance learning makes it possible to offer universal access with high quality and marginal increases in cost. Is it hard to do? Yes! Does it require major restructuring of institutions and revision of policies and procedures? Yes! But, it is all doable. And, some would say, at this juncture in our country's history, it is probably mandatory.

We are now facing the most serious challenges to higher education in the past 40 years. The budgets of almost every state are in serious deficit. Campus buildings are in disrepair, infrastructure needs to be improved, large numbers of senior faculty are preparing to retire, and we are likely to face a significant increase in student enrollments resulting from the downturn in the economy.

This is a time that calls for new thinking about the organization and operation of all of our higher education institutions. It is very likely that there won't be sufficient resources to continue to operate them in the way we have in the past.

This new book on *Distance Education*, therefore, appears at an ideal time.

It is certainly not coincidental that a book on distance learning was authored by an educator from Maine, whose credentials in this field are impeccable. Judith Johnson has had an intimate relationship with distance learning in Maine, as well as a wonderful opportunity to view its development across the nation and the world.

In the mid-1980s Maine began the process of developing the first statewide, comprehensive distance learning network in the United States. Launched in 1989 as the Education Network of Maine (EdNet) with considerable publicity and expectation, it enrolled over 1,500 students in its first semester of operation, making it the 4th largest "campus" in the University of Maine System (although it was not a campus in the traditional sense).

Maine showed the way for many educators struggling to make sense of new technological developments across the United States and in other parts of the world by providing a working model for the use of "mass *access* technologies for education" (e.g., television [broadcast, closed-circuit, two-way], the Internet, the Web, e-mail, fax, phone, etc.) and how they could be used in new ways to serve people of all ages wherever they lived and worked.

Most importantly, as more students enrolled each year, this new educational initiative demonstrated that educational *costs* could decline as enrollments increased.

Judith Johnson, because of her expertise in assessment, was one of the pioneers in the development of Maine's distance learning network. In the first year of operation of the Network (1989), and each year thereafter for nearly a decade, she was asked to conduct a survey of the success of distance learning students in relation to students in traditional classroom settings. The results of these studies documented that distance learning students did as well or better than students in "regular" classrooms. In addition, her reports provided a wealth of information about the profiles of the students that were attracted to distance learning. This demographic information became enormously important to higher education planning in Maine, and was very helpful to planning that was just beginning in other states.

Finally, as we strive to address the great educational challenges we are facing today, we need to be better informed about the tools which are available to address them. The Pony Express tried to address its need for change, primarily revolving around productivity issues, by running horses faster or longer. They were simply not aware that other people were developing the telegraph.

Our nostalgic attachment to campuses and higher education traditions must not prevent us from embracing the need for change in education and from using the massive technological tools which will allow us to re-define how we address the issues of access, quality, and productivity.

In this book Dr. Johnson has pulled together the research and case studies to provide a comprehensive picture of the evolution and current status of distance learning. This book needs to be studied by policy makers and educators who are attempting to grapple with the realities of 21st-century higher education. It is not intended to be a roadmap. It is much more. It is a creative architect's rendering of what the future structure of higher education may look like, and it provides useful examples of how to get there.

—George Connick

Preface

As I write this preface, I am reminded of the following quote, which I read back in 1998 when I began thinking seriously about writing a book on distance learning.

> Studying distance learning is somewhat like chasing quicksilver: the pace of change in the field is so rapid—both because of changes in technology and in the organizational arrangements for delivering it—that establishing a solid base of information will be a never-ending task. (Phipps, Wellman, & Merisotis, 1998, p. 28)

Despite this admonition, I decided to proceed. I taped the quote, printed in large bold type, to the wall just above my computer. As I wrote, I saw it happening—everyday, something new. But I also knew that the topic about which I was writing had a beginning and that is where I started.

A number of books have been published on distance education over the past decade, but most cover only one or two aspects of the enterprise (e.g., the technology, teaching techniques, the learner, or organization and administration). This book is a treatise-of-sorts, covering everything from distance education's beginning to its future. It is a comprehensive look at distance education, all in one volume. I begin with a thumbnail sketch of the history of distance learning, going back to its earliest forms, even before the advent of technology as we know it today. In Part I the reader is guided through the evolution of distance education via a trip around the world. Part II describes some of the standouts in distance education: Maine's system, Oregon's system, Western Governor's University, and Britain's Open University.

In Part III, Teaching at a Distance, the reader will learn about two of the most central and important aspects of distance education—pedagogy and student support services. Four abbreviated case studies are presented that illustrate real-life examples of how this new way of educating students is working. The reader will learn about the important aspects of the design and delivery of distance education, and ingredients for an effective course are presented. In Part IV the topics of assessment, evaluation, standards, and accreditation are addressed. The book concludes with a summary, lessons learned, and a discussion of what the future will surely bring.

This book is intended for a variety of audiences. First, the book is written for institutions and individuals exploring the topic of distance learning. Readers will find the text helpful in deciding how to move forward in the development and delivery of distance education courses and programs. Second, the book is written for faculty and staff involved in or interested in becoming involved in this enterprise. Many resources (i.e., examples, definitions, case studies, instruments, and guidance) are provided for faculty that will assist them in effectively teaching courses at a distance.

Third, the book is an excellent textbook for upper-level undergraduate and graduate-level courses related to technology and learning. For example, courses such as teaching and learning with technology, foundations of distance and open learning, teaching teachers how to use technology, information technology and society, and the challenges of the information age, are but a few. Because of its comprehensive nature, everything students need is found in its pages. Enjoy the journey!

Acknowledgments

There are so many individuals to whom I am grateful, beginning with Dr. George Connick, who wrote the Foreword for this book and who hired me to do my very first distance education evaluation years ago. Dr. Pamela MacBrayne carried on what he began, contracting with me to conduct research and evaluation of the University of Maine's distance education arm through its many iterations. Working with both George and Pam was always a pleasure.

I am indebted to many generous individuals who took the time to meet with me and share their experiences about distance learning. Among them, Dr. Miriam Luebke, Dr. Patrick Wiseman, Sue South and Dr. Andrew Weil, Dr. Jon Schlenker, Dr. Stephen Ehrmann, Dr. Arthur Chickering, Glenn LeBlanc, and Alan MacLean, without whom this book would not have been possible. I am grateful to all the people, institutions, and organizations that allowed me to include descriptions, illustrations, and materials to enrich the content of the book. These include the University of Maine System, Oregon Colleges Online, Western Governor's University, Britain's Open University, WebCT, Blackboard, Inc., Mary Lampson, Molly K. Burke, Laurie and Jim Ollhoff, Cynthia Hook, Sally Johnstone, Kelli Dutrow, Kathryn Wade, and Dr. Bruce Landon and his research team. I wish to acknowledge the folks at the American Council on Education, the American Federation of Teachers, the National Education Association, and the Western Cooperative for Educational Telecommunications for granting me permission to reprint documents on standards.

I am grateful to Kimberly Spencer for her assistance in transcribing many of the interviews I conducted and for typing some of the supplemental documents for the book.

I wish to express my appreciation to Dr. Richard L. Pattenaude, President of the University of Southern Maine (USM), and Dr. Joseph S. Wood, Provost and Vice President for Academic Affairs at USM, for granting me a sabbatical during the summer so I could devote my time to writing.

It is with deep appreciation that I acknowledge my former graduate assistants, Kathrina P. Hilinski and Joan Freedman, who spent endless hours looking through piles of paper to find all the references cited in the book. They provided great assistance in the compilation of the reference list, permission credits, and other administrative tasks. They are a great pair with whom to work. I am also indebted to Kathryn Smith, another former graduate assistant, who gathered, read, and reviewed hundreds of research articles for the book.

I am especially grateful to Brian Ellerbeck, Executive Acquisitions Editor for Teachers College Press, for his support and timely responses to questions I had along the way. It has made all the difference for me.

Finally, I want to acknowledge, with heartfelt gratitude, the love, support, and encouragement given to me by my partner, David L. Silvernail (a.k.a. "Opa"), and my family, Lara and Arthur Anthony, Louis Talarico, III and Lesley Robertson, Ross and Amy Talarico, Tom and Mary Beth Johnson, Linda and Roger Bishop, and my mother, Virginia Johnson, and my late father, Thomas B. Johnson, Sr. I would like to thank several special friends, Bill and Sheri Crittendon, Bob and Jolene Lemelin, Norma Kraus Eule, Pete and Mildred Hinkle, and Sandy Armentrout and Dick Barnes, for their ongoing interest in this book writing project. And, I would like to remember the late Dr. Ronald Nuttall. He was a wonderful friend and advisor. How lucky I am to be surrounded by so many nice people. Thank you all!

PART I

The Age of Technology: What Is Distance Education?

Distance education often is defined simply as a form of education in which learner and instructor are separate during the majority of instruction. But unlike independent or self-directed study, distance education usually implies the presence of an institution that plans curriculum and provides resources and services for its students. For years limited to correspondence courses, radio, and broadcast television, distance education has come of age in the past 5 to 10 years with the advent of new telecommunications and information technologies. These have led distant learners and their instructors into new possibilities for interaction and information access. Adults, particularly, find distance education, with its savings in commuting time, an easier fit into busy lives. Adults are comfortable, too, with the independent structure of the distant classroom and are more likely to possess the self-motivation to focus on educational goals away from a campus setting. Fitted with the new technologies, distance education offers greater opportunities to individualize instruction, as communication between student and instructor broadens beyond face-to-face dialogue and a particular time. Distance education, then, becomes as inclusive or as personal as the individual and instructor elect (Community College of Maine, 1991).

The Congressional Office of Technology Assessment defines distance learning as the "linking of a teacher and students in several geographic locations via technology that allows for interaction" (Daniel, 1997, p. 15).

While these two definitions are typical of what Americans think of as distance education, others in the world define it more elegantly. For example, a definition that comes from South Africa is not only longer, but richer.

> Distance education is the offering of educational [programs] designed to facilitate a learning strategy which does not depend on day-to-day contact teaching but makes best use of the potential of students to study on their own. It provides interactive study material and decentralized learning facilities where students can seek academic and other forms of educational assistance when they need it. (Daniel, 1997, p. 15)

Underlying all these definitions is the concept that students are not face-to-face with an instructor and use some type of technology in the learning process.

During the past 2 decades, with the advent of distance education and technology, pedagogy has changed. At first with interactive television (ITV), for example, the pedagogical tools were similar to those used in the classroom, only the instructional mode of transmission was the television. During the late 1990s and into the 21st century, dramatic changes and improvements have been made in distance learning, with sophisticated technological advances contributing to an enhanced educational experience for its audiences. The rate of change has been greater than in any other phenomenon in education. And, technology has forever changed the way educational institutions do business.

When we look at how technology has changed education, we have only to explore a few of the tools commonly used today. For example, electronic mail (e-mail), computer conferencing, and the World Wide Web strengthen interactions between faculty and students, especially shy students who are often reluctant to ask questions in class, and commuting and part-time students who have fewer opportunities for interaction. E-mail is a way students can interact with the course instructor as well as with other students in the class. Online communication among students facilitates study groups, collaborative learning, problem-solving, and assignment discussions.

New technological tools are undeniably empowering and motivational, and access to them makes learning more diverse and fun. Schools and colleges have a responsibility to provide students with the opportunity to gain the skills necessary to be competitive in today's world, and the use of technology is one of those skills.

Gaines, Johnson, and King (1996) state that although new technologies are infiltrating new areas, such as music, art, and industrial/vocational education, they are "functionally different than a decade ago" (p. 74). Special needs students benefit considerably from new technologies that have made learning more accessible, adapting to individuals' unique learning needs. New technology cultivates active learning, provides new ways for students to learn, and renders a more authentic, outcome-driven, performance-based type of learning.

"Whether we love it or fear it, the future is digital," exclaimed Maine's Governor Angus King in his State of the State speech in January 2001 (Williams, 2001, p. D1). Others have revealed similar sentiments. "Love it or hate it, educators concur that technology has had a major impact on higher education, and that adopting the new tools is mandatory" (Hendley, 2000, p. 4). In the move toward technology and distance education, instructors must learn new techniques to ensure that students have a meaningful learning experience. Rather than standing in front of a room full of students and lecturing, the faculty member must adopt a role as coach or facilitator, encouraging participation and keeping discussions focused. Students, as well, must develop new strategies and skills for learning in a new environment (Schuell, 2000). Those who take online courses must be computer literate and able to maneuver through the course. With user-friendly courseware like WebCT and Blackboard, most students with any basic computer knowledge find they are able to catch on quickly. Links and point and click formats make moving through the course easy (White, 2000). Critical to the success of students new to online learning

is an orientation to what activities they may expect in these courses. Students should be updated on how to post e-mail messages, how to enter chat rooms, how to participate in conferencing and make contributions to bulletin boards, and how to use word processing programs to cut and paste or add attachments to e-mail. Students should be informed about how to send class assignments electronically; most of all, they should be exposed to any special software the institution uses for online learning. More on this in Chapter 10.

Sally M. Johnstone (2000), founding director of the Western Cooperative for Educational Telecommunications (WCET) at the Western Interstate Commission for Higher Education (WICHE), quotes John Seely Brown, chief scientist at Xerox Corporation, who said:

> the World Wide Web will prove to be as revolutionary as electricity. . . . When electricity became widely available, people changed their behaviors. They altered when they slept, when they worked, and even what their jobs were. (p. 20)

This same phenomenon is already occurring in higher education. With the increasing availability of distance learning technologies, students are altering when they sleep, when they work, and when and how they take classes. And, unlike the early forms of distance education where isolation and separateness prevailed, students are now able to benefit from an educational experience that may be even more engaging and fulfilling than that of face-to-face learning (Carnevale, 2000b; Fraser, 1999; Johnson, 2000; Saba, 1999a). One of the unanticipated positive outcomes of distance learning, especially in online courses, is increased communication and interaction. The "single most important element of successful online education is interaction among participants" (Kearsley, 1997).

Students in an online course are anywhere and everywhere, and participating anytime and all the time. By design, communication and interaction predominate. Technology allows the shy student to cast an opinion without anxiety or embarrassment. It allows the student with a disability to participate without judgment from other classmates. It makes education possible for the single mother who works during the day, takes care of her children when she is not at work, and wants to participate in a course after her children are in bed. It gives the busy executive access to courses that will keep him or her current in the field without having to take time away from a, sometimes, unforgiving schedule. "Technology is a great equalizer" (Coombs, 2000, p. 3). Indeed, distance learning "minimizes discrimination and prejudice that arises naturally in face-to-face settings" (Kearsley, 1997). Technology offers faculty new ways to reach and teach formerly unreachable students. It makes teaching and learning a more creative endeavor for both the teacher and the learner. The tools and pedagogy that are available through this new medium are changing and improving at a remarkably rapid pace and make the whole education enterprise more innovative and exciting for those who partake. Surely as we progress to the future, and as faculty experiment with their teaching methods, we will continue to see more and more new tools, pedagogy, and ways of delivering education for the 21st century.

CHAPTER 1

The Evolution of Distance Learning in Higher Education

Distance learning's past has emerged into a new entity. In the past decade, higher education has taken on tools for learning faster than at any other time in its history. Here we look at the beginning of distance education, its present, and our predictions for the future.

THE PAST

Distance education, in some form, has been around for decades. Before 1900, the communication system of the Roman Empire set the stage for distance learning, long before the idea of such a phenomenon was conceived. Inventions during this time of the printing press and the postal service made possible the printing of many copies of learning materials to be distributed to many individuals. Correspondence education began toward the end of the 19th century, and in the 20th century, radio, telephone, cinema, television, programmed learning, computers, and the Internet all became tools of the new method of distributing education (Daniel, 2000).

Australia and New Zealand

In the 1930s, radio was first used to broadcast educational programming to schools. Television became a medium of choice for distance education in the 1960s, and today with the power, speed, and versatility of the Internet, courses are offered anytime, anywhere.

During the 1930s radio as a medium was used to deliver educational programming in Australia and New Zealand by the Australian Broadcasting Company (ABC). In addition to program broadcasts, the ABC provided financial assistance to the schools for the purchase of radio receivers. "In 1935, 21 percent of all Australian schools were making regular use of radio . . . [programs]. By the mid 1950s usage had risen to 90 percent" (Teather, 1989, p. 504).

In 1956, television was introduced in Sydney and Melbourne to deliver educational programming to schools. The programs were used by teachers to supplement their curricula and to provide access to experiences that were beyond the resources of the schools (Gilmour, 1979). More comprehensive programs in math and science were developed and broadcast to schools to address a teacher shortage in these subjects. In the 1960s and 1970s, television broadcasting in Australia increased significantly, and by 1972 more than 90% of all schools in Australia were receiving and using both enrichment and subject-specific television programs.

In the 1960s, when the Open University (OU) was being developed in the United Kingdom, Australia had four universities that were providing opportunities for part-time higher education study using distance learning. At Massey University in New Zealand, approximately 12,000 students were enrolled in several hundred courses. In the 1980s, more than 35,000 students were taking distance education courses in Australia from approximately five universities and 30 colleges. In 1961, due to a short supply of evening classes at the University of New South Wales, lectures were broadcast over radio to part-time adult students in their homes. Problems arose with this arrangement, however. The University's radio station obtained a license to broadcast, but the "transmission frequency allotted . . . was beyond the tuning range of an ordinary radio receiver, so students had to have their receivers modified" (Teather, 1989, p. 506). But this did not solve the problem completely. The power provided to the University radio station (which was about half the power of a nearby non-University station) did not allow for clear transmission of the audio. Thus, students ended up hearing only half of the transmission. To remedy these problems, the University established centers where students could gather to listen to broadcasts and have discussion groups afterward. Those who could not attend the sessions were mailed broadcast tapes. By 1966, the University added television programming to its radio programming to offer courses to extension centers. The courses were delivered using a combination of the two media and supplemented by notes and diagrams that were mailed to students before the broadcasts. Student-led discussions and live seminars supported the learning activities. This arrangement became known as the Division of Postgraduate Extension Studies, and by 1982 more than 2,300 students were enrolled in the broadcast courses. An additional 2,700 participated in courses in which audio- and videocassettes of the same courses were offered.

Eventually distribution of higher education courses in Australia and New Zealand became satellite-based. In 1985 and 1986, domestic Australian communication satellites were launched and educational networks were established.

The United States

Educational broadcasting in the United States evolved in a similar fashion. In the 1920s, unsuccessful attempts were made to develop broadcasting for educational and cultural purposes and to reserve some radio channels for educational uses. It wasn't until the 1950s, when states were faced with shortages of teachers and school facilities, that instructional television was seen as a way to ease these problems. "Local and state educational authorities established stations using the reserved channels" (Lyle, 1989, p. 516). The broadcasts were used to support classroom instruction, and most programs were developed and produced by local teachers. With the passage of Title VII of the National Defense Education Act of 1958, educational broadcasting increased and appropriations by

the legislature provided support for projects in education. However, when school enrollments began to decline in the 1970s and teachers were in surplus, the broadcast medium for instruction declined as did local production of programs for schools.

With respect to higher education, universities were among the first to have radio stations back in the 1920s. University extension programs were broadcast using these radio stations and have continued ever since. Television became the medium of choice for the broadcast programs in the 1960s. Many college and university systems developed televised curricula to provide access for more individuals and to reduce pressure on the physical plants. Systems and consortia alike cooperated to deliver courses to the public. A 1979 survey by the Corporation for Public Broadcasting (CPB) and the National Center for Educational Statistics (NCES) "found that 25 percent of the nation's colleges and universities offered courses for credit over television and 36 percent of them used broadcast television to supplement instruction" (Lyle, 1989, p. 516). A major turning point in the distance education enterprise came in 1981 when Walter H. Annenberg announced his $150 million gift over 15 years for the development of university-level television programming. The CPB was chosen as the agency to oversee the planning of the programming that would be funded under this gift.

The United Kingdom

While these developments were occurring in the United States and Australia, the United Kingdom officially opened the Open University in 1971 (Cathcart, 1989). Primarily a correspondence institution, OU used correspondence materials and textbooks as its major resources along with television broadcasts. The institution was open to any and all who wished to partake of its educational opportunities. Working closely with the British Broadcast Corporation, OU paid for its own production costs using revenue from the government's department of education and science.

When the United Kingdom's Open University achieved higher ratings for its teaching of Engineering than Oxford, Cambridge, and the Imperial College, London, it was a sign that what had begun 30 years earlier as a radical and suspect initiative for second-chance students had now become a well-respected university. (Daniel, 2000)

Other Countries

The success of OU prompted other countries to adopt its model and establish their own open universities. For example, in 1972 Spain created the Universidad de Educación a Distancia using radio broadcasts. Holland offered multimedia courses to its citizens via television, and in 1977 Norway established an Institute for Distance Education that coordinated and produced integrated multimedia courses on topics of concern to its citizenry. Eventually Norway's live broadcasts were recorded and distributed to interested constituencies on cassettes. Their purpose came to focus more on the materials than on the broadcast. Likewise, Sweden's Utbildningsradion, established in 1978, became responsible for preparing learning systems and producing audiovisual educational media. Its main priority was to produce programming for underserved, disadvantaged groups (e.g., the mentally and physically challenged and individuals with limited education). In addition to its broadcasts (both television and radio), all programs were available on cassette, along with educational materials to make up learning packages. These were distributed to learning resource centers across Sweden.

These efforts and others were part of the foundation for today's distance education, an evolution in the making. While some of the programs and projects in broadcast education may not have been deemed overly successful at the time, "research and experience leaves no doubt that educational broadcasting can, particularly within multimedia systems, be an effective educational instrument" (Lyle, 1989, p. 516).

As Sir John Daniel (2000), Vice Chancellor of Britain's Open University, asserts:

... whereas in 1990 only a small proportion of traditional universities offered any distance learning courses, by the year 2000 very few did not have such offerings. Today no self respecting university president can admit to not offering courses online.

(For a comprehensive account of early educational broadcasting, see chapters by Inquai, Hurst, Teather, Lyle, Hill, Cathcart, and O'Brien in Eraut, 1989.)

TODAY

Distance learning is the most significant phenomenon occurring in higher education today. Everywhere one looks, whether in community colleges, 4-year institutions, Ivy League colleges, research institutions, or technical colleges, distance education is on the rise, and the rise is occurring at a rapid pace. Distance education and technology are major factors in the contribution to current and expected changes in the postsecondary education enterprise.

Distance education is expected to grow at a compound annual growth rate of 33 percent, according to International Data Corporation. Analysis predicts that distance education demand will increase from five percent of all higher education students in 1998 to 15 percent by 2002. [Indeed] . . . the reported growth rates (from 1999–2000 to 2000–2001) range from 200 percent (Pennsylvania State University's World Campus) to over 1,000 percent (University of Maryland's University College) today. (Oblinger, Barone, & Hawkins, 2001, p. 11)

Never before in the history of higher education has there been a change that has had such an impact on those involved in this enterprise. According to Peter Drucker, "Universities won't survive. The future is outside the traditional campus, outside the traditional classroom. Distance learning is coming on fast" (Gibson & Herrera, 1999, p. 57).

The idea and advent of distance education have been instrumental in producing a range of emotions in those involved in higher education. Many faculty are resistant; some are confused; others are excited about the new realm of possibilities for their teaching. Some worry about the future of their livelihood; others see this change as an opportunity to expand their pedagogy and teaching opportunities. Critics of distance education say that this mode is inferior to the more traditional face-to-face, campus-based learning, where discourse is spontaneous and interactive, and where the faculty can see the students and pick up nonverbal body language such as facial expressions. Skeptical faculty argue that part of the learning experience is the connection made between student and student, and student and professor, or the experience of community. However, "in all fairness, there are few studies that measure the effectiveness of textbooks and lectures as an educational delivery system" (Oblinger, Barone, & Hawkins, 2001, p. 19). But because of the newness of technology and the uncertainty of its use in educating students, institutions are held captive by questions related to its use.

Proponents of distance learning, on the other hand, argue that distance education technologies allow for increased access to a variety of courses. Distance education offers the student more convenience in scheduling classes, decreases travel time to and from a campus, and allows for student control over when participation in classes will occur (Johnson, 1999a). Furthermore, distance learning technology, such as the Web, is

> the first medium that honors the notion of multiple intelligences—abstract, textual, visual, musical, social, and kinesthetic. Educators can now construct learning environments that enable [a student] to become engaged in learning any way the student chooses. The anytime, anyplace nature of the Web allows students to spend as much time as they need searching for information, running simulations, or collaborating with peers. (Oblinger, Barone, & Hawkins, 2001, p. 5)

Some have found that this new way of delivering higher education is just as good as traditional ways, and maybe even better (Daniel, 2000; Johnson, 1999b). In fact, as Sir John Daniel (2000) stated in a speech to attendees at the Taiwan Conference on Distance Learning:

> Open universities have learned how to carry out distance education successfully at scale and I emphasize that this is not merely a technological success. Through the principle of course team we have become better at teaching than conventional universities, on both academic and pedagogical grounds.

Some say that students in distance education courses are more engaged with the learning process and that interaction happens more than in traditional face-to-face courses (Carnevale, 2000b; Marchese, 2000). Researchers also have found that distance education is "more effective than the classroom lecture and the traditional relationship between student and faculty member" (Oblinger, Barone, & Hawkins, 2001, p. 6).

A large body of research touts that there are no significant differences between the learning outcomes of distance education and those of classroom-based education (Epper, 1996; Oblinger, Barone, & Hawkins, 2001; Weigel, 2000).

> [But] why [argue some] hold up lecture-based classroom education as the benchmark for evaluating new educational delivery systems? . . . If there is no significant difference between distance education and classroom-based education, advocates of distance education should hardly trumpet this claim; they should be deeply troubled by it. How could they think of making the status quo the standard for evaluating learning technologies that have so much more to offer? (Weigel, 2000, p. 12)

With distance learning technologies, teachers can develop new teaching methodologies rather than adapting old pedagogy to their distance courses. The Web is a "fundamentally new medium for education with the potential to birth new pedagogical methods" (Weigel, 2000, p. 12).

Charles M. Cook, director of the New England Association of Schools and Colleges' Commission on Institutions of Higher Education, comments on distance learning. He asserts that this mode of delivery "can provide a more active learning environment for students than traditional education by engaging the student with interactive technology, instead of relying on a professor's lecture" (Carnevale, 2000d). He feels that this type of educational delivery is more learner-centered than traditional delivery. In fact, in a survey of faculty, findings revealed that they "believed web-based courses do a better job of giving students access to information, helping them master the subject, and addressing a variety of learning styles" (Oblinger, Barone, & Hawkins, 2001, p. 19).

> The Web . . . can also be a great new medium for deeper forms of learning. . . . The beautiful thing is that today's technologies, with their incredible abilities to connect, search, engage, and individualize, to prompt performance and assess understanding, are—in the hands of a teacher with the right ambitions—terrific enablers for [deep learning]. (Marchese, 2000, p. 4)

Distance education serves the needs of not only the traditional-age college student, but also the most rapidly growing segment of the population, adult learners over the age of 35 years who have full-time jobs, families, and limited discretionary time. A report by the American Council on Education Center for Policy Analysis and Educause (Oblinger, Barone, & Hawkins, 2001) cites seven distinct audiences for distance learning: corporate learners, professional enhancement learners, degree-completion adult learners, college experience learners (or the traditional student), precollege (K–12) learners, remediation and test-preparation learners, and recreational learners (Oblinger, Barone, & Hawkins, 2001).

Distance education has touched a majority of institutions of higher education in the United States over the past 5 years. *USA Today* (Snapshots, 2000) reports that 75% of U.S. institutions of higher education now offer distance education courses and programs, and 35% have accredited distance education programs. It appears, however, that public institutions are using the distance mode of delivery much more than are private institutions.

In 1997, 79% of public 4-year institutions and 72% of public 2-year institutions offered distance education courses, compared with 22% of private 4-year institutions and 6% of private 2-year ones (Carnevale, 2000a, p. A57). Currently, institutions with more than 10,000 students (87%) are more likely to offer distance education courses than those with between 3,000 and 10,000 students (75%), or those with fewer than 3,000 students (19%) (Carnevale, 2000a, p. A57). These numbers are likely to increase substantially over the next decade with all the advances in technology and the growing demand by the public for convenient and flexible educational opportunities.

In this age of technology, future college students (e.g., today's children) have and are using computers in their schools. "Today's students, increasingly comfortable with technology, expect online resources (a digital library, Web resources, simulations, video) as part of the learning tools and learning experience" (Green, 1997, p. 4). In fact, colleges and universities of today are "dealing with the first generation of students who have never known life without PCs (created in the '70s) or the Internet (largely a '90s phenomenon)" (Oblinger, Barone, & Hawkins, 2001, p. 26). Students entering higher education today have the knowledge and skills to use technology that exceed those of faculty and staff working in higher education (Bleed, 2000). Students are not only computer literate, they are "technophilic" (Cini & Vilic, 1999, p. 38).

Over the past 2 decades, communication using information technologies has gone from using overhead projectors, audiovisual media, slides, and the viewing of prerecorded public television programs, to the delivery of instruction using interactive technologies and asynchronous modes, with degree programs offered to students worldwide. Changes in technology today are constant, and faculty, staff, and administrators must keep pace with new technologies to ensure that their students receive the best that education has to offer.

PART II

Distance Education:
East, West, and Across the Sea

It is happening in Maine—it is happening in Oregon and many places in between. From Florida to Canada, distance learning is woven into the fabric of higher education. Look to the east of the United States and you will find it in Great Britain and Europe, and to the west, in Hawaii and Asia. To the south, distance education is in South America, Africa, and Australia. Distance education has made its way around the globe, and as has been illustrated here, every day more institutions are adopting technology to deliver education anytime, anywhere.

Part II presents four distinct examples of distance education, both in the United States and abroad. The examples illustrate various approaches to the delivery of distance education used in Maine, Oregon, the western United States, and Great Britain. The examples are intended to provide the reader with successful foundational principles of distance education, while also demonstrating that approaches may be very different.

Chapter 2 provides a look at distance education in the University of Maine System. Original research conducted by the author over the past 15 years is presented and offers a context in which the reader may view the evolution of distance education in Maine. Often cited as a "model for the country," Maine's

distance learning endeavor was among the first in the country.

Chapter 3 describes the unique features of the distance education Community College System in Oregon. The reader will learn how the system was created, what its purpose is, what it offers students, and how students benefit from the online features. The chapter includes a tour of the system with a student to see, firsthand, how important many of the attributes of the system are, and to get an idea of how a student can use the system to benefit her own particular educational needs.

Chapter 4 presents an approach to distance learning that involves many institutions and states. Known as Western Governor's University (WGU), this "institution" took resources from already existing institutions and brought them together to provide access to courses around the country for students anywhere. The development of WGU is described, as are the pitfalls and setbacks it faced along the way. Advantages and disadvantages of this competency-based educational institution are offered.

Chapter 5 describes Britain's Open University, which has been in existence since 1969. A model for distance education, Open University's progression is traced from 1971 to the present.

CHAPTER 2

Distance Education in Maine:
Design, Evolution, and What Is Happening Now?

"As Maine goes, so goes the nation." This sentiment has been used for decades to predict presidential election outcomes, but it also can be used in the recent past and the present to summarize the movement in distance education. While policy makers and administrators in many parts of the United States were discussing the use of technology in education, the state of Maine began, more than 2 decades ago, to deliver college courses and programs using interactive educational technology.

THE 1980s AND 1990s

In the early 1980s, the University of Maine System began delivering college courses using a two-way video and two-way audio interactive television (ITV) system. During that time, the University's ITV system used a combination of microwave signals, fiber optic cabling, and local cable television to broadcast live instruction between on-campus studio classrooms and four or five off-campus remote classrooms. A typical scenario is outlined in Figure 2.1.

Like faculty at other institutions venturing into the delivery of distance learning, the University of Maine faculty sought to replicate the traditional classroom experience using the ITV system. That experience included a teacher-centered approach where the professor lectured to students and encouraged questions and interaction via telephone or microphone. Using the traditional classroom model helped to legitimize use of a new technology.

In the mid-1980s, the University of Maine ITV system was expanded to connect electronic classrooms located at each of the seven University of Maine campuses with more than 70 remote sites around the state.

Figure 2.1. ITV Vignette

Professor Sherman arrives at the broadcast classroom at 7:45 a.m. to teach his scheduled 8:10 a.m. introduction to psychology class. The professor is greeted by Wally Matthews, broadcast technician, who is responsible for everything that goes on in the control room during the class. Wally and Professor Sherman discuss any last minute changes in class protocol, and the professor makes his way to the podium at the front of the classroom, arranges his materials, and hooks his microphone to the lapel of his jacket.

At 8:00 students begin arriving at the studio classroom to take their seats at tables that are situated in view of one of four television monitors positioned around the classroom. There are four microphones on each table for use by students who wish to speak. Meanwhile, at four remote sites beyond the campus boundaries, students arrive at their respective locations to view the course simultaneously on television monitors in their classrooms. Because the ITV system is two-way audio and two-way video, students in the remote sites and those in the broadcast site will be able to speak with and see each other. A camera positioned at the rear of the broadcast classroom captures the professor—full face—as he delivers his lecture. In an effort to engage remote site students, Professor Sherman often looks into the camera lens, giving the impression that he is visually interacting or making eye contact with these students. Wally, who sits in the control room, monitors the four remote sites for questions or comments from students. When a student pushes the table microphone control button to speak, Wally switches the audio and video to that site so the professor and all students can see and hear the student.

In 1988, the system was again expanded and became an entity known as the Community College of Maine (CCM). This expansion came after several years of planning and after inequities in educational opportunities for Maine citizens became apparent. Maine has a large geographic area, larger than the other five New England states (New Hampshire, Vermont, Connecticut, Massachusetts, and Rhode Island) combined. While a large part of the population lives in the central and southern part of the state, almost

> two-thirds of the population lives beyond a reasonable commuting distance to a University or Technical College campus. Those students undeterred by distance still must contend with harsh winter weather, secondary roads and minimal public transportation in their efforts to get to a campus. (Community College of Maine, 1990, p. 1)

The CCM plan called for the development of a telecommunications system that would make use of existing campuses, off-campus centers, and high school sites, and link them by fiber optic cable, point-to-multipoint microwave, and satellite transmission. Through the use of electronic classrooms, interactive courses were delivered to students in rural areas around the state. This eliminated the need for travel to a campus to take college courses. A provision for student support services was made by the off-campus centers.

The mission of the CCM was to encourage access to higher education for older, part-time, and commuter students. In the early 1990s, the system was again expanded to a configuration that included the seven campuses, 10 centers, and more than 100 sites, with an interactive television system that broadcast to homes, offices, and the more than 100 sites. Shortly after this model was implemented, the system began to deliver asynchronous courses to provide more options for students, better accommodate students' work schedules and family responsibilities, and increase access to higher education for Maine citizens. With this mode of delivery, students were provided more flexibility in the pace and time at which they participated in courses. Soon, not only older, part-time, commuter students were enrolling, but also traditional students. "In Maine, distance education is more than a convenient way to attend college; it has solved a very old problem for many of Maine's people—educational access" (CCM, 1991, p. 3).

The CCM soon became known as the Education Network of Maine (ENM) and, along with the delivery of courses from its base campus in Augusta, began to broker courses from the other six University of Maine campuses located in Farmington, Fort Kent, Machias, Orono, Presque Isle, and Portland/Gorham. Additionally, the ENM offered a degree program in library sciences from the University of South Carolina.

As leadership changed within the University of Maine system (UMS), changes also were made in Maine's distance education delivery system. The ENM no longer was considered an "educational institution"; rather it became a delivery system without academic rights, a vehicle for the delivery of courses and programs that originated at the seven University of Maine campuses. Known as UNET (University of Maine System Network for Education and Technology Services), this entity was responsible for providing assistance to faculty in the development and adaptation of their courses to the distance mode, for all the technological aspects of delivery, for student support services, and for other functions. UNET staff consisted of 87 full-time equivalent specialists, including Web course designers, network managers, video editors, and student support counselors, all of whom worked with faculty to improve existing distance courses and create new ones (Daviss, 2000). By the spring of 2001, UNET (then known as the University College) made available eight associates degrees, six baccalaureate degrees, three masters degrees, and 13 graduate and undergraduate certificates. More than 175 courses were offered, with about a third delivered over the Internet. The remaining courses were delivered using interactive television, videotape, computer conferencing, or some combination of these. More than 7,000 students were enrolled in the courses, and degree and certificate programs.

In the late 1990s, with the introduction of compressed video, students and faculty had yet another option for distance delivery. While compressed video has its advantages (e.g., professor has control of all functions of the compressed video system, video interactivity, and image previewing capacity), it is not without limitations. For example, only 12 to 15 students can fit into most compressed video classrooms; there is no capacity for tape recording a class; and faculty members must learn how to operate the system and must do so during the class. The instructor may designate a student to operate the system, but in that case, the student-designee must focus part of his or her attention on that responsibility and may miss part of the content of the class. The system is voice-activated for switching from one site to another; thus, when one student begins to speak in a remote site, the video is switched to that site so the student may be seen. To ensure that collisions will not occur, a communication protocol must be established before the start of the course. (See Chapter 6 for more information about compressed video.)

TODAY: THE STATE OF DISTANCE LEARNING IN MAINE

The UMS University College now offers courses via ITV and online. Interactive television courses are broadcast live by faculty from the university campuses to centers and sites across Maine. Students attending classes at these sites view the class on TV monitors and interact with the instructor and other students using a toll-free classroom telephone. Compressed video, available only on the UMS campuses, allows two-way video interaction. Many ITV courses use computer conferencing to deliver course materials, hold class discussions, and encourage interaction.

Online courses generally do not require scheduled classroom attendance; however, some online courses require occasional on-site attendance for meetings and proctored exams. These courses use computer conferencing (e.g., Blackboard or WebCT), e-mail, and the World Wide Web for communication, research, and information resources. Students who do not have access to the Internet from home can participate in these courses from the computer lab at their local Maine University center or site.

ITV and online courses may use videotapes for part or all of the course material; others may include streaming video and/or audio technology, enabling students to view and/or listen to the class on a multimedia PC connected to the Web.

All courses offered are from regionally accredited institutions within the University of Maine System or the Maine Technical College System, and carry college credit.

In Fall 2001, University College offered 171 courses, with 7,789 students enrolled across the state.

Research and Evaluation

Over the past 15 years, much research and evaluation have been conducted on interactive distance learning in Maine. These two activities went hand in hand with this relatively new mode of course delivery. Beginning in the mid-1980s, the University of Southern Maine (USM), a divided campus located in both Portland and Gorham, began delivering a limited number of courses over its interactive television system. Using a combination of microwave signals, fiber optic cabling, and local cable television systems, live instruction was broadcast from the on-campus studio classroom in Gorham to two remote site classrooms, one approximately 12 miles from the studio, and the other about 40 miles away. Instructors provided live in-class instruction to students in the studio classroom, and students in the remote site classrooms received the same instruction simultaneously via television monitors in their remote site classrooms. Within a year, an interactive two-way video system was added to these televised courses, which allowed students and instructors to see each other. During this time, a third remote classroom also was added.

One goal of the new ITV system at USM was to improve on the 1970s models of telecourses, in which most courses were not interactive and the pedagogy of choice was generally lecture. Likewise, evaluation study designs were used that allowed the examination of variables that were left unstudied in the 1970s and early 1980s, or where study findings were inconclusive (See Brenden, 1977; Carver & Mackay, 1986; Chu & Schramm, 1967; Denton, 1985; Ellis & Mathis, 1985; Harold, 1967; Hult, 1980; Johnson et al., 1985; Porter, 1983; Silvernail & Johnson, 1987; Thorman & Amb, 1975; Zalatimo & Zulick, 1979).

Based on these early studies, there were two factors that may have contributed to the inconclusive findings. One main factor was the purpose of instructional television systems (ITS), and the second was delivery mode(s). For example, ITS were designed for many different purposes, including preservice and continuing education, undergraduate and graduate education, and skills training. In addition, a variety of modes were used (e.g., closed-circuit television, satellite transmission, videotapes, and interactive television). Consequently, some of the differences in the findings may have been attributable to differences in purposes and comparisons among delivery modes.

However, the problems with these earlier studies went beyond purpose and mode. Many of the early studies used designs that included samples of students from different age groups, with different abilities, and with different reasons for taking a distance education course. This resulted in comparisons between nonequivalent groups. Furthermore, most of the early studies lacked the use of a control group, "precluding appropriate comparison between control and experimental groups" (Silvernail & Johnson, 1990, p. 2). Additionally, adequate controls for course content and instructional style were absent. "The major problem [in researching the topic] has been matching the television and live instruction groups according to instructor, course content and materials, and classroom environment" (Hult, 1980, p. 5).

University of Southern Maine

Evaluations of distance learning courses at USM were designed to address early study deficiencies. One of the first studies conducted, in 1989, was a controlled experimental study in a college-level psychology course. The study was designed to assess the impact of two-way interactive televised instruction on student achievement and attitudes, using equivalent control and experimental groups, with the same instructor, instructional mode, and course content for students receiving live in-class instruction and those receiving instruction by interactive television.

A combination of course grades; end-of-course evaluation data; SAT verbal scores, considered a proxy for student ability (Sternberg, 1984); and student opinion surveys were used to assess achievement and attitudes for the 112 students involved in the study.

The findings from this study suggested that the interactive television section was as effective as the traditional classroom setting. Further, the live and remote sites of the ITV section appeared to be similar. The students in both sections reported positive attitudes toward the professor's style of instruction, the course content, and their level of achievement (Silvernail & Johnson, 1990).

A similar study conducted by the author in the late 1980s used ITV to deliver college calculus to Maine high school students at their high school, while college students on the University's campus received the course live. We were trying to assess the viability of using ITV to provide access for high school

students to courses unavailable at their schools. Interaction between the high school students and the college students and professor on campus was accomplished using a dedicated telephone line.

The two-semester calculus course was taught by a university professor in a studio classroom and simultaneously broadcast to undergraduate students enrolled at two off-campus center classrooms and to the high school students in their school classroom. A total of 28 students were involved in the study, 17 undergraduate college students and 11 college-bound high school students. Evaluation methodology for the study included analysis of student performance and assessment of attitudes.

While not statistically significant, the high school students performed better academically than the college students. All students reportedly had positive attitudes toward the medium of instruction and the instructor's teaching style. The high school students felt that taking the college-level course was probably a more positive experience than taking the same course at the high school level would have been. They also seemed to appreciate the opportunity to experience a college-level course taught by a college professor. All students had the advantage of the availability of videotapes for their personal review. This option made the technical difficulties experienced at the high school site more palatable. Although use of the telephone system for voice interaction somewhat interfered with the fluidity, spontaneity, and level of interaction experienced by the high school students, course ratings were generally positive (Johnson & Silvernail, 1989).

Community College of Maine

While USM was using distance education technologies to deliver courses on a limited basis, the President of the University of Maine at Augusta, Dr. George Connick (see Foreword), proposed a more extensive system to reach well beyond its campus. The new system was proposed to address a need in Maine to provide greater access to a college education for all Maine citizens, including those who lacked adequate preparation for the University. Known as the Community College of Maine, this entity had as its mission to serve rural adult students whose access to college courses was either limited or nonexistent. In addition to academic instruction, the CCM also provided student support services.

The CCM significantly increased access to educational offerings in isolated areas of the state. The College's ITV offerings reached into communities that previously had had no formal contact with higher education. Persons once isolated from a college education could now enroll in college courses, both graduate and undergraduate, and matriculate in an associates degree program. During its inaugural year (1989), more than 2,500 students registered for courses.

Unlike USM's system, the CCM's ITV system was a two-way audio and one-way video system. The CCMITV system connected electronic classrooms located at each of the seven University of Maine System campuses with more than 70 remote sites. From each campus, the classroom signal was broadcast by means of interactive fixed service microwave from one transmitter to multiple antennae at the various receive sites. Students at the remote ITV classrooms were taught by a professor who was simultaneously teaching a classroom of students on campus, much like the USM model.

Eleven university off-campus centers and more than 60 high school sites throughout the state served the bulk of students enrolled in the CCM. The off-campus centers not only served as receive sites for instruction, but also coordinated registration, academic advising, admissions, financial aid, and other services for students at the centers and high school locations in their region.

Along with a more extensive delivery system came a more comprehensive evaluation plan. Because questions about educational quality, student learning, and student evaluation of distance courses had begun to surface, the author designed studies to attempt to address some of these questions. Although student achievement had been studied by researchers (e.g., Creswell, 1986; Silvernail &Johnson, 1990; Johnson & Silvernail, 1989; Silvernail, 1985; Stover, 1986; Wergin, Boland, & Kaas, 1986; Whittington, 1987), studies of the impact of student motivation and student satisfaction on the evaluation of ITV courses were few. Thus, a study was designed, using a survey methodology (Appendix A), to examine the effects of distance, motivation, and satisfaction with course content and medium instruction on student evaluation of ITV courses.

The study sample consisted of 1,520 students enrolled in 31 courses at 36 sites throughout the state of Maine. Most of the students were female and adult students, and 80% had full- or part-time jobs.

Path analysis procedures were employed to examine the direct and indirect effects of four independent variables on students' evaluations of their ITV courses: (1) student satisfaction with the course, (2) student satisfaction with the medium of instruction, (3) student motivation, and (4) distance traveled. The findings confirmed that course evaluations are most affected by students' satisfaction with the course and with the ITV system. This was not surprising, as student evaluations of courses are based on students' perception of the effectiveness of course delivery and satisfaction with their opportunity to have a positive learning experience (Baird, 1987). Motivation had a small but significant effect on end-of-course evaluations, but the effect was indirect through the satisfaction variables. There were no effects related to distance. This finding was in direct contrast to findings of earlier studies that revealed a direct positive correlation between distance and course evaluations (Silvernail, 1985; Silvernail & Johnson, 1989). That is, the further from a campus the student lived, the more favorable were his or her evaluations of the course and the ITV system (Johnson & Silvernail, 1994).

Study of the CCM ITV system continued through the 1990s. We studied first-time and returning faculty perceptions of their teaching experience using ITV. We looked at the impact of the ITV system on faculty instruction. And, we continued to evaluate the effectiveness of ITV in the delivery of courses to college students. In every study, we tried to examine at least one new variable or twist in addition to continuing with our evaluation of student satisfaction and achievement.

In Fall of 1990, we designed a seminal study to compare the quality of ITV instruction with traditional classroom instruction in equivalent courses. Nearly 300 students enrolled in six courses delivered over the CCMITV system and 158 students enrolled in six live equivalent courses were studied. For each ITV course, there was a live equivalent course, taught by the same professor. Forty-five sites were represented for the ITV courses (41 receive sites and four campus origination sites).

Satisfaction with courses, professors' organization and delivery, and the ITV system were studied.

We also looked at student achievement. In four of the six sets of courses, ITV students achieved significantly higher grades than students in the equivalent non-ITV courses. All students were satisfied with the courses, but ITV students did not rate the instructors' preparation and effectiveness as positively as did non-ITV students. This may have been because ITV students did not have as much contact as non-ITV students with the professors or because they did not appear to receive as much feedback from the professors as did the non-ITV students. However, all students, both ITV and non-ITV, appeared to be satisfied with course presentation, clarity of assignments, and faculty use of instructional aids.

While the findings from a study such as this added evidence and support for the premise that ITV is not only a viable option for the delivery of higher education, but an effective means by which access may be improved for various populations, it also underscores the importance of faculty attention to those students with whom they are not face-to-face (Johnson, 1991c).

USM and CCM Faculty

Faculty studies were conducted during the late 1980s and early 1990s. The author and several colleagues designed studies to examine faculty expectations about what ITV teaching would be like, perceptions and attitudes toward ITV teaching and course delivery, satisfaction with technical support, and what instructional strategies they used. We were also interested in finding out what motivated faculty to choose to teach a distance education course when there clearly was no institutional requirement to do so.

Study findings confirmed faculty expectations. Faculty expected that preparing and teaching an ITV course would be more time-consuming and would involve more work than a non-ITV course, and it did. Not expected, and truly a bonus of teaching on the system, was that they gained insight into their teaching and, in fact, felt that using the ITV system helped them to improve their teaching strategies and style. Faculty felt that they had to be more organized, and the technology available to them increased their desire to try new teaching methods. Tools, which included a character generator and overhead camera, enhanced the presentation of course materials. Furthermore, because all classes were videotaped, not only

did students benefit, but faculty could review the tapes as well and assess their own performance and techniques.

Reasons faculty chose to teach an ITV course included the innovative and challenging nature of this new approach. They were also motivated by monetary rewards (faculty received a one-time stipend to develop and prepare a course for ITV, and each course counted as double in the faculty member's course load). Many faculty were interested in making their courses more accessible to students who were not able to attend campus-based courses, and some faculty cited departmental need as a reason for teaching ITV courses.

Interaction with students in remote sites seemed to be somewhat of a problem. And, as a result of the lack of personal contact, more supervision was needed for students at these sites. Faculty concern about student performance, however, proved unwarranted. Students at remote sites performed as well as and sometimes better than students at the origination site. Additionally, faculty adjustment to this new medium of instruction was easier than expected.

Over the next 5 years, several more faculty studies were conducted (Bay, Johnson, & Silvernail, 1988; Johnson, 1990a–e, 1991a–f; Johnson & Silvernail, 1990; Silvernail & Johnson, 1992). Some of the more interesting findings include the following:

- Faculty saw ITV teaching as an opportunity to reach a more diverse student population.
- Faculty saw improvements in their course organization as a result of teaching an ITV course, and many said the experience had caused them to try new teaching methods.
- Faculty said that instructional aids actually enhanced presentation of course materials, and they found the technical support and training they received adequate.
- Overall, they liked the opportunity to use advanced technologies that encourage self-analysis of teaching techniques and methods.
- Faculty were consistent in their articulation of what would make the system better, including two-way video, microphones for students to use rather than a telephone system, more efficient mail or delivery system for assignments and course materials, and more training for first-time instructors.

- Most faculty felt that they had made substantial changes in the way they presented course materials over ITV.
- Fewer than half of the faculty studied felt that classroom interaction was adequate, and only half felt that opportunities to interact and communicate with students were sufficient.
- Some faculty reported that their ITV students never said a word during the entire course and that unless they required that attendance in remote sites be taken, they never really knew whether students were present or not. Furthermore, because few students interacted, they said that it was difficult to gauge student learning.
- Despite some of the problems inherent in teaching over ITV, nearly all faculty wanted to continue this practice.
- Faculty who had taught more than once reported seeing improvements in the technology since beginning to teach on the system, and many felt that student interaction had increased somewhat. (It was hypothesized that this may have been a result of faculty becoming more skilled at encouraging this activity.)
- Nearly all returning faculty said that their course organization and teaching methods had improved as a result of using the technology.
- However, concerns remained about student attendance in remote sites, interaction with students, and some logistical aspects.
- Another concern raised by these instructors was that of student evaluation of the course and faculty. Some felt that their evaluations from students in remote sites were not as positive as the ones they had received from students in traditional courses.

In an effort to study this concern over faculty evaluations, we designed a study (Silvernail & Johnson, 1992) to look at the impact of ITV instruction on student evaluations of their instructors. Past research had revealed that "the amount of interpersonal contact between students and their instructors, and the accessibility of instructors, has an impact on student evaluations of their instructors" (Silvernail & Johnson, 1992, p. 47). Given that ITV teaching in the early days lacked personal contact and may even have contributed to the inaccessibility of the instructor, faculty had reason for concern. However, a search of the research literature at that time failed to uncover research that explicitly examined the relationship between students' perceptions of ITV and their evaluation of instructors. Furthermore, virtually no research could be found in which the relationship between teaching style and end-of-course evaluations was examined. Our study was designed to begin to close these gaps. The study included two professors who had very different teaching styles as measured by the *Canfield Instructional Styles Inventory* (Canfield, 1980). The two faculty members team-taught an interdisciplinary course. The first instructor's style was labeled instructor-oriented. Characteristic of this style was encouragement of competition among students, an emphasis on lecture, and placing responsibility for learning on the student. The second instructor had a student-oriented style in which cooperative learning was encouraged, demonstration and direct experience were used as the primary learning tools, and the major responsibility for student learning was assumed by the professor.

Student evaluations were correlated with their perceptions about the effectiveness of ITV. Students were categorized by the rating they gave to the ITV system as an effective medium for course delivery. About half of the students rated ITV as an ineffective way to deliver the course, and the other half said it was an effective delivery system. Despite their views of the effectiveness of ITV, there were no significant differences in the way the two groups rated the professors. However, students who viewed the ITV system as effective were also significantly more satisfied with the amount of interaction they had with the professor, and they felt that they had ample opportunity to ask questions during class time, more so than students who found the ITV system ineffective. The overall course rating was higher for students who rated ITV as effective. We concluded that although students may not have been excited and satisfied with the technology, this did not appear to have an impact on the way they rated faculty performance, but it did affect ratings of course-specific factors.

The Education Network of Maine

During the early 1990s, the CCM was updated and expanded to include all seven University of Maine (UM) campuses as broadcast origination classrooms, 10 off-campus UM centers, and more than 100 sites located in offices, schools, churches, libraries, and community organizations. The two-way audio and one-way video interactive television system was used to broadcast courses to the more than 100 sites and to students' homes. In 1996, the ENM began to offer courses asynchronously, defined as "not at the same time." Asynchronous instruction, then, is instruction in which the teacher and students use various technologies to communicate and complete course activities anytime and anywhere, but not necessarily at the same time. This type of instruction provided more options for students, better accommodated students' work schedules and family responsibilities, and increased, even more, access to higher education for Maine citizens. Asynchronous courses afforded students more flexibility and more convenience in their course taking. Asynchronously delivered courses differ from ITV in that students can access the courses from their homes or offices—anytime—rather than traveling to a site or center at a specified time, which is the expectation and requirement for an ITV course.

The first courses offered asynchronously were business courses, Principles of Marketing (PM) and Operations Research (OR). The first course, PM, was delivered exclusively over the World Wide Web. The second course, OR, was delivered using videotapes, with half the class sessions held over ITV every other week throughout the semester. Students in OR were expected to view certain videotaped lectures and complete assignments in a study guide prior to attending each ITV session. Students in the PM Web course were expected to participate in the class regularly, but at their convenience through computer conferencing from home or a center. Students could meet all course requirements using Internet resources. All lecture materials were included in the course syllabus so students could read them off-line if they so chose.

As was the practice in Maine, these courses were evaluated (Johnson, 1998) using a survey methodology (Appendix B). We studied student satisfaction and achievement, and began to explore student learning styles and preferences. Results from these evaluations were far superior to past evaluations we had conducted.

In the course, students were predominantly female, and the mean age was 35 years. The majority of students took the course from their homes. Students were very satisfied with the quality of the lecture materials, with the way in which the professor organized the course online and with his teaching style, attentiveness, and responsiveness to them. They felt that the technical, content, and moral support they received was very satisfactory. The pace of the course was appropriate. The logistics were well organized, and the interaction students had with each other was valuable to their learning experience. They felt "connected" to others in the course. The overall satisfaction with the course was high. Nearly 50% of the students passed the course with an A, B, or C. Approximately 26% of the students did not finish the course or withdrew, and more than 20% received an incomplete grade that subsequently was completed to the satisfaction of the professor.

As in PM, OR students were older (mean age was 33 years), and two-thirds were female. Students were very satisfied with the quality of the audio and video on the videotapes, the instructor's responsiveness and feedback, and the organization and pace of the course, and they too felt "connected" to other students taking the course. Overall, students were satisfied with the course.

In an effort to begin to examine learning styles and preferences of students taking distance education courses, we conducted a preliminary study of these students' learning styles and found that more of the students were independent in the way they approached the course. That is, they were happy studying alone and did not need immediate feedback from the instructor on their work. However, the majority of students in both courses felt that class discussion was an important part of the learning experience. Most classified themselves as good readers and had confidence in their ability to manage their own study schedule.

University of Maine

In 1995, a behavioral sciences external (BEX) degree program was launched at the University of Maine. The program was delivered asynchronously with periodic campus meetings in the form of planning seminars. A small cohort of seven students enrolled in the first round of the program, taking their courses from either home or a center. Because of the small number of students enrolled and the unique qualities of the program, an in-depth telephone interview evaluation methodology was used with all seven students. Interviews averaged 45 minutes, and an interview protocol (Appendix C) was developed to explore all aspects of the course and learning experiences.

The findings were mixed; that is, while there were many positive outcomes, questions were raised about various aspects of the program. For example, students were very enthusiastic about the opportunity to complete a degree from the University of Maine on their own time and at their own convenience. Most of the students were unable to take college courses otherwise because of family and job responsibilities and/or distance to a UM campus. Students found the courses intellectually challenging and felt that the time spent on them was well worth their effort. Many said the delivery mode was superior to other courses they had taken face-to-face. They felt that "this delivery mode fosters individuality, allows flexibility, forces students to be accountable for their learning, and demands self discipline and independent learning" (Johnson, 1997b, p. 8). Students cited many benefits from having taken the courses in the BEX degree program. Among them were the development of better writing skills, new research skills, and improved computer skills. They learned patience, perseverance, and self-control, and they gained an increased understanding of technology. While four of the students felt that the teaching approach in the courses was excellent, two felt that the teaching was nonexistent—that is, they had to do all the learning on their own.

Due to the newness of the program, many of the kinks had yet to be worked out. Course requirement details were unclear, there were some problems with the technology, especially in inclement weather (i.e., telecommunication towers were down), and a few students were not as proficient using the software as they needed to be, and thus some of their work appeared to be "lost in cyberspace." Several suggested that more technical support would have contributed to their success in the courses. Also, faculty feedback in some of the courses was not as frequent as students had hoped. Program ratings were average (3.1 on a 5-point scale with 5 being excellent). The technology received a rating of 3.0 on the same scale; however, the instructional materials were rated 4.1. Despite some of the problems and frustrations students experienced, all students said they wanted this program to continue and more like it to be offered. They felt that as the program grew, the problems would be resolved. They were willing to be patient in exchange "for the convenience, flexibility, and access to higher

education that [the program] gave them" (Johnson, 1997b, p. 12). Based on the interview data, the author made five recommendations.

Recommendation 1: The program and other external degrees are needed to serve students in rural Maine. Continue the program and use the feedback received through these interviews to improve the delivery.

Recommendation 2: A solid support system must be put in place to assist these students, who, for the most part, are faced with independent, isolated learning.

Recommendation 3: Because of the nature of an external degree, the feedback mechanism needs to be strong. Whether by e-mail, phone, fax, or postal mail, all students, both distant and face-to-face, need immediate and frequent feedback on the work they do. Feedback is a very important part of the education process.

Recommendation 4: Regularly scheduled visits to sites by faculty to meet with students would enhance the educational experience for students enrolled in the program. Two informal sessions per semester are recommended. One should occur near the beginning of the semester and the other shortly after the mid-semester point.

Recommendation 5: Program policies need to be clearly stated in writing so students, faculty, and administrators are all operating within the same context and under the same policies. (Johnson, 1997b, pp. 13–14)

University of Maine System Network for Education and Technology Services

In 1998, as change came to the University of Maine System, distance education once again changed. This time the change cast distance learning into a new role with a new mission. The ENM no longer had the rights of an educational institution; rather it became purely a delivery system. With this change came a name change as well, the University of Maine System Network for Education and Technology Services. This new entity had as its mission to deliver courses and programs that resided at the seven University of Maine campuses. UNET staff became responsible for assisting faculty in developing and adapting courses to the distance mode. They also were charged with maintaining and administering all aspects of the technology and providing student support services, among other things.

By the spring of 2001, UNET was delivering eight associates, six baccalaureate, and three masters degree programs, and numerous undergraduate and graduate certificates. One-third of all courses offered were Internet courses, and the balance used ITV, videotapes, computer conferencing, compressed video, or some combination of these. Evaluation studies continued and a new focus became important, the study of student learner preferences.

In 1999, one such study was conducted (Johnson, 2000). Twenty-one courses were included and 166 students participated. The methodology for this study included mailing a questionnaire and a Johnson Learner Preference Scale (Johnson, 1992a, b) for completion by students. The questionnaire asked the usual things: questions about demographics, satisfaction with the courses, technology, and instruction, and about student access to and understanding of the technology used to participate in and complete the courses. The Johnson Learner Preference Scale (JLPS), developed between 1985 and 1990, was used to examine student learning styles and preferences. Briefly, the JLPS was designed to measure the learner preferences of college-level students and adults. The scale measures learner preferences with regard to learning styles, academic self-confidence, and sources of academic motivation. It focuses on how students approach learning, how they interact with instructors and with each other in learning situations, and what motivates them to learn. The scale identifies six learner preferences: enthusiastic learner, grade-conscious learner, collaborative learner, confident learner, reticent learner, and structured learner. Figure 2.2 defines each of the six learner preferences.

Findings were similar to those in past studies. Students were older (mean age was 34) and mostly female. The majority of students took the course from their home, with approximately 10% using site or center computers to complete the course. About one-third of the participants were full-time students. Two-thirds of the participants had never taken a course asynchronously before the current one; however, most said they were comfortable using the technology. Students generally felt the pace at which the

Figure 2.2. Johnson Learner Preference Scale

LEARNER PREFERENCES

Enthusiastic Learner—This individual is enthusiastic about learning. His/her motivation stems from a genuine desire to learn for the sake of gaining new information about a variety of topics. This person is fully involved in courses and has a high interest level.

Grade-Conscious Learner—This individual is performance-oriented and is driven by external signs of success such as grades in class. Although this person is interested in gaining knowledge, he/she places a great value on the grade he/she earns.

Collaborative Learner—This individual is a collaborative or cooperative learner. Participation in group activities such as projects and/or discussion is important. This person is confident in his/her own ability to learn what is important, and may take a leadership role in groups.

Confident Learner—This individual is confident about his/her abilities, tends to set realistic and attainable goals, and usually accomplishes them. This person expects to be successful in most learning situations.

Reticent Learner—This individual is reserved or guarded as a learner. Although this person may have something to offer in class, such as a question or comment, he/she may tend to remain silent.

Structured Learner—This individual is eager to learn and needs a high level of structure and organization. He/she depends on authority to provide that structure and organization, and prefers to have information imparted from an authority figure rather than seek it on his/her own.

course was delivered was about right, and they were satisfied with the level and type of interaction they had with the professor and other students. The professor, for the most part, provided timely and useful feedback to students on their coursework. The communication vehicle of choice was e-mail.

With respect to learning styles, students scored highest on the confident learner preference. None of the participants were identified as structured learn-

Figure 2.3. University College University of Maine System Distance Learning Homepage

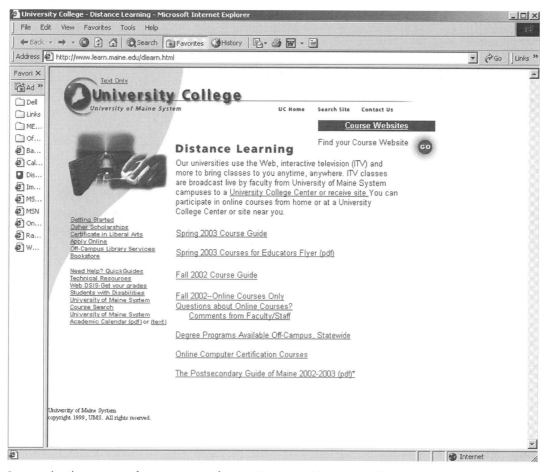

Reprinted with permission from University of Maine System. Web site: http://www.learn.maine.edu

ers, and only a few scored high on the collaborative and grade-conscious learner preferences. Regardless of their learner preference, student grades were similar. A number of interesting findings were revealed about students' learner preferences. First, it appears that most of the distance learners in this study were independent in their learning style. They preferred working alone rather than in groups. They felt confident about their abilities to achieve success, and they preferred courses that allowed them to pursue their own interests. Due to the nature of distance education courses, this is a positive finding. Students must be able to work on their own and must be able to manage their time since the structure of a set course time is usually absent.

University College of the University of Maine System

Today, yet another iteration of the Maine distance learning system has been established. University College, as it is called, is the distance education arm of the University of Maine System. Its web site, http://www.learn.maine.edu, offers many links where students can get help in a variety of areas. Course listings are posted on the home page (Figure 2.3) each semester, along with links to getting started.

From its beginning, distance education in Maine has evolved and grown to match the technology. Truly a model for the nation, Maine was a pioneer and George Connick was instrumental in leading the way.

CHAPTER 3

Distance Education in Oregon: Community College System

In August 1996, Oregon formed a statewide coalition of community colleges to create a strategic plan for distance learning, Strategic Plan of the Oregon Community Colleges for Distance Learning (SPOCCDL). Creators of the plan set out to "establish a common vision, define strategic directions, and identify implementation strategies for the coordinated delivery of distance learning services throughout the network of Oregon community colleges" (Baker, 1997, p. 4).

OREGON COMMUNITY COLLEGES FOR DISTANCE LEARNING

A committee was formed to develop the plan. Members of the committee included faculty, chief administrative officers (both instructional and student), learning specialists and librarians, and the Director of Distance Education for the Oregon Community Colleges.

The committee developed a vision statement to guide the development of the plan.

To foster effective learning that surmounts time, place, and barriers by providing comprehensive access, educational excellence, equity of opportunity, and responsiveness to educational needs for all Oregonians through collaborative partnerships among Oregon's community colleges for the development of distance learning policies, implementation of cooperative distance learning procedures, and delivery of community college instructional programs and services that combine the best technology practices with the best teaching and learning practices. (Baker, 1997, p. 4)

Defined as a "work in progress," the plan was developed using a broad framework so that future growth and additional detail could be added as distance education was implemented. A complete copy of Oregon's strategic plan may be found at http://occdl.chemeketa.edu. Click on DL Resources, then SPOCCDL Plan, then SPOCCDL to view the document (see Figure 3.1.).

Oregon Community Colleges Distance Learning is a group of 17 Oregon community colleges and two Washington colleges that have worked together for 19 years to present distance education courses to over 198,000 students. Originally, all offerings were telecourses, but as the number and variety of distance learning courses increased, so did the modes of delivery. Now courses are delivered via online or modem, live interactive to satellite campus classrooms, interactive CD, mail, videotape, cable, and telecourse, and some employ mixed modes. Students are able to complete an associate of arts Oregon transfer degree entirely by distance delivery. Two member colleges have other 2-year degrees available also. Since distance education courses require only a minimum (or no) on-campus attendance, they have become one of the most popular alternatives to traditionally taught courses. The classes are academically equivalent to on-campus classes, and most will transfer to other community colleges and 4-year institutions. During a typical term, more than 70 different telecourses, over 300 modem/Internet-based classes, about 20 live interactive courses, 30 videotaped classes, and other distant options are offered, including interactive CD, courses by mail, and independent study.

Member colleges include:

- Central Oregon: www.cocc.edu
- Chemeketa: www.chemeketa.edu
- Clackamas: www.clackamas.cc.or.us

Figure 3.1. Oregon Community Colleges Distance Learning Homepage

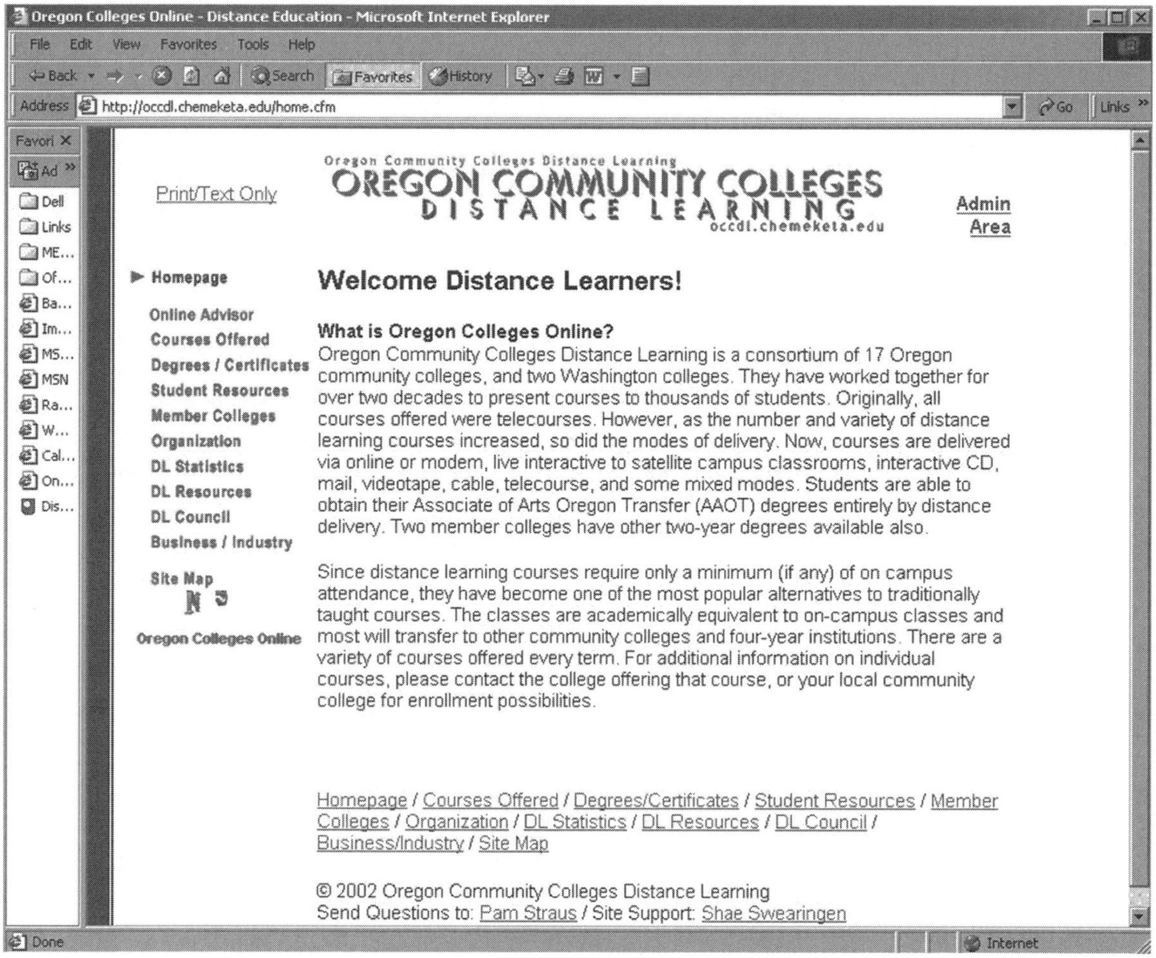

Reprinted with permission from Oregon Department of Community Colleges and Workforce Development. Web site: http://occdl.chemeketa.edu

- Clark: www.clark.edu
- Clatsop: www.clatsop.cc.or.us
- Columbia Gorge: www.cgcc.cc.or.us
- Klamath: www.kcc.cc.or.us
- Lane: lanecc.edu/distance/distance.htm
- Linn-Benton: cf.lbcc.cc.or.us/disted
- Lower Columbia: lcc.ctc.edu
- Mt. Hood: www.mhcc.cc.or.us
- Oregon Coast: www.occc.cc.or.us/ldist.html
- Portland: www.distance.pcc.edu
- Rogue: www.rogue.cc.or.us

- Southwestern Oregon: www.southwestern. cc.or.us
- Tillamook Bay: www.tbcc.cc.ot.us
- Treasure Valley: www.tvcc.cc
- Umpqua: www.umpqua.cc.or.us

An Online Advisor on the web site supports an electronic advising service for both distance and traditional students. The online service has a number of topics from which students may choose. When one clicks on "enter," an opening screen tells a little about how to use the service and includes a list of member colleges of Oregon Colleges Online (see list above). Topics covered by the electronic advising service include general information as well as:

- Information about Oregon Community Colleges
- Choosing a college
- Choosing your major
- Getting started
- Transfer credit
- Financial aid
- Personal development
- Career center

A visit to the "getting started" link, for example, outlines the basics of what a student needs to know to get started in college, including the application process, placement assessment requirements, how to develop an educational plan, and how to register and pay for courses. The "financial aid" link gives students ideas about what types of aid are available to them and various payment options. Students are advised to contact their financial aid office for more information. In addition to obtaining general information about Oregon Community Colleges, students may request information specific to their needs by going to the Online Advisor, signing on, and asking for information tailored for their own personal experience. This web site may serve as a model for providers of distance education who need to think about how students will use it to get the information they need. Providers may use this model as they create their own set of links to ensure that students are able to maneuver through the site in an easy and straightforward way.

Important also are tools to assist students in assessing their own skill levels. A section within the Oregon Community Colleges Distance Learning web site covering student resources includes "Student Guidelines" (Appendix D) and a survey entitled, "Are Distance Learning Courses for Me?" (Appendix E). Students are encouraged to read the guidelines, which address topics directly related to distance education courses. Completing the survey will help them to assess whether distance education is for them.

The site also offers resources for faculty to use when designing their courses to meet the needs of learners. For example, one of the distance learning resources entitled "Effective Course Elements" (Appendix F) offers tips on what to include in the course,

elements that have proven effective in distance education courses. There is advice about what should be included on a syllabus (orientation), how to encourage interaction (interactivity), effective teaching methods (presentation strategies), learning strategies (active learning), activities for students (research), and suggested assessment tools (outcomes assessment). All information and suggestions in this section are based on research by distance learning organizations. In addition to "Effective Course Elements," Oregon Colleges Online presents a section entitled "Distance Learning Course Design Considerations" (Appendix G) in which effective principles for designing a distance education course are outlined. The document is based, in part, on "Principles of Good Practice for Electronically Offered Academic Degree and Certificate Programs." This article may be found on the Western Interstate Commission for Higher Education web site, http://www.wiche.edu, by clicking on Publications, then on Educational Technology, and finally on Good Practices in Distance Education.

A TOUR OF OREGON COLLEGES ONLINE WITH AMY

Amy has made a decision that she wants to return to college. She completed 1 year of study in her home state of Minnesota, but recently married and has moved to the west coast where her husband will attend medical school. When Amy began her college education 3 years ago, she thought she wanted to become a teacher; however, now she is not sure. Amy has secured a full-time job as a manager in a retail store in Oregon. Her job, while demanding, will allow her time to take some courses at one of the community colleges in Oregon. After contacting the Admissions Office of one of the community colleges, she has decided that taking courses online may best fit the demands of her current lifestyle. She is advised by the Admissions Office to visit the "advising service" on the web site for Oregon Colleges Online. Here is what she finds.

Amy goes to http://occdl.chemeketa.edu and sees the "Welcome Distance Learners!" screen (see Figure 3.1). She clicks on "Online Advisor" on the left of the screen and is linked to a screen entitled Oregon Community Colleges Online Advisor (Figure 3.2). Here she clicks on the "customize" icon and

Figure 3.2. Oregon Community Colleges Online Advisor

Reprinted with permission from Oregon Department of Community Colleges and Workforce Development. Web site: http://occdl.chemeketa.edu

Figure 3.3. Oregon Community Colleges Online Advisor—Customize

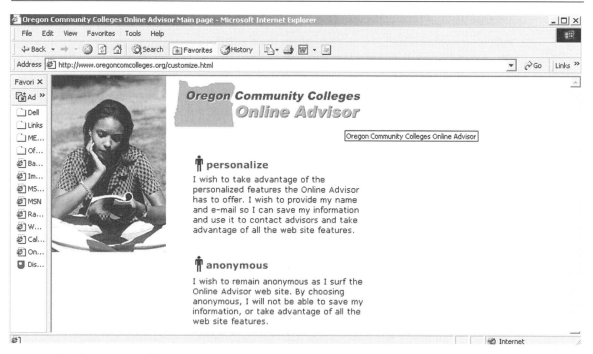

Reprinted with permission from Oregon Department of Community Colleges and Workforce Development. Web site: http://occdl.chemeketa.edu

is linked to another screen, which offers her two choices: to "personalize" or to remain "anonymous" (Figure 3.3).

Because she wishes to remain anonymous at this time, she clicks on "anonymous," which takes her to a questionnaire that asks for information about her educational needs (Figure 3.4). Amy fills in the information as requested and submits it for analysis. Within a few seconds another screen ap-

pears, which gives Amy the results of her "advising session" (Figure 3.5). This gives Amy some general information about what would best fit with the information she has provided in the questionnaire. Amy's information seems to fit best with the general studies degree program. Her next step is to submit a transcript of her past college courses to see which ones will transfer to the Oregon community college she selects. She is also encouraged to com-

Figure 3.4. Oregon Community Colleges Online Advisor—Anonymous

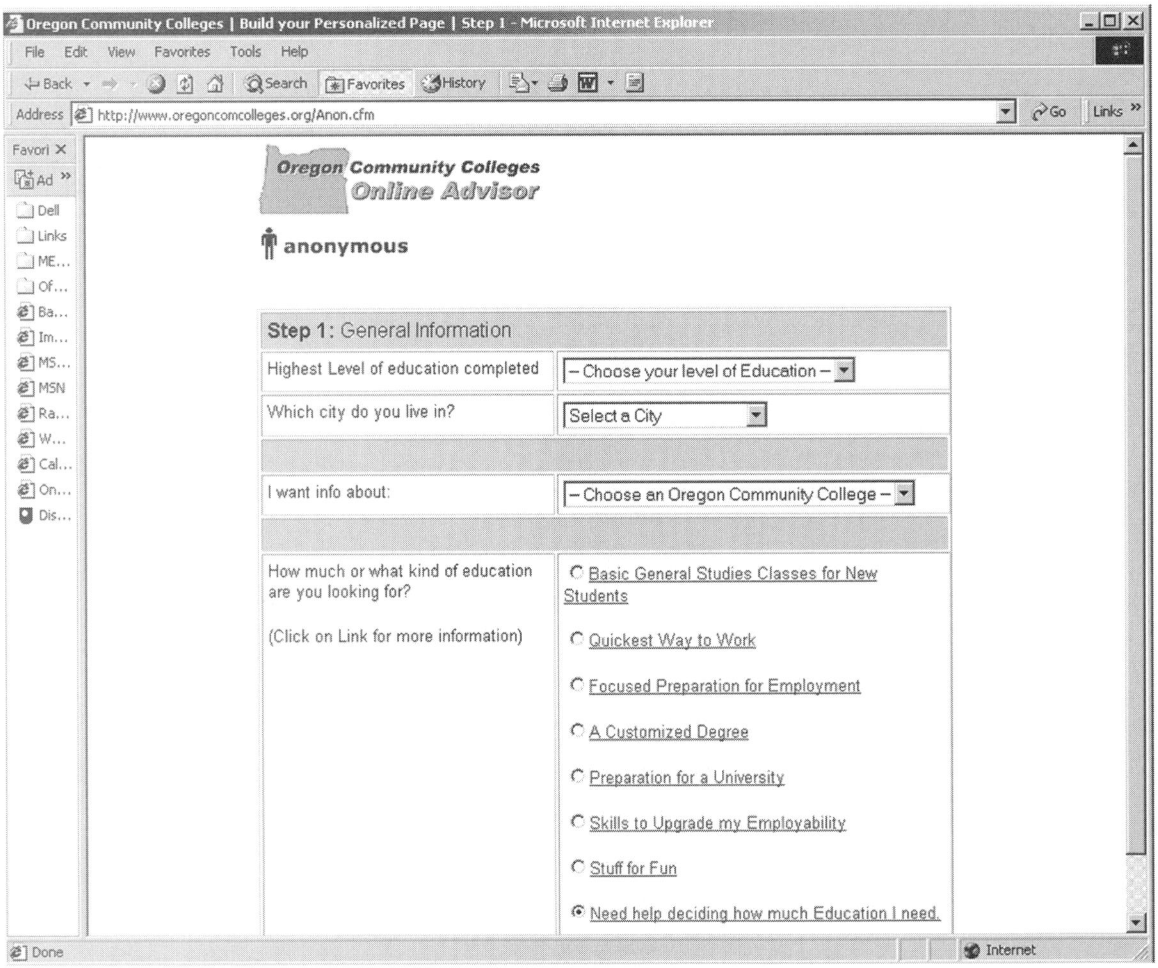

Reprinted with permission from Oregon Department of Community Colleges and Workforce Development. Web site: http://occdl.chemeketa.edu

Figure 3.5. Oregon Community Colleges Online Advisor–Results

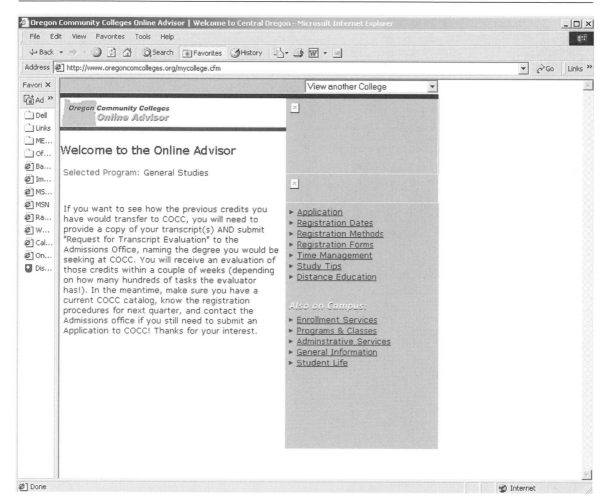

Reprinted with permission from Oregon Department of Community Colleges and Workforce Development. Web site: http://occdl.chemeketa.edu

plete an application and register for courses. Since Amy has decided that she wants to complete the courses through distance education, she clicks on the "Distance Education" option and is taken to another screen (Figure 3.6). Next she clicks on "Distance Education at Central Oregon," which appears at the bottom of the screen. Another screen appears that presents options for "Online Course Tool Help" for both faculty and students. Amy

chooses "Help for students taking Open Campus courses" (Figure 3.7). Another menu of student help options appears, and Amy is able to navigate through the various choices to better prepare her for what lies ahead.

Oregon's web site makes it simple for prospective students to get the information they need to make informed educational decisions. The site is easy to navigate, with links provided to information

Figure 3.6. Oregon Community Colleges Distance Education Information

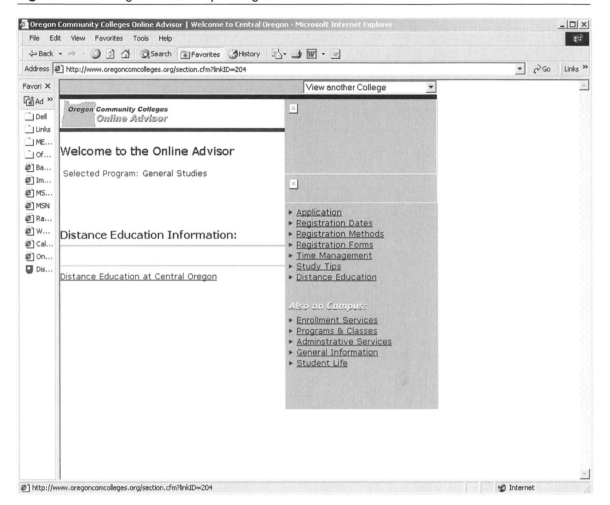

Reprinted with permission from Oregon Department of Community Colleges and Workforce Development.
Web site: http://occdl.chemeketa.edu

on many topics. This is appealing to a student like Amy who wants a one-stop approach. She can learn about Oregon's programs and courses, apply, register, and take courses without ever having to visit a campus. More and more, students are demanding this type of access, and more and more institutions are providing it.

Figure 3.7. Oregon Community Colleges Help for Distance Learning Students

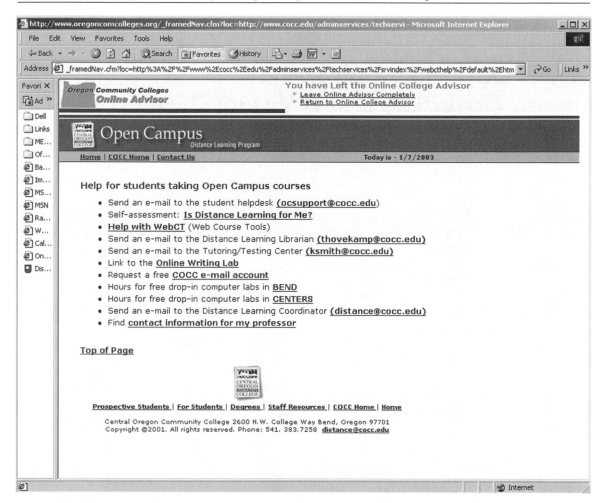

Reprinted with permission from Oregon Department of Community Colleges and Workforce Development. Web site: http://occdl.chemeketa.edu

CHAPTER 4

Western Governors University: Nineteen Governors and a Virtual University

Western Governors University (WGU), incorporated in 1997, offered its first programs in the summer of 1999. Developed as an institution that would cater to the needs of its learners, the university offers competency-based degrees and certificates as well as providing opportunities for students to take distance education courses from participating institutions. Described as a "real university, . . . without a physical campus . . . [and] no limits, [students can] take some of the best courses from institutions all across the country, all without ever leaving home" (Western Governors University, 2001). WGU takes advantage of what technology offers to provide educational opportunities to students who want an alternative to the traditional campus-based classroom experience. Students who enroll at WGU are allowed to set their own schedule and work at their own pace. Students are assigned an advisor/mentor with whom they can consult as they progress through a program. Participating states are presented in Figure 4.1.

The September 1997 issue of *The Technology Source* portrayed WGU as

> a watershed for higher education, combining the accreditation and prestige of the traditional university with the speed and connectivity of modem technology. In addition, WGU has taken a step that could affect the future of higher education—it is decoupling sit time from a diploma. WGU staff members will assist students in putting together an academic program combining online courses with residential classes at one or more traditional institutions, but for students to receive a degree from WGU, they must demonstrate that they have acquired a set of specific competencies as determined through a battery of assessments. WGU

will not award degrees based upon credit hours. (Morrison, 1997, p. 2)

The methods used by WGU, however, have been used by higher education institutions for decades (i.e., correspondence courses and use of the College Level Examination Program (CLEP) tests to earn college credit). So although WGU's approach is seen as a new way to offer degrees, some question whether WGU is actually doing anything new (Young, 1999).

Western Governors University was established to "revolutionize the way colleges compete for students, the way professors teach, and the way education is measured" (Blumenstyk, 1998, p. A21). Onlookers watched as administrators and organizers faced many challenges with regard to accreditation, faculty, and curriculum. The first of these challenges involved growth. It was predicted that the virtual WGU, in its focus on accommodating part-time and nontraditional learners, would have difficulty dealing with "the flood of campus-bound 18 to 24 year olds" (Blumenstyk, 1998, p. A21). However, the 18- to 24-year-old students did not come. Rather, the average age of students is around 40, and 85% of enrolled students work full-time. Most students have families, some college experience, and significant life experiences. In May 2001, 500 students were enrolled, an increase of 150% from 2000. There are more than 1,000 courses available to students from institutions around the United States and Canada (Morrison & Mendenhall, 2001)

When WGU opened, two pilot programs were launched. One program enrolled students in an associate of arts degree, while the other offered a cer-

Figure 4.1. Participating Western Governors University States*

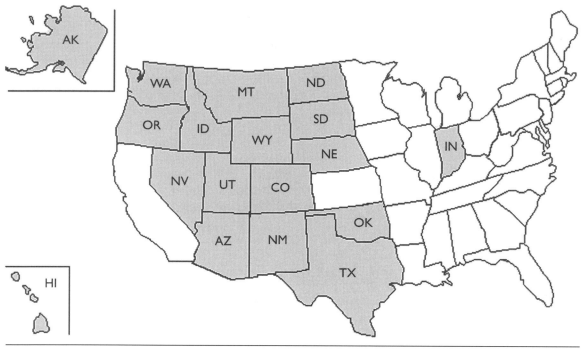

* *Note:* Guam, a participant, is not shown on this map.

tificate in electronic manufacturing technology. The programs provided courses via computer or other technologies to fewer than 100 students who were eligible to take a series of competency tests toward receiving such degrees or certificates as defined by the WGU. These programs were considered to be a "crucial first test of the public's reaction to its competency-based degrees, as well as how well it handles the myriad logistics involved in serving a far-flung student body" (Blumenstyk, 1998, p. A22). The first graduate of WGU completed a competency-based master of arts degree within a 16-month period.

WGU has articulation agreements with eight institutions in the United States. On the horizon are agreements with community colleges whose associate degree recipients will be able to transfer to WGU's baccalaureate degree programs. WGU also has 22 major corporate and foundation partners who support the mission and vision of the institution.

WGU is a nonprofit corporation, governed by a 14-member board and a National Advisory Board comprising executives from corporations such as

Microsoft, Novell, and International Thompson. WGU receives donations from these companies as well as from fund-raising efforts. The institution set a goal of raising $10 to $12 million in 1999 and 2000 and more than $30 million by 2003. WGU's business model consists of three parts: (1) an electronic clearinghouse through which established colleges or companies market their distance learning courses, (2) a vehicle for delivering training to corporate employees, and (3) an institution that awards degrees and certificates to students who can demonstrate that they have mastered specified competencies in academic technical fields (Blumenstyk, 1998).

The competency program, being the most controversial element of WGU, is expected to involve only a fraction of the students. A projected 95,000 students is expected by 2008, but only about a fourth of those will be pursuing a competency-based certificate or degree. Planners are hopeful that WGU will be making a profit by 2005, with revenues of $126 million.

In the design stage, various universities and companies were expected to provide services for WGU, such as online access to bookstores, online registration, library access, and other traditional services. An online catalog would list courses being offered, both in high-tech (e.g., Internet) and low-tech ways (e.g., using the postal service). Help would be available for students in determining whether the programs and courses available through WGU were right for them. A web site would provide links to resources designed to assist students in their decisions about whether to enroll and how to identify competencies required to complete a certificate. It would be easy for students to connect with the registrar, the bookstore, or library. This catalog would charge corporations and colleges to advertise their courses. It also would be instrumental in creating a market. Not only would students have access to thousands of educational opportunities, but they also would be guaranteed the services provided by WGU.

One of the obstacles WGU faced early on was that of gaining accreditation. On November 27, 2000, WGU was granted Candidate for Accreditation status. This was a significant step toward full accreditation and WGU was one of only a few online, virtual universities to achieve such status (Carnevale, 2000e). Over the next year, WGU would undergo "extensive evaluation and prepare a self-evaluation report" for the Distance Education and Training Council (DETC). The DETC's goal is to promote sound educational standards and ethical business practices within the distance study field. Founded in 1926, the DETC serves as a clearinghouse of information about the distance study field and conducts accreditation reviews of prominent distance learning institutions throughout the world through its independent Accrediting Commission. The seven-member Commission was established in 1955 and gained federal recognition in 1959. It is a nationally recognized institutional accrediting agency approved by the U.S. Department of Education and by the Council for Higher Education Accreditation. Today, more than 2.5 million Americans are enrolled in more than 70 DETC-accredited institutions (Western Governors University, 2001).

In June 2001, it was announced that the competency-based WGU had received accreditation from the Accrediting Commission of the DETC, a major milestone for the institution. Cited as an historic moment for the DETC, Executive Secretary Michael P. Lambert stated that "WGU is an outstanding in-

stitution that is blazing new trails for all of higher education" (from Press Release 6/13/01).

Another obstacle WGU faced was to gain access to federally sponsored financial aid programs. The existing rule was that "institutions that offer[ed] more than half of their courses by correspondence or distance learning [could not] participate in the programs" (Blumenstyk, 1998, p. A23). However, by 2000, WGU "secured access to federal financial aid for its students. WGU [was] named by the U.S. Department of Education as one of the first technology-based learning institutions in the country to provide financial aid to distant students" (www.wgu.edu/wgu/union/aid.html).

WGU has many advantages for students. First, in many states, public colleges and universities are at or near their full capacity. To accommodate more students, states would have to spend millions of dollars on new buildings and facilities. WGU is a university that does not have or need a physical campus. Second, it provides access to millions of people who do not live within reasonable commuting distance of a college campus. Third, WGU provides courses from dozens of institutions across the United States and around the world. Fourth, students decide what it is they want or need to accomplish; it is a student-centered university. Using a combination of knowledge and skills gained through a variety of ways (i.e., on the job, through courses taken, or just throughout their lives), individuals are able to obtain a competency-based degree or certificate. "Competency-based education awards degrees based on students demonstrating what they know and can do rather than by accumulating a certain number of credit hours" (Western Governors University, 2000). Choice, convenience, flexibility, value, and access are all part of the WGU experience. "With the use of technology to overcome the barriers of distance and time, WGU makes gaining a college degree possible for more people than ever before" (www.wgu.edu/wgu/about/students.html).

From a business perspective, member institutions are free to charge out-of-state tuition if they so choose. Some professors worry that an institution's decision to participate in WGU may be based on how much profit they believe they will make rather than on the quality of the faculty and instruction (Blumenstyk, 1998, p. A24).

WGU's chief academic officer, Dr. Albrecht, feels that fields that require licensure, such as business, nursing, and engineering, lend themselves well to competency-based degrees and certificates. However, he also recognizes that WGU was "created by politicians and has had little visible input from traditional academics. 'As new degrees and programs are added, . . . more academics will be recruited' [he states]" (Blumenstyk, 1998, p. A24).

Students who intend to earn a competency-based degree or certificate are required to go through an application process. Application forms are available online at WGU's website (see Figure 4.2; http://www/wgu/edu), and students must complete and submit an online application. If a student's native language is not English, he or she also must submit results from the Test of English as a Foreign Language. A score of 550 or above is required for nonprovisional admission. WGU has rolling admissions so one can submit an application at any time. Students must be at least 16 years of age to apply.

Requirements for admission to degree programs include either a high school diploma or proof of ability to succeed in college-level courses, an interview with an admissions counselor, a transcript of coursework completed within the past 5 years, and completion of a preassessment. In addition to these requirements, those seeking a bachelor's degree must submit a transcript of all past college coursework. Students seeking a graduate degree also must present proof that they have received a baccalaureate degree from an accredited institution. Students apply to a specific program or, if unsure which program would be beneficial, may apply with undeclared student status.

Once the application has been processed, the student is notified of his or her acceptance or rejection. For those who are accepted, two interviews are scheduled in which questions are answered and an academic action plan is developed. A student who is

Figure 4.2. Western Governors University Online Application

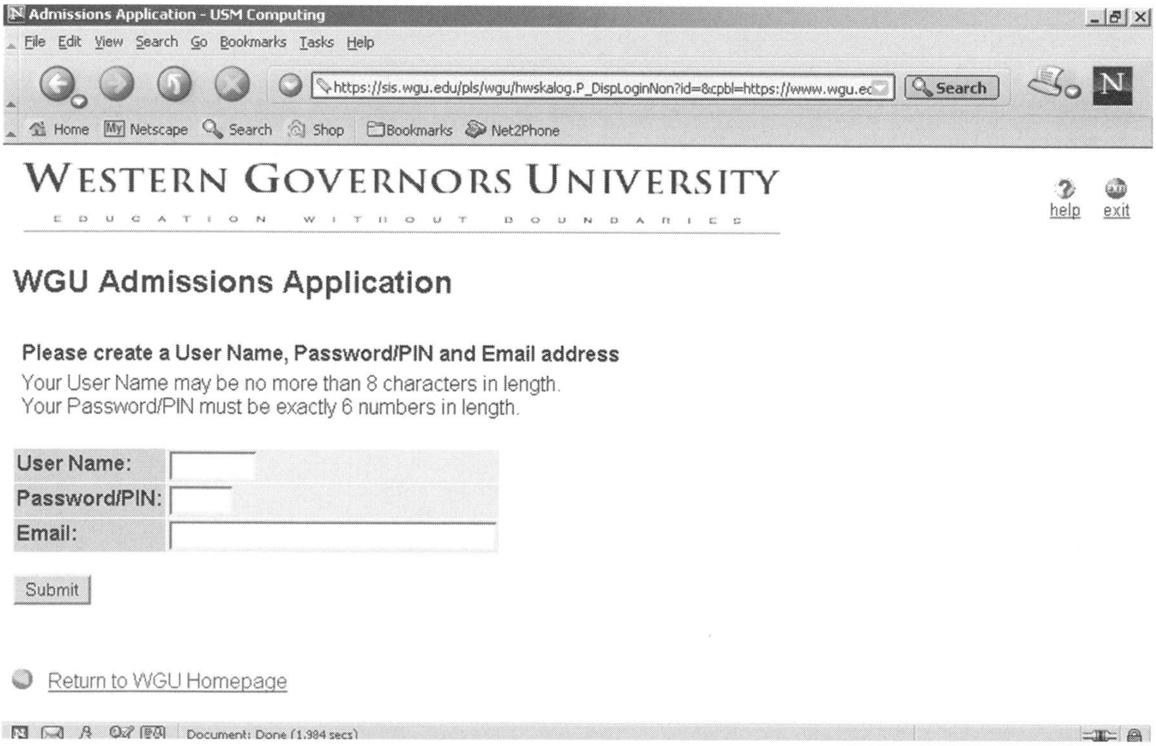

Reprinted with permission from Western Governors University. Web site: www.wgu.edu

not accepted is notified of the reason(s) and given suggestions about how to prepare to reapply. Prospective students are encouraged to visit WGU's web site for information about a number of topics. The Guide to the WGU Web Site (www.wgu.edu) is presented in Appendix H.

Much progress has been made since WGU began operation. The institution has received full accreditation, and enrollments, while fewer than predicted, are increasing. Many will be watching WGU over the next few years to see how well this type of virtual university does.

CHAPTER 5

Open University: A Model for Distance Education

The Open University (OU) is Britain's largest university, with more than 200,000 people studying its courses. Since its establishment by Royal Charter in 1969, it has opened the door to higher education for more than 2 million people. "The OU offers anyone and everyone the opportunity to study anything from a short course to a Ph.D., all on a part-time basis and all in their own home" (www.open.ac.uk). The Open University's mission statement reflects its continued commitment to students. Its four guiding principles are:

- Open as to people. The OU is open to everyone regardless of background or previous education.
- Open as to places. The OU is open as to the places where individuals study (in the United Kingdom and elsewhere, at home, work, or during temporary travel away from home).
- Open as to methods. The OU is committed to developing new and excellent methods of teaching to support student learning at a distance. OU uses the newest technology wherever appropriate.
- Open as to ideas. The OU is fully involved in UK research and development. OU is a lively learning community dedicated to expanding and sharing knowledge.

OU courses are designed for students studying in their homes or workplaces, in their own time, anywhere in the United Kingdom, Ireland, throughout Europe, and often further afield. Courses use a range of teaching media—specially produced textbooks, television and radio, audio- and videotapes, computer software, and home experiment kits. Personal contact and support comes through locally based tutors, a network of 330 regional study centers in the United Kingdom and overseas, and annual residen-

tial schools. Advisors located at regional centers assist students in a number of ways: by talking to them about their experiences and expectations, by sending them diagnostic materials to help them assess their preparedness, by giving them details of any suitable local courses or taster sessions, by telling them where they can see examples of OU course materials, and by inviting them to any open days or induction meetings the region holds.

Undergraduate courses are open to all regardless of education qualifications. The OU takes special responsibility for making higher education accessible to people with disabilities; currently some 6,200 of its students belong to this category.

The majority of OU students are working toward a BA/BSc degree. Teaching and research higher degrees are also available.

- The OU has 125,000 undergraduate students and 40,000 postgraduate students.
- In addition, 44,000 "study packs" were sold in 1999 to people who wanted to study an OU course without formally enrolling.
- Almost 80% of undergraduates are in paid employment while studying.
- About one-third of first-degree graduates since 1973 have held less than the minimum entry requirements for a traditional university.
- The largest number of students are in the 25–45 age range, but there are many outside that. The oldest OU graduate ever was 94, and the youngest was 18.

Apart from those studying for degrees, many OU students follow courses related to professional development. These often lead to certificate or diploma qualifications. Others just study individual courses to update their qualifications or fulfill personal ambitions.

The OU offers 300 undergraduate and postgraduate courses in arts, modern languages, social sciences, health and social welfare, science, mathematics and computing, technology, business and management, education, and law. The success of OU rests on four pillars:

1. high-quality, multimedia learning materials, developed by teams of academics and experts
2. personal support to each student from a living, breathing human being who knows the student's name and aspirations
3. efficient logistics and administration
4. teaching that is rooted in research

It is possible to achieve a degree through the OU in 3 years, studying full-time, but most undergraduates combine part-time study with work or family responsibilities. The average time taken for a degree is 6 years. The average cost of this is about £3,500. Many students' tuition is paid for by their employers.

More than 150 OU courses use IT to enhance learning in various ways, including virtual tutorials and discussion groups, electronic submission (and marking) of assignments, multimedia teaching materials, and computer-mediated conferencing. OU students read more than 170,000 e-mail and computer conference messages each day. Five OU courses are delivered via the Internet. OU researchers have developed new applications of IT to learning: the "virtual field trip" for Level I science students, and an Internet stadium capable of hosting mass audience events with up to 100,000 participants. More facts about the OU may be found in Figure 5.1.

NEW TECHNOLOGY

Since it was founded, the Open University has always sought to make use of whatever technology is most appropriate for its educational objectives and best meets the needs of its students.

As technology develops, the University continually reviews and revises its methods and systems. The convergence of computer technology and telecommunications is presenting both challenges and opportu-

Figure 5.1. Facts About the Open University

- In October 1998, the Open University collected over 100,000 examination scripts from 400 centers in 94 countries
- The Open University has awarded over 250,000 degrees
- There are more than 8,000 tutors in the Open University learning system
- More than 30,000 studying at the Open University are located outside of the United Kingdom
- The Open University is in the top third of all UK universities for the volume and quality of research
- The Open University plays a major role in training future researchers
- Gender is 50:50
- Disability and ethnicity reflect the United Kingdom's population
- 7,000 students are over the age of 60

(Facts taken from Daniel, 1998)

nities, which will radically change the way the OU teaches in the future. It also will present dilemmas about access for students—always a factor that the University has to consider very carefully.

Historical Background

When the University began teaching in 1971, the main technologies it employed were radio and television.

In the first technology foundation course, students were lent a cassette recorder to enable them to listen to audiotapes. Nowadays it is assumed that almost every home has at least one cassette machine, and the teaching advantages of tape replay over broadcast radio are such that almost all University courses now use audiotapes.

Video has followed a similar route. When this technology was first introduced, the OU made video replay machines available in its study centers. Students who missed a television broadcast could watch it on tape at the study center. As ownership of video machines became widespread, the University withdrew from providing machines and now expects students to make their own arrangements. Although broadcast television is still important and widely used, some courses now provide their audiovisual component entirely on tape.

Computer Provision

The University initially provided terminals in study centers, linked to its own mainframe computers. Students needed to reserve time on these machines to carry out practical work and assignments.

As the concept of mainframe and terminal was replaced by the rapid development of networked personal computers in the 1980s, the University moved to its present policy of home-based computing. Today there are some 62,000 OU students—more than the entire student population of most universities—taking courses that require the use of a computer. Thousands more use computers for research, writing assignments, and e-mailing tutors.

Most computers are provided by the students themselves. The University has encouraged suppliers to offer machines at favorable prices and has set up a subsidized plan to provide students receiving a financial award low-cost access to computing equipment.

Investment in New Technologies for Teaching and Learning

Considerable investment in the development of new technologies for teaching and learning has taken place over recent years. The University has initiated a major investment program under the title INSTILL (Integrating New Systems and Technologies into Lifelong Learning). This has seen an investment from reserves of £10 million over a 5-year period. Currently, development is being funded through the Program for Embedding Learning Technologies.

The Knowledge Media Institute

The creation of the Knowledge Media Institute (KMi) was a key aspect of the INSTILL program and recognized the need for the Open University to be at the forefront of research and development in the area of knowledge media.

The term "knowledge media" refers to the process of generating, understanding, and sharing knowledge using several different media, as well as understanding how the use of different media shapes these processes. Knowledge media encompasses a number of technologies, including Internet-enhanced collaboration media, multimedia environments for disabled learners, intelligent agents, organization memories, digital documents, scientific visualization and simulation tools, and representation of knowledge of both a formal and informal variety.

KMi comprises about 40 people, 70% of whom are funded by external grants. The Institute is truly interdisciplinary, including researchers in communication technologies, multimedia, human–computer interaction, cognitive science and knowledge representation, and management.

There are currently about 30 ongoing projects, developing and applying technologies for knowledge media for a wide range of users and with a wide range of partners. Industrial sponsors include major blue-chip companies such as British Telecom, British Petroleum, Apple Computers, Sun Microsystems, and IBM, as well as institutional funding bodies such as the Engineering and Physical Sciences Research Council (EPSRC) and the European Community. The KMi also works closely with the local community—for example, local charities and schools—and with other parts of the Open University. In particular, staff members are involved in over 20 course teams.

More details on KMi activities can be found on OU's web site at http://kmi.open.ac.uk.

Teaching via the Internet

The extraordinarily rapid development of the Internet—the global network of computer networks—is comparable to the invention of the printing press in the way it is revolutionizing human communication. Instant access to other network users, anywhere in the world, and to vast quantities of computer-stored information, is literally changing people's lives.

Like most other universities, the OU was an early user of the Internet. Members of staff actively participate in the worldwide academic dialog that the Internet facilitates. There also have been pilot projects enabling students to use Internet facilities—for example, for literature searches. The Internet has become an additional strand in the teaching strategy of many courses, as students become increasingly able to make use of computers and modems from their homes.

The University also has set up FirstClass, an electronic conferencing system, which allows students in more than 150 courses not only to send e-mails but also to join discussion forums where ideas are shared by displaying messages to all participants. Twenty thousand mail messages and more than 150,000 conference messages are read each day.

Some courses are being offered via the Internet. Two computing courses were among the first, and a taught Masters in Open and Distance Learning has been available since 1997. Personal tuition is pro-

vided via the Internet, as well as course materials and other learning resources. A major new course that teaches in this way is T171 You, Your Computer and the Net, which is taught entirely online—there is no face-to-face interaction (see Figure 5.2). Each student has a personal tutor available via electronic mail and is a member of both a tutorial group and a team working on collaborative assignments. Studying the course involves communication with tutors and fellow students via e-mail and conferencing. At the core of the course is a dynamic web site to which only registered students have access. All of the specially prepared teaching and assessment

Figure 5.2. Open University: You, Your Computer and the Net

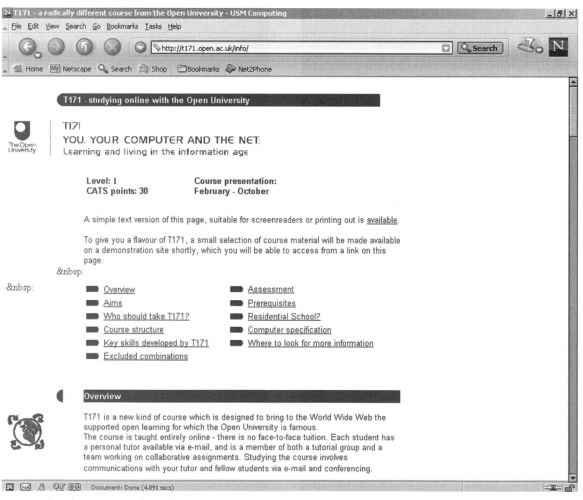

Reprinted with permission from the Open University. Web site: http://t171.open.ac.uk/pres

material is published on this site, which grows and develops as the course progresses (web site: http://t171.open.ac.uk/pres/).

Using Personal Computers for Teaching and Learning

Many courses have incorporated innovative computing elements into their teaching strategies. M206 Computing: An Object-oriented Approach, a radically innovative and practical computing course, registered 5,100 students in the United Kingdom and Europe for its first presentation in 1998. It is prob-

ably the biggest object-oriented computing course in the world, and in November 1998 it received a medal from the British Computer Society as a full Award Winner in its IT Awards project (web site: http://mcs.open.ac.uk/m206_info/).

S103 Discovering Science (see Figure 5.3) is a wide-ranging course that introduces important scientific concepts and develops the skills needed to study science successfully. It introduces the disciplines of biology, chemistry, earth science, and physics, and shows the links between them. As well as using the more traditional media, S103 makes extensive use of interactive CD-ROMs and computer-mediated

Figure 5.3. Open University Discovering Science Course

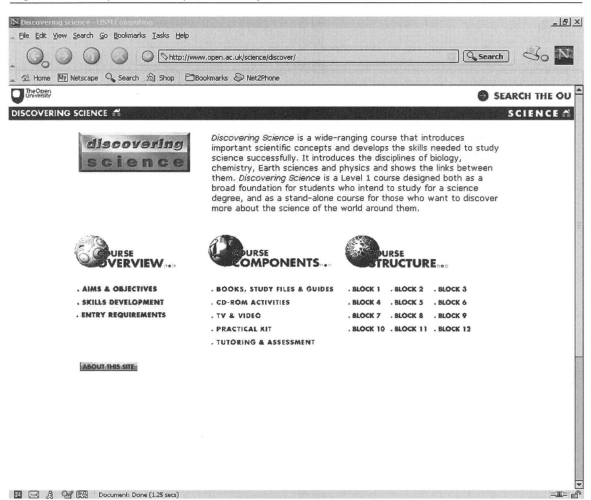

Reprinted with permission from the Open University. Web site: http://www2.open.ac.uk/science/s103

conferencing (web site: http://www2.open.ac.uk/science/s103/).

Satellite and Digital Broadcasting

The University's immense resources of course materials, and its expertise in distance teaching techniques, have made it a natural partner in a number of developments to offer education via satellite and digital broadcasting.

PALACES

The PALACES (Public, Associate Lecturers, Alumni Customers, Enquirers, Students) program is developing a world-class web presence for the OU that is radically changing the interface between students, tutors, and the University. Many administrative functions, such as registration for courses, residential schools, and examinations; access to personal and academic information; and provision of study calendars, handbooks, and assignment guides, are being put online.

Electronic Assignments

A system allowing students to submit assignments electronically has been implemented and is being further developed. Students submit their assignments via a web page or e-mail, their tutor collects them via a web interface, marks them on screen using specialist marking software, and then returns them to the system via the web interface. The system automatically processes the score given for each assignment, recording it on the student's assessment record, and returns the assignment (along with scores and tutor feedback) to the student electronically.

Presence on the World Wide Web

Up-to-date information about the Open University can be found on the World Wide Web at http://www.open.ac.uk/ (see Figure 5.4). This site contains many of the examples mentioned above, as well as an account of the Open University's teaching methods and full descriptions of all its current courses.

In the areas contributed by the academic units, there are many examples of current research activities.

Special areas of the web site are reserved for students and staff members, and there are plans to develop this further as a major element for communication within the huge OU community.

SERVICES TO DISABLED STUDENTS

The Open University's unique system of study, which combines supported open learning with a wide range of multimedia learning materials, makes it particularly accessible to disabled students. With nearly 7,700 students with a disability taking its courses and using its study materials in 2001, the OU is Europe's leading provider of higher education for disabled people.

The OU has pioneered a supported open learning system that has brought its courses within the reach of the entire adult population. The OU way of study is an integrated mix of correspondence texts, radio and television programs, audio- and videocassettes, computing and computer-mediated communication, residential schools, "home kits" for practical work, and teaching and counseling support, all delivered through a network of over 300 local study centers.

It is the University's policy to encourage disabled people to study with the OU and to provide them with the necessary support and facilities to do so on equal terms with other students whenever possible. The OU is an equal opportunities institution and welcomes applications for admission to its academic programs from all sectors of society.

Disability Statement

Under the Disability Discrimination Act of 1995, universities are required to publish Disability Statements every 3 years outlining their policies and services for disabled students. Their main purpose is to inform prospective and existing disabled students of the services and facilities available to them and of the institution's policies and plans for future provision.

The OU's first Disability Statement was published in January 1997. The discussion here provides an

Figure 5.4. Open University Homepage

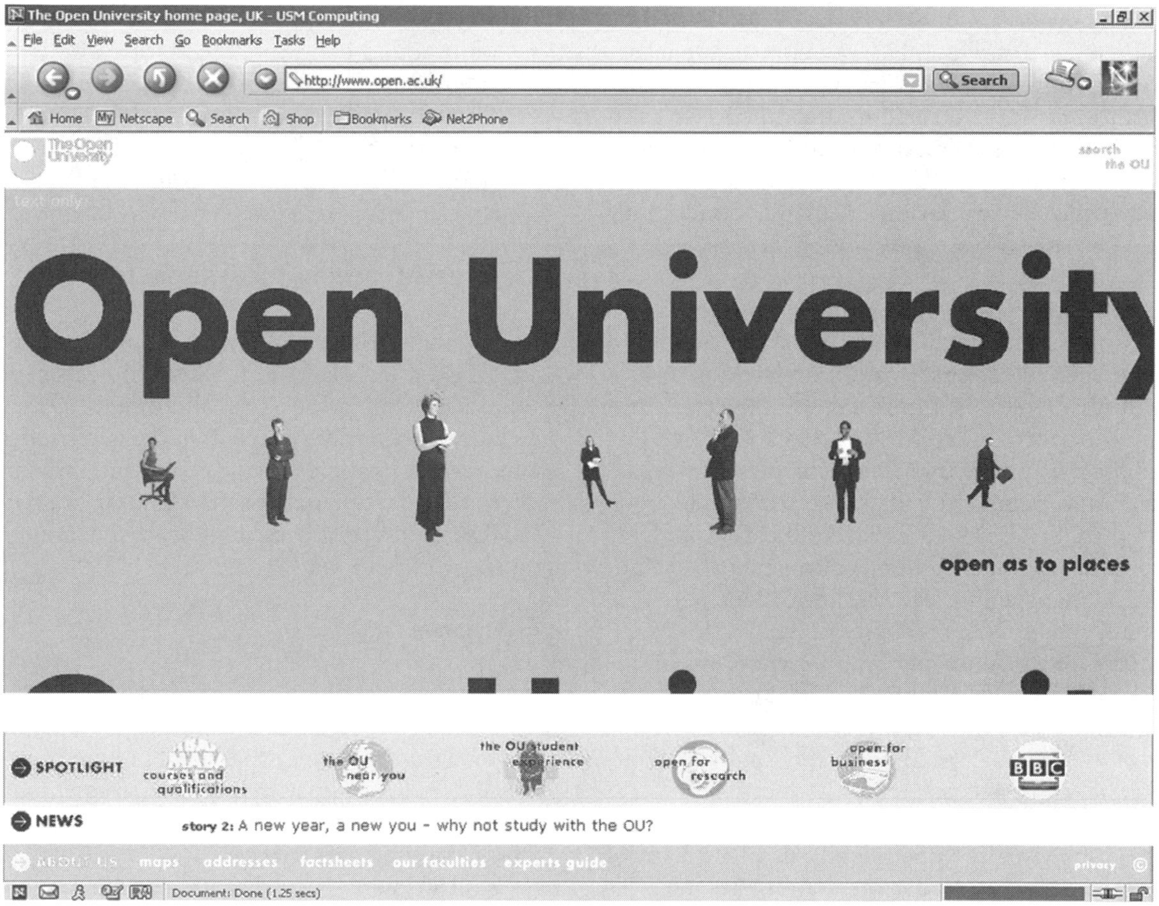

Reprinted with permission from the Open University. Web site: www.open.ac.uk

accurate summary of the contents of the current statement. A copy of the full Disability Statement is available in large print, on tape, in Braille, or on computer disk from the Office for Students with Disabilities, The Open University, Milton Keynes, MK7 6AR.

Admission to the University

Admission to the OU in general is based on the "first come, first served" principle. In certain circumstances, however, places in courses can be reserved for disabled applicants, usually where it can be shown that an applicant would be seriously disadvantaged

educationally by having to wait an additional year. All admissions inquiries should be referred to the Special Needs Team in the nearest OU regional center. The United Kingdom is divided into 13 OU regions, with regional centers in London, Oxford, Bristol, Birmingham, Nottingham, Cambridge, Leeds, Manchester, Newcastle, Cardiff, Edinburgh, Belfast, and East Grinstead.

Services to Students

The University has developed a wide range of services for disabled students. These generally are coordinated by the Office for Students with Disabilities at Walton Hall, but other regional and central OU departments also are involved in organizing and providing services.

When they reserve a place in a course, applicants are asked to indicate whether they have a disability or health problem that might affect their OU studies. If they answer "Yes," they are asked to provide more information on their circumstances and to specify which of the various available services they need—helped if necessary by staff in their nearest OU regional center.

Advice and counseling are available to all OU applicants and students through services organized by OU regional centers. In addition to normal tutorials and day schools, tutors can ask for extra tutorial sessions for individual students experiencing particular difficulties. Home visits also can be arranged, and many students make use of telephone tutorial facilities. Deaf and hard of hearing students are provided with communication support, including sign language interpreters, lip-readers, note takers, and, subject to availability, induction loops.

Access to a study center may present problems for a student with a disability. Regional centers try to ensure that disabled students are allocated to suitable study centers depending on their individual circumstances and needs.

Special weekend residential "study skills" courses are held for visually impaired and deaf and hard of hearing students to introduce new students to the OU's study system and to help them to develop a range of basic study skills. OU staff also are encouraged to attend. The courses are not compulsory but are extremely popular. Costs are borne by the University.

For many disabled students, conventional course materials are inappropriate (e.g., printed texts for someone who is blind). The University has developed a range of alternative materials to meet the needs of students with disabilities, as follows:

- Audiocassette versions of printed course material for use by visually impaired and other print-disabled students. The material is recorded at the OU's Audio Recording Center at Walton Hall by volunteer readers (many of whom are members of the relevant course teams).
- Transcripts of radio, audio, television, video, and CD-ROM material for use by deaf and hard of hearing students.
- Television programs with Ceefax subtitles.
- Subtitled course videos (available at present only in certain courses).
- Comb-bound course material for those with impaired manual dexterity.
- A limited Braille service (mainly labels for audiocassettes).
- Digital audio/electronic versions of printed course material (new service under development).

Examinations and Assessment

Services include alternative or modified assignments, if aural, visual, or mobility problems make the set assignments impossible. Examination facilities include examinations taken at home, alternative format question papers (Braille, tape, and large print), alternative format answers (Braille, tape, amanuensis, disk), extra time, rest breaks, and examinations taken over more than 1 day.

Equipment

A range of equipment is available on free loan to students, including radio aids and text telephones for use by hard of hearing students, "talking" scientific calculators for those with impaired vision, and computers with word processing software for students who have difficulty writing.

Students with severe disabilities can receive a professional assessment of the possible benefits of assistive IT hardware and software (e.g., a PC with synthetic speech output for someone who is blind, or voice recognition software for someone unable to use a keyboard) for carrying out study activities such as producing written work, reading, note taking, or operating a computer. In most cases, the University will pay for the provision of equipment recommended for individual students, as well as the cost of training through a special Access Technology Loan Scheme run in conjunction with the National Federation of Access Center, a network of some 30 colleges and other educational institutions in England, Wales, and Scotland that specializes in support for disabled students.

Residential Schools

Some disabled students find attendance at a residential school very difficult or impossible. In these

Figure 5.5. Open University Special Services to Students with Disabilities

Disabled Students Receiving Services in 2002	Number
Tapes (in place of printed texts)	1023
Transcripts	1068
Comb-bound materials	900
Personal radio aids	112
Interpreters, etc.	37
Access technology	135
PCs with word processing software	35
Talking calculators	50
Text telephones	30
Hearing support weeks	22
Special format examination papers	563
Special format examination answers	732
Students requiring an assistant at summer school	349
Students requiring advice before allocation to a summer school	1174

Reprinted with permission from the Open University.

cases, exemption is normally granted. For the most part, however, disabled students are encouraged to attend, and every attempt is made to allocate them to the most appropriate university campus. Where appropriate, disabled students may take an assistant (or have one provided by the University), at no extra cost, to enable them to participate fully in the academic and social life of the school. A wide range of equipment can be provided, such as wheelchairs and bed boards.

"Hearing Support Teams" are provided for hearing-impaired students at Level I course summer schools in certain weeks and at specific sites. These include sign language interpreters, lip-readers, note takers and VDU equipment, and keyboard operators. The VDU facilities are used to provide students with a screen-based text summary of lectures and group sessions as they take place.

A range of specialist notes and publications also are available for OU teaching staff and students, providing information and practical advice on student support and study.

A regular news magazine, *Open Links*, is sent twice a year to all disabled students who wish to receive it. This is a forum for students' views and ideas as well as a source of information on matters of particular interest. The Open University's Students' Association offers considerable support to members with disabilities (see Figure 5.5). It aims to ensure that there is a student coordinator in each region who will offer advice on transport, help at summer school, and other assistance. (Text taken from www.open.ac.uk/factsheets with permission to reprint and/or modify.)

Over the past 3 decades, the OU has become an impressive distance learning institution in terms of academics, access, and services. Of all the distance education institutions the author has studied, the OU is head and shoulders above the others in services to students with disabilities. The institution can and does serve as a model to those who are beginning their journey toward distance education organization. Even more it would benefit distance or traditional institutions to observe OU's work with students with disabilities.

PART III

Teaching at a Distance

Many universities and colleges in the United States began exploring the delivery of courses and programs using distance education technologies during the 1980s and 1990s. Factors such as changing demographics and the demand for broader access to higher education by a new student population have prompted institutions of higher education to establish electronic distance education systems to meet new demands. Web-based and technology-enhanced education is evolving at a rapid pace, and many students are learning more and learning better than they ever did in the traditional classroom. Distance learning "may provide a competitive or even superior way to learn for many students" (Armstrong, 2000, p. 23). "Online learning . . . allows for differentiation of institutions, learning styles, and pedagogy. The variations provided by online learning will not only rival—but are likely to surpass—the diversity of types of institutions that currently characterize American higher education" (Oblinger, Barone, & Hawkins, 2001, p. 2). Teaching and learning at a distance may, in the not so distant future, be the standard against which traditional face-to-face instruction and learning is measured (Chaffee, 2001; Cox, 2000; Truman-Davis, Futch, Thompson, & Yonekura, 2000).

CHAPTER 6

Pedagogy: What Works?

Pedagogy is defined by *Webster's II: New College Dictionary* (1999) as "the art or profession of teaching; preparatory instruction or training" (p. 809), a simple definition that is not terribly descriptive. A look in *Roget's II: The New Thesaurus* (1995) gives us a little more—"The act, process, or art of imparting knowledge and skill: education, instruction, pedagogics, schooling, teaching, training, tuition, tutelage, tutoring" (p. 716). In education, we use the word *pedagogy* to refer to the tools a teacher uses to impart knowledge and skills. Tools such as written curricula, tests and quizzes, presentations, and question/answer interaction often are used. Demonstrations, science fairs, problem-solving exercises, puzzles, projects, and research are contained in many teachers' toolboxes. Until the 1980s, the majority of pedagogy was limited to the classroom where face-to-face teaching and learning occurred. Classroom instructional tools such as the chalkboard, overhead projector, and hands-on work were used by instructors to convey the knowledge they wished students to acquire.

On the following pages, are descriptions of many of the pedagogies currently used in distance learning. Where appropriate, a vignette, illustrating the use and meaning of the term, is presented. Pedagogies fall into four categories and are presented in four sections. In the first section, synchronous pedagogy will be featured, with asynchronous pedagogy in the second section. The third section presents general terms that are applicable to all distance education pedagogy. And, in section four, two popular course management systems will be detailed. At the end of this section, you will find a table that compares the applications of five different course management software packages and information about a web site for comparing over 50 courseware systems.

TALKING ABOUT ...
SYNCHRONOUS PEDAGOGY

Synchronous pedagogy describes a type of two-way communication with virtually no time delay, allowing participants to respond in real time.

Broadcast Video

Found mainly in interactive television courses, this medium allows students and faculty to see each other during classes delivered over an ITV system.

Broadcast Video Vignette. David likes to take ITV courses delivered by the state university. Being a recreational learner, he has always dabbled in education for education's sake. He has chosen ITV courses because he lives in a rural area 200 miles from the campus. David is in his 50s and has a good job with the local electric company. At this stage in his life, he has no desire to relocate, nor does he wish to attend the community college located a little closer to his residence. One of the sites for the university's ITV courses is located at the high school in his town. The courses, which are mostly delivered in the evenings, are first- and second-year courses. Some high school students who are qualified to take more advanced courses also participate in the offerings. Although David has his bachelors degree, completed some 30 years ago, he finds that taking courses in a variety of areas is personally rewarding. His desire to take courses stems, in part, from a curiosity about many disciplines outside of the major he studied long ago. David is a lifelong learner, and ITV gives him an opportunity to pursue any area he wishes.

Compressed Video

Compressed video is an economical way to transmit video images using telephone lines. A digital transmission process is used to send the video signal. The information to be transmitted is compressed into a fraction of its original bandwidth by a codec, (i.e., a piece of coding and decoding equipment used to convert and compress analog video and audio signals into digital format for transmission and back again to analog signals upon reaching their destination). Because of the amount of bandwidth used, the signal is not as clear as full-motion video, and quick movements often appear jerky or blurred. Two or more locations can participate in a conference at one time; however, all connections between locations are programmed into a central computer and established in advance. During a conference or class, video and audio from all sites are transmitted to a central control unit. This unit selects one video image and sends it back to all sites, resulting in every site seeing the same image on its remote monitor. Switching from site to site is triggered automatically by the loud and consistent audio. However, a cough (which may be loud, but not consistent) will not trigger the video switch, nor will the whispering conversation of two students (which may be consistent, but not loud). Faculty who use the compressed video medium are advised to establish protocols for speaking to manage the interaction between sites. (See "Tips for Managing Your Conference" in Appendix I.)

Interactive Television (ITV)

ITV courses originally were offered as a way to increase access to students who were not able to attend classes on campus. Generally, the configuration of an ITV course consists of an instructor and a classroom of students who are located in a broadcast location, usually on a college campus. There are remote site classrooms, usually two or more, situated in areas away from campus. The interactivity dimension of the course may be audio and video, or exclusively audio. A variety of communication devices may be used to interact. For example, some ITV classrooms employ table microphones; others use microphones that are mounted on classroom walls; and some use the telephone as the means of communication between remote and broadcast locations. All students in all locations usually can see the instructor (one-way video), but some systems support two-way video in which the instructor can see students in remote sites, and students in all sites can see each other. Instructional tools such as monitors, front face cameras, overhead cameras (used as overhead projectors), the traditional chalkboard, and other traditional tools used in face-to-face classrooms are frequently found in the ITV classroom. In some instances, techniques and pedagogy used in the ITV classroom closely parallel those used in the face-to-face classroom.

ITV Vignette. Professor Ross has been asked by his department chair to teach a biology course for nonmajors over interactive television because of the shortage of science courses available to high school students in some of the remote areas of Minnesota. This will be the first time Dr. Ross has used ITV as a medium of instruction. He is excited about the prospect of learning new teaching techniques using this technology, but is also apprehensive because his biology course has a laboratory component as well as lecture. In addition to learning about all the applications of the ITV system, he must create ways for students to complete labs at a distance. In his discussions with fellow science professors, he develops lab exercises that students can carry out at home with materials he will mail them through the postal service. One of the labs involves the irradiation of sunflower seeds over different periods of time. The purpose of the assignment is to study the effect of irradiation on the plants' growth rate. Interestingly, he thinks that students completing this exercise will have an advantage over students who might be doing the experiment in a typical lab class that meets a couple of times a week. The at-home lab allows students more opportunities to gather data and witness the process on an ongoing basis.

The lecture component of the course is similar to a traditional face-to-face class, with meetings three times a week over the interactive television system. While Professor Ross feels that teaching this introductory-level course to nonmajors using ITV technology will be successful, he also feels that those who teach science courses with labs will have to be innovative in their approach (example adapted from Carr, 2000b).

Real Time

An application in which information is received and immediately responded to without any time delay is described as real time. Also referred to as synchronous, this system keeps regularly occurring events in timed intervals in step using some form of electronic clocking mechanism.

Telecourse

A telecourse is a coordinated learning system based on a series of television programs. A telecourse is supplemented by printed materials (text, study guide, readings) and local faculty involvement in the form of lectures and/or consultation. Telecourse programs may be viewed in a variety of ways. Most are broadcast over local cable stations. Program tapes are also available for viewing on local campuses or at the colleges' outlying centers. A few colleges have tapes available for checkout. Students also may have the option of renting tapes from outside agencies.

Two-Way Audio

Instruction that is transmitted via any means that supports two-way communications, including ordinary phone lines, is characterized as two-way audio. Two typical configurations are: (1) an instructor in one location creates a virtual class comprising students phoning in from many locations, and (2) an instructor in one location creates a virtual class comprising one or more physical classrooms. Each physical classroom may have 10 to 20 students present. Physical classrooms generally are managed by a nonacademic proctor who is responsible for carrying out the instructor's physical tasks by proxy. Most two-way audio conferencing employs new technologies to permit conversations to flow simultaneously in both directions.

Two-Way Video

This form of distance education is similar to one-way video except students are almost always grouped in one or more classrooms. Students may interact with the instructor and members of the parallel physical classrooms. This approach employs standard television studio and transmission technology to extend the traditional small to mid-size classroom mode. New technologies permit participants to see both sides of the video transmission simultaneously.

Two-Way Video and Two-Way Audio

This format uses interactive video in which all sites are in visual contact with one another. Some form of audioconferencing is used for real-time verbal interaction.

Videotape

ITV courses frequently are videotaped so students who miss a class or wish to review a particular session are able to do so by using the taped version of the class. Some institutions videotape on-campus courses and send them to off-campus centers where students may take the course without attending the on-campus class. When ITV was relatively new, many faculty worried that the taped version of their courses would be used to replace them, which, in most cases, it did not. Although the videotapes are the property of the institution, there is still some controversy over who owns the content of the videotapes.

TALKING ABOUT . . . ASYNCHRONOUS PEDAGOGY

Defined as "not at the same time," asynchronous communication and course distribution is a thing of the present and future.

Asynchronous Instruction

When a course is delivered asynchronously, the instruction is delivered at one time and students can participate at another time. Teachers and students use a number of technologies to communicate and perform the tasks of the coursework in asynchronous "classrooms." For example, e-mail may be used for communication between students and their professor, and among students. Listservs, computer conferencing, virtual chats, and electronic bulletin boards are other tools most frequently used in asynchronous courses.

Asynchronous Vignette. Anna is a single mom with two children who are in middle school. She works at City Hall as a receptionist in the Tax Office. Anna wants to be a teacher's assistant in the school her children attend. Although she has completed 30 credit hours of coursework at the local community college, she needs another 30 credits to get her associates degree and the job. Because her children are becoming increasingly involved in after-school activities, it is becoming more difficult for her to get to class in the late afternoon or evening when the courses are offered. She is exploring other options that will make study more convenient and practical for her. In a meeting with a counselor at the local community college, Anna was told about distance learning opportunities. With asynchronous courses, she will be able to continue her current job, maintain her involvement with her children, and work toward her associates degree without attending classes on campus. She will be able to complete her coursework at her own convenience in the comfort of her own home. Asynchronous learning will make the difference for Anna between realizing her educational goals and not.

Forums

Also referred to as discussion boards or electronic bulletin boards, forums are information services that can be reached via computers connected by modem and/or the Internet. With these services, users can gather information, place and read electronic messages from other users, and download files. Students can access and contribute to discussion boards or forums any time, day or night. Most often used in asynchronous courses, forums may be used effectively with large groups of students. The discussion is threaded and remains online until faculty delete it.

Students who enroll in courses online that use these pedagogies have an advantage over students in traditional face-to-face courses. They develop better writing skills and participate more in their learning. "Proponents of writing-across-the-curriculum . . . have been saying that students learn when they formulate their ideas in writing" (Lang, 2000, p. 21). Writing is an inherent part of taking an online course, especially when bulletin boards and forums are used. Although not spontaneous in nature, these discussions encourage thoughtful reflection and response by the participants. It is important for the professor to stipulate expectations about participation in forums. That is, students must use correct grammar, spelling, and sentence and paragraph structure. It is important that students know this, because online discussions become part of the permanent course record and will have some weight in the grading scheme. As Lang (2000) states:

> In an online discussion . . . writing is very much dialogical. In addition to the instructor, there is an audience of peers whose role is not to evaluate for a grade but to explore and develop ideas together. This communicative purpose in the writing process is what many composition teachers aim for in having students share their writing in small groups, for there students take more care with—and therefore think more carefully about—writing that has a real purpose for a real audience. Online, that purpose and that audience are an integral part of the environment. (p. 23)

The forum can help in community building as well. Students and faculty can post pictures of themselves along with brief biographies. This helps everyone get to know a little about the others in the class and become somewhat acquainted.

Ottenhoff and Lawrence (1999) propose some tips for a successful forum.

1. Remember that an online forum requires instructors and students to make clear and explicit comments.
2. Faculty should have excellent skills in course management and should understand a variety of teaching techniques.
3. Faculty who facilitate online forums not only should have mastery of the subject matter, but should be well versed in effective pedagogy.
4. Faculty should be aware of "best practices" and adopt them in their instructional practices.
5. Organization is key to a smooth journey through an online course.
6. Feedback on students' participation and work should be prompt and frequent.
7. Faculty should find a way to assess how the course is going. A mid-course online discussion is one way to get feedback from students in the class.
8. Faculty should be present, that is, make their presence known without being intrusive or overbearing. Feedback and comment are two ways to do this.

Forum Vignette: Introduction to Business. Communications is taught over the Internet every semester at Robertson University. The course, which is required in the business management major, usually has an enrollment of about 50 students each semester. Professor Louis began teaching this course in the early 1980s using the interactive television system. With the advent of the Internet and more requests by students for more flexibility, Dr. Louis agreed to teach the course online. When he introduced the Internet version, there were some glitches, and it took a few semesters before he was able to perfect the course. Now in its third year online, the course is one of the most popular among students.

One of the main activities of the course is, as the title suggests, communications. Therefore, there are a lot of assignments in which students demonstrate various types of communications they have learned in the course. Professor Louis uses a web forum for most of the activities and assignments he requires of his students. All papers are posted online in the forum, and students view the papers of their peers regularly. All responses to assignments are part of the public forum as well. The professor finds that over the course of the semester, students' writing improves significantly. He attributes this to the public nature of their assignments and to the writing practice. Students are motivated to do their best work because they know that peers as well as the professor will be critiquing it. The forum also gives each student a chance to see how others respond to the same assignment and get ideas about styles that are different from their own. An important motivation for students to participate in the forum is that their participation is part of their final course grade. A final assignment that Dr. Louis and his students find useful is a public reflection by all students on the process of using the forum in their learning.

Online Courses

These are courses that use the World Wide Web as the primary delivery mode. A textbook may or may not be required; all other materials, as well as communication with the instructor, are provided through the course web site. Critical to the success of an online course is an interpersonal approach. This means that faculty must manage the course effectively, giving prompt feedback and attention to all students, and students must be responsible for their participation and involvement. The term *web-based instruction* often is used interchangeably with online courses.

Streaming Media

Streaming "refers to synchronized video, audio, graphics, and animation sent over the Internet or over campus networks, where personal computers play the media streams directly" (Sircar, 2000, p. 54). Streaming video and audio often are used to create a more enhanced course content presentation. Movies, video clips, audio speeches, and other streaming media are used by faculty who wish to provide a more interesting and dynamic educational experience. Information presented in a variety of ways helps students to better understand the material. The use of streaming media is closing the perceived gap between face-to-face and online learning.

> By integrating streaming media in a Web-based framework to deliver critical components of a consistent teaching technology, we get a pedagogical solution to removing the difference between learning in class and learning at a distance. If both on-campus and distance education implements the same instructional technology, resulting in equivalent performance, then Web-based streaming as a delivery method becomes a key factor in the design of content. (Sircar, 2000, p. 56)

To access streaming media, one must download a streaming system such as *RealPlayer*. Because of the high-speed Internet connection that is required, those away from university campuses do not experience the same effect of streaming media as those who are participating in classes on campus. However, with the implementation of Internet2, these modalities will become a reality for more learners, wherever they are located (Campbell, Lum, & Singh, 2000).

Streaming Media Vignette. Modern History is being offered this semester using a computer-enhanced format. Mr. Bishop, an adjunct faculty member, has taught the course for the past 20 years over ITV. However, this semester the course will be delivered over the Internet using streaming media to make the course more interesting and real to students. The period of time on which he will focus will cover the years between 1960 and 1970. Much of the content of his course will focus on the events surrounding the assassinations of John F. and Robert F. Kennedy and Martin Luther King, Jr. Mr. Bishop will use King's famous "I Have a Dream" speech in his course and, because of the streaming media, students will have an opportunity to hear it over their computers. In addition, video clips of the political activities of both Kennedys will be used to make the learning experience more interesting and real to students.

Most students who enroll in Mr. Bishop's course will participate using university computers on campus as well as those located in remote university sites or centers. However, Maggie Kate has a cable modem at home and Linda has a DSL line; thus, these two students will be able to participate from their homes. Cable modems and DSL lines provide high-speed access to the Internet. Unlike Maggie Kate and Linda, most students access the Internet from their homes via modems, which require relatively low bandwidth. With this type of connection, the learning experience will not parallel that in which high-speed Internet connections are used on campus computers.

Videoconferencing

Video technology and telecommunication networks are used to link individuals for videoconferencing. This takes place in "real time." That is, participants are present in various locations at the same time, and a live video link displays their images on monitors in each location's classroom. Telecommunication allows for their verbal interaction, while the video technology displays their presence. Faculty have found videoconferencing useful when they must be at conferences away from campus and still want to conduct their class during that time. Another important use of this medium is when a guest speaker is not able to be physically present but his or her presence may be possible using videoconferencing. Access to guest speakers, experts in the field, or co-instructors enhances the quality of the learning experience.

Videoconferencing also is used in the rapidly growing field of telemedicine. Doctors are able to "see" their patients over the Internet for consultation. Doctors also are able to read X-rays online and discuss patients with local health care providers. Likewise, the judicial system increasingly is using

videoconferencing to reduce the cost involved in transporting prisoners to courthouses for arraignment. The arraignment can be done on site using a videoconferencing system located in the jail. This system also is being used in scientific laboratories and offices around the world to make the world a smaller place where people from anywhere can participate in meetings, research, and education.

Videoconferencing Vignette. Dr. Hinkle teaches several courses in the library sciences program at his university (vignette adapted from Carnevale, 2000f). Recently Professor Hinkle found that he had to travel to France during the spring semester to attend an important meeting on the latest technology for library management. This year, the research conference did not coincide with the institution's break, and thus he would have had to cancel two classes in order to attend the research conference and the meeting. Luckily his institution has an Internet-based videoconferencing system that is both inexpensive (about $7,000) and of high quality. Because of this technology, the professor will be able to conduct his classes while he is away, using the videoconferencing system and an Internet connection in France at the conference. These connections are usually available in most hotels.

Virtual Chats

A virtual chat is a real-time interaction that occurs online between two or more computer users. The messages are typed into a computer, and all who are present in the chat can see and respond to the messages as they appear on the screen. Chats are most effective with small groups of students rather than large numbers of individuals. Forums would be a better choice if a large number of students were involved in a discussion. Frequently used in online courses, chats are also common among computer users for socializing and meeting people on the Internet.

Some professors have found that students who are enrolled in asynchronous courses prefer not to have the virtual chat as part of the pedagogy used. This is in part because students who choose a web-based or asynchronous course do so for the flexibility it offers. Chats tend to constrain that flexibility and require the online presence of students in the course at a scheduled time (Carr, 2000a). However, for courses that are computer-enhanced, a virtual chat may work very well.

Virtual Chat Vignette. Dr. Anthony's graduate-level Introduction to Counseling Techniques course has an enrollment of 20 individuals. In the past, she has taught the course in a traditional face-to-face setting; however, because of the number of students who live away from campus, she has been asked to teach the course online. Given the nature of the course, Dr. Anthony has found it necessary to use some synchronous methods for groupwork. That is, five groups of four students are required to participate in two virtual chats a week. During these chats, students complete exercises in group counseling. They take turns serving as the facilitator of the group. An assignment Dr. Anthony uses in her face-to-face classes concerns problem solving. She develops scenarios in which patients have come to the counseling center for help. The patients present symptoms of depression or other clinical disorders, and students must discuss how to deal with these patients. Each group is given a different scenario to discuss and solve. "Asking [20] students to respond individually to one scenario or topic . . . may result in thoughtful responses from the first three responders and 'I think so, too' from the remaining [17]" (Pierce, 2000, p. 21). Each group will make a summary presentation of their project to the rest of the class using an online forum. Presenting provocative problems and asking students to discuss approaches they would use to assist patients in dealing with their disorders, using a virtual chat, works equally well online and in the traditional classroom setting.

During the course, students will have some flexibility in the times they schedule their own group's chats. Most groups are finding that evening chats are most convenient, and at the beginning of the semester they set up the times at which they will meet. Dr. Anthony may be present for the chats or she may opt to review the content of each virtual chat at a time other than when groups are scheduled. Either way, all chat discussions are archived and remain part of a permanent record for the course so they can be reviewed later. One important thing Dr. Anthony considers is that, if students have a question about the content of an assigned chat, she must be available to clarify anything that needs clarification or students will end up spending important time trying to figure out what exactly Dr. Anthony meant. A phone number or information about where she may be reached when the chat is scheduled is important information for students to have.

TALKING ABOUT . . . GENERAL DISTANCE EDUCATION PEDAGOGY

Many technologies are used in both synchronous and asynchronous courses and programs. The pedagogy presented in this section is applicable to both delivery modes.

Audio Bridge

This specialized equipment interconnects three or more telephone lines to enable conference calls. The bridge is usually operator assisted, and the equipment most often is provided by companies specializing in bridge services. Students may opt to use this medium as a way to conduct groupwork with their peers. A faculty member might want to use an audio bridge to have a real-time discussion with students who are enrolled in an online course.

Browser

A browser is a software package that interprets HTML or XML code to produce World Wide Web graphics, animation, and sound on a computer. Browsers such as Netscape® and Internet Explorer® are used both for World Wide Web content and for university or corporate intranet content.

Computer Conferencing

An ongoing computer conversation with others in different locations, using text, is known as computer conferencing. It can be done synchronously, so that messages appear as they are being keyed, or it can be done asynchronously, where messages are keyed and stored for later use by the receiver or sender.

Electronic Mail

Also known as e-mail, electronic mail is a fast, easy, and inexpensive way to communicate with individuals or groups on networked computers and computers equipped for Internet access. Besides basic correspondence, most systems allow the user to send attachments and files to others.

Electronic Medium

Electronic media include all technologies used in distance education. The World Wide Web, computer conferencing, listservs, and e-mail are examples of electronic media. Electronic media are used for communication as well as for the distribution of class handouts, notes, and other instructional materials. They are used for communication among participants in distance education courses, as well as for completing assignments and activities for these courses.

Full-Motion Video

Full-motion video is a standard video signal that can be transmitted by a variety of means, including television broadcast, microwave, fiber optics, and satellite. Compressed video enables full-motion signals to be stored and transmitted more economically than does full-motion video.

HTML

HyperText Markup Language (HTML) is a code in which World Wide Web pages and interactive CDs are written. It has some of the characteristics of printed matter and also links to other web pages. It does have some shortcomings, one of which is that it is difficult for most faculty to use because of the technological sophistication it requires as well as the time-intensive nature of the task.

Hyperlinks

Hyperlinks are URLs or e-mail addresses with built-in programming that takes the user to the site when its address is clicked. Hyperlinks usually appear as underlined text in web pages, but also may consist of icons or image maps.

Images

Prints, charts, tables, illustrations, and other still pictures that are reproduced using digital technology are referred to collectively as images. Formats such as Graphics Interchange Format (GIF) or Joint Photographic Expert Group (JPEG) are used because of their compatibility with the Web. Faculty use images to visually enhance the content of a course; however, because downloading images requires a high-speed Internet connection and a Pentium-class computer, faculty should use them judiciously to avoid creating a problem for students whose access may be limited. Some web sites allow students to request a text-only version of the content by clicking on a "text only" icon.

Internet

The Internet is a worldwide network of computer networks. It is an interconnection of large and small networks around the globe. The Internet began in 1962 as a computer network for the U.S. military and over time has grown into a global communication tool of many thousands of computer networks that share a common addressing scheme.

Internet2

Internet2 is a consortium that includes more than 180 universities interested in establishing high-speed networks and in creating research and education applications for those networks to run. Occasionally, it hosts musical exchanges that could become commonplace on the public Internet by 2003 to 2005. By then, the commercial Internet is expected to be as fast as today's Internet2 networks, which are used only for research and education (Olsen, 2001).

Instructional Multimedia

This term describes computer-based training that incorporates a mix of media. Media elements often include sound, animation, graphics, video, and text.

Listservs

Listservs are asynchronous. Using e-mail, anyone who subscribes to a particular listserv can participate in discussions about topics of interest around which the listserv is developed. When individuals subscribe to the listserv, they become part of a mailing list. When anyone on the mailing list contributes to the listserv in the form of an e-mail, the content of the e-mail is automatically sent to all subscribers. Participating in a computer conference is similar to participating in a listserv, except that the former may be either synchronous or asynchronous.

MOOs

Multiple-user Object-Oriented environments (MOOs) are online meeting places. Consisting of online communication systems and graphic interfaces, they make ideal distance education classrooms (Young, 2000c). These vehicles for communication made their debut in the 1970s when kids played a fantasy game online called Dungeons and Dragons. Adapted for education, faculty have continued to use MOOs for instruction and discussion online. Differing from the virtual chat, MOOs consist of many chat rooms where students can visit and interact. Still images and video clips often are incorporated in the discussions. Movement from one room to another is accomplished by clicking on icons. Pictures used in these discussions enhance what otherwise might be more mundane.

MOOs were developed by two faculty members at the University of Texas at Dallas. They wanted to create an online meeting place where their students could interact. "At its best, . . . the software can provoke discussions that are richer than traditional class sessions. It [is more like] the intense late-night coffeehouse intellectual discussion [about which most faculty fantasize]" (Young, 2000c). A MOO system, *enCore Xpress* "is distributed free of charge online, provided that users agree to share any improvements they make to it" (Young, 2000c).

PDF

Portable Document Format (PDF), by Adobe, looks like printed matter. It is used on the Web to deliver text and graphics. To use PDF, one must download the Adobe Acrobat Reader plug-in.

PowerPoint

Often used for conference presentations, lectures or demonstrations, PowerPoint is a Microsoft® software package. Faculty can save PowerPoint presentations on the Web, and they can be downloaded by students or others using a web browser.

Print Medium

Print is the foundational element of distance education programs and the basis from which all the other delivery modes have evolved. Print formats include textbooks, study guides, workbooks, course syllabi, case studies, tests, and other resources.

Teleconference

A teleconference is a simultaneous conference to multiple sites distributed via audio (phone or other audio). Satellite videoconferences and videoconferences using compressed video sometimes are referred to as "teleconferences." A foreign language professor may want to use the teleconference to engage students in a conversation using the foreign language. This allows the professor to test students' pronunciation and conversational skills (Young, 2000a). To facilitate this medium, institutions must offer toll-free numbers so that student expense will be minimized.

World Wide Web

Loosely used, the WWW (or Web) refers to the whole constellation of resources that can be accessed using gopher, FTP, HTTP, Telnet, Usenet, WAIS, and other tools. The WWW is a hypertext-based, distributed information system originally created by researchers at CERN, the European Laboratory for Particle Physics, to facilitate sharing research information. The Web presents the user with documents, called web pages, full of links to other documents or information systems. Selecting one of these links, the user can access more information about a particular topic. Web pages include text as well as multimedia (images, video, animation, and sound). Servers are connected to the Internet to allow users to traverse, or surf, as it is called, the Web using a web browser.

TALKING ABOUT . . . COURSE MANAGEMENT SYSTEMS

Putting a course online and managing the related activities has been made easy with the recent development of course management systems. Improvements and upgrades have made newer versions of these systems easier to use, and time and experience have proven to be the elements that have put them into nearly every distance learning enterprise. Two of the most frequently used courseware packages in American universities and colleges are WebCT and Blackboard. However, there are numerous other packages that are being adopted by institutions.

Because of the numerous available choices, users are faced with choosing the one that best suits their needs. Some institutions have integrated several courseware packages into their distance delivery systems, while others have adopted only one. Different packages offer different features, and it is up to those who will use the courseware packages to select the one or ones that work best for their courses. One of the most important features to consider is the ease with which the package may be used, both by faculty and by students. One should be able to navigate a course using the familiar point and click feature. Aesthetics play an important part in the desirability of a courseware package as well. Do the graphics and format allow faculty to create a course and instructions that reflect their own style? And, are there provisions for assessment, evaluation, and student support? Is the programming language appropriate for applications such as chat rooms, forums, e-mail, transfer of audio files, and the administration of quizzes and exams? Courseware reliability and speed are two other factors to consider when choosing a package to use.

Because of the many systems that are available, it would be impossible for an individual or institution to research, consider, and compare all the features of a system before selecting the right one. A web tool with which to compare online educational delivery applications is available for exactly that purpose. Developed and designed by the project team of Bruce Landon, Ph.D., of Douglas College, British Columbia, the site, www.edutools.info, helps educators evaluate and select online delivery software. Once at the site (Figure 6.1), click on "Compare Products," then on "Compare all products by all features" and a comparison grid will appear.

The project team includes Landon, Randy Bruce of Kwantlen University College, and Amanda Harby of the Centre for Curriculum Transfer and Technology. The analysis describes and compares the following applications:

- Technical specifications
- Instructional design values
- Tools and features
- Ease of use and accessibility
- Potential for collaboration
- IMS metadata standards compliance

In this section, WebCT and Blackboard will be highlighted. Using Landon's comparative tool, a comparison of five online course software packages also will be presented. Landon and his team provide a comprehensive table that compares all features, tools, and technical information of the software and applications they review. To view the table, the reader may go to the web site noted and follow the links as described above. It is worth the trip!

WEBCT

What Is WebCT?

WebCT is an integrated learning environment that is used by over 1,500 colleges and universities worldwide. WebCT is more than just a course tool used to facilitate distance learning. It is a flexible, integrated environment where students can combine course experiences with the real-world communities of work and play. The environment is composed of a number of elements that will help the student be successful in both current coursework and lifelong learning opportunities. The elements of the integrated learning environment include:

- The WebCT course platform—The platform is the interface in which faculty create and present courses to students. The platform includes many educational tools to assist students in communicating and collaborating with fellow students and faculty, and enhancing the learning experience.
- My WebCT—In version 3.0 and higher, all students are provided with a front page that will list all their WebCT courses, links to the e-Learning Hub, and links to academic support resources.
- e-packs—All the major college textbook publishers have created textbooks and supplemental material that is integrated into the course platform. If students are taking a WebCT course with pub-

Figure 6.1. A Web Tool for Comparative Analysis of Online Courseware

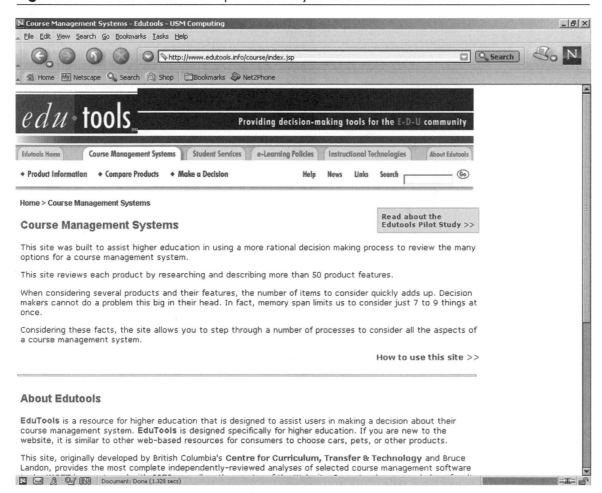

Reprinted with permission from Bruce Landon, Ph.D. Web site: www.edutools.info/course/index.jsp

lisher content, they will need to purchase an access code, just as they would purchase the textbook.

- The e-learning hub (Figure 6.2) is the place where students can find all kinds of people, ideas, and tools to make life as a student easier and their studies more interesting. This is where students can touch resources located in all the places that hold information—teachers, classes, departments, campuses, and the worldwide learning community—and use them for the course.

How Does WebCT Work?

WebCT provides step-by-step instructions to students on how to get started and how to navigate through the software for a course being taught using WebCT. Explanations about such things as access codes and solutions to commonly encountered problems also are provided.

The WebCT e-learning hub provides students with tools and human resources to enhance their learning experience. The e-learning hub fosters in-

Figure 6.2. WebCT Course Management System e-Learning Hub

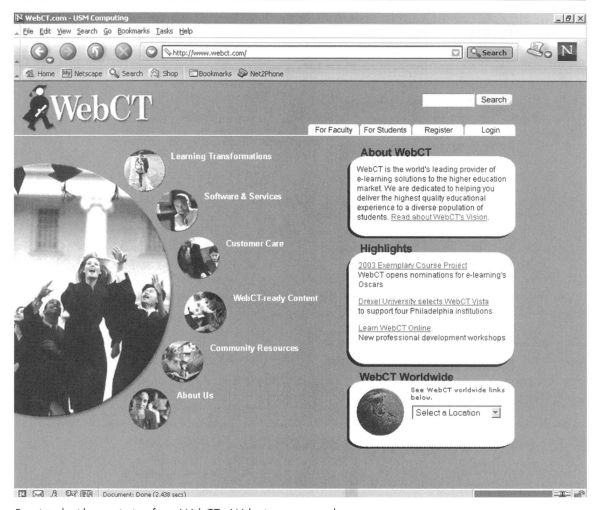

Reprinted with permission from WebCT. Web site: www.webct.com

quiry, encourages discourse, facilitates collaboration, and spurs active learning. The boundaries of the classroom are expanded so that students can:

- Explore content provided by WebCT partners and contributed by community members
- Connect with others through discussions and debate
- Create connections to the career marketplace
- Learn to be a successful distance learner and find out how to use the resources of the Internet for academically associated pursuits

- Explore communities related to academic interests
- Become a member of the community to fully utilize the hub's resources
- Receive learning support through question and answer services
- Enjoy a more satisfying learning experience through enhanced interactions with faculty and fellow students

The e-learning hub also can be used with courses that do not use WebCT for course delivery. Some of the features available include a student resource center in which career services, financial aid, and academic support are offered. In addition to academic resources, the WebCT e-learning hub offers many nonacademic resources. A career center provides guidance in writing a resume and cover letter, and it allows students to conduct a job search and learn interviewing skills. Information about opportunities for study or work abroad, as well as how to decide whether graduate study is the right choice, are part of the e-learning hub.

WebCT student resources include tips on how to study effectively, guides to better writing and Internet research, and information about how to be a successful online learner. Students actually may earn an entire degree online using WebCT. In fact, WebCT's online course management system is being used by the colleges and universities governed by the Tennessee Board of Regents. Students are able to take classes and earn their degrees online through any of the 19 institutions in the Tennessee system (Ludwig, 2001).

WebCT has many resources for students, similar to what would be found on a university campus. There is academic support that includes a writing center, a research center, and a study skills center. An online student orientation provides students with guidance on how to use the online course tools and how to be a successful student, and library resources that are specifically related to being an online student. There is extensive information about how to use the tools that are available through WebCT and a student resource center where students can ask questions.

WebCT is full-range software that provides resources not only for students, but also for faculty and administrators. Faculty resources include information about assessment and evaluation, communication and collaboration, content and course management, and pedagogy and how to use it to complement the faculty member's teaching style. There are resources that faculty can use to plan their course, including discussions about the advantages and disadvantages of putting a course online. Appendix J, "WebCT Tools and the Good Teaching Principles They Support," provides a look at each WebCT tool, examples of how it is used, which of the Principles of Good Practice (Chickering & Gamson, 1987) the tool facilitates, and the learning styles that it enhances. Other resources include Internet and computer survival basics, WebCT user

case studies, and current research articles on the use of WebCT.

WebCT resources to aid both the teacher and the learner include:

- Getting started with WebCT
- Campus success stories
- User guides and instructional documentation
- Online teaching and learning resources
- How to obtain training
- The WebCT exchange and workbench
- Academic support on the Web
- Effective online learning
- How to use WebCT
- Information about the technological aspects of WebCT
- Academic e-learning communities
- How to ask questions about online teaching and learning using WebCT

WebCT provides user guides and instructional documentation, with tutorials for both faculty and designers. Also available and downloadable are student handouts that explain basic concepts such as e-learning and how to log on to a WebCT course. For faculty there are also newsletters, training modules, and a calendar of training events offered by WebCT. WebCT eXchange provides faculty tools with which to create quizzes, in addition to showcasing courses of all kinds so they can see and share ideas about what makes a good WebCT course.

Information is provided about how to keep the server running in an efficient and reliable way. Administrators may use WebCT to view resources applicable to the administration of an institution and course delivery. Examples of exemplary institutions using WebCT offer a look at how these institutions have implemented the software from an administrative as well as a pedagogical viewpoint. Interface information is provided, and products to be released in future years are presented. WebCT also has a question center where Dr. C (Figure 6.3) answers queries regarding anything not already explained on the web site.

Academic e-learning communities are highlighted in many disciplines, including arts and media, business, computer science, education, engineering, English, hospitality, humanities, journalism, library science, medicine, sciences, social sciences, and world

Figure 6.3. WebCT Course Management System Ask Dr. C

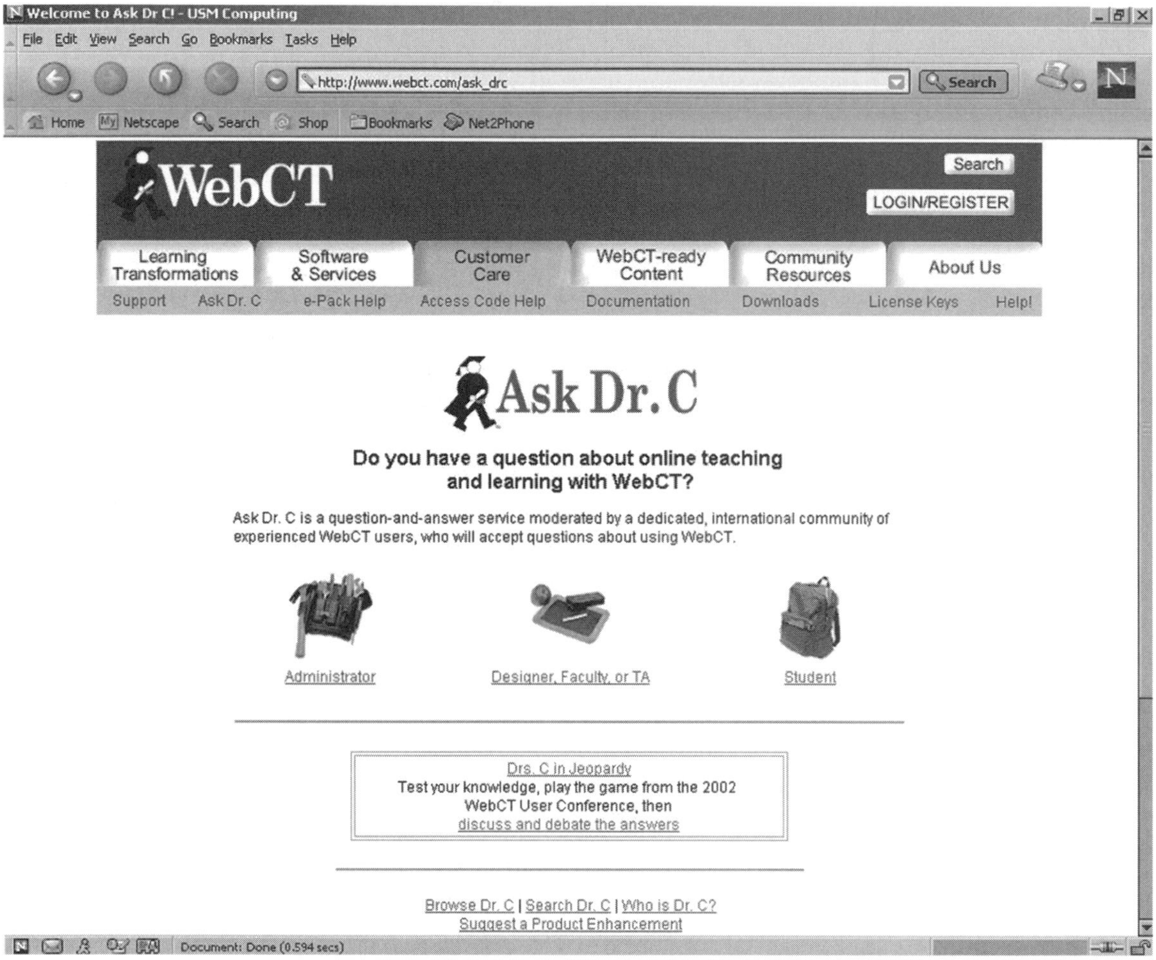

Reprinted with permission from WebCT. Web site: www.webct.com

languages. In addition, there is a faculty resource center, a student resource center, a tutoring network, and professional associations and service groups (i.e., National Foreign Language Center, Teaching, Learning and Technology Group, and National Association of Student Personnel Administrators). More information about WebCT is available at www.webct.com. (Information about WebCT modified and reprinted with permission from www.webct.com).

BLACKBOARD LEARNING SYSTEM

What Is Blackboard Learning System?

Blackboard Learning System* is the comprehensive and flexible e-learning software platform developed for educators to enhance their teaching and learning environments through the use of the

*Information courtesy of Blackboard, Inc. and the University of Maine University College, www.blackboard.com and www.learn.maine.edu. (Reprinted with permission. More information about Blackboard is available on their web site.)

Internet. While bringing courses online is still one of the most critical components of the e-learning system, many institutions also recognize that the Internet can do much more for their academic programs and communities. Blackboard Learning System is the first platform in the academic market to deliver a course management system (Figure 6.4), customizable institution-wide portals, online communities, and an advanced architecture that allows for web-based integration with multiple administrative systems.

Blackboard Learning System allows institutions, faculty, and students to:

- Access academic, personal, and social content through the institutional portal
- Deliver course materials and learning via the Internet
- Create effective academic and social communities
- Increase their access to relevant educational content
- Provide educational information services
- Reach a broader base of students, alumni, and communities

Institutions around the world use Blackboard to supplement traditional classroom learning and deliver quality distance learning.

Figure 6.4. Blackboard Course Management System

Reprinted with permission from Blackboard Inc. Web site: www.blackboard.com

Built from the ground up for education, Blackboard Learning System has evolved from the course management system originally developed in conjunction with faculty members at Cornell University. The platform has been refined through 3 years of continual innovation and feedback from its user base. As of June 2000, Blackboard's software products and web services reached more than 3,300 colleges, universities, K–12 schools, and other organizations in every U.S. state and more than 100 countries.

How Does Blackboard Work?

Blackboard operates using either Netscape or Internet Explorer. The browser must accommodate both JavaScript and Java. Students can download a free copy of Netscape for use on home computers from the Netscape site (http://www.netscape.com).

Students who do not have a home computer will find access in their institution's computer center or at public libraries that have a web connection. To access the course, a student must have a University e-mail account. This is usually set up automatically after the student registers for the course in which Blackboard is used. Technology support is offered for anyone who encounters a problem logging on to the system. Once the course begins and after logging into the site, students will find a menu, which will allow them to navigate the course (Figure 6.5).

Clicking on the "course" tab takes students to a menu (see Figure 6.6) which includes "announcements," where updates, reminders, and other such messages are found. Both current-day and previous messages may be posted throughout the duration of the course. "Course information" displays information typically found in the syllabus, such as homework

Figure 6.5. Blackboard Course Announcements

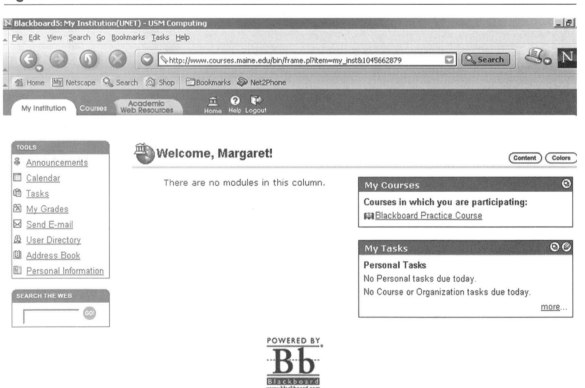

Reprinted with permission from the University of Maine University College.
Web site: http://www.courses.maine.edu

assignments, required readings, labs, projects, and lectures. "Staff information" includes information about the instructor and other course staff, including e-mail addresses, telephone numbers, office hours, and personal biographies. The "course documents" area is used to hold the majority of information that will be delivered online, including all relevant documents like course outlines, handouts, lecture materials, and related readings. Daily and weekly assignments are posted in the "assignments" area and may contain links to tests, quizzes, and surveys. The "communica-tion" area is where the communication tools are found. These may include discussion boards, virtual chats, group pages, rosters, and e-mail tools, depending on what the instructor chooses to use. An "external links" or "resources" or "web sites" icon is where students find the URLs their instructor has posted to assist them in accessing web resources. And, finally, "student tools" include such things as a digital drop box used to submit assignments to the instructor, a course calendar, a grade book where students may view their grades, an "edit home page" feature, a

Figure 6.6. Blackboard Practice Course Welcome Screen

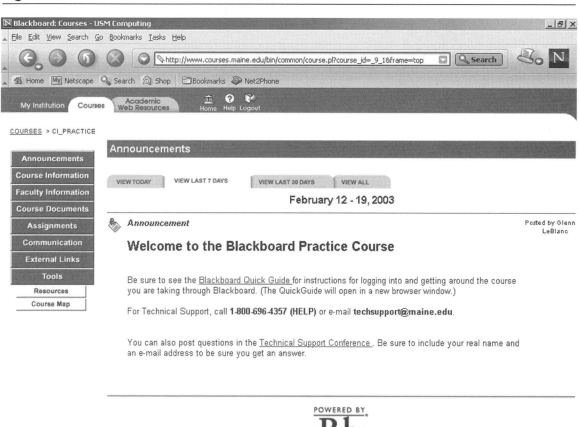

"change password" function, and an "enter or change your e-mail address." By clicking on these icons, students are able to navigate freely around the course. Information about how to view and download course materials, use the discussion board, check and send e-mails, and use the drop box to submit assignments is provided online within the course site.

Many faculty like to assign project work to small groups of students. To join a project group, students may click on "communication," then "group pages," then the group in which they are planning to work. Once in, they will be able to use a number of communication tools whose access is limited to members of the group.

Instructions about how to access quizzes, tests, and surveys are located in the course site as well. Once a student opens a quiz, he or she must complete it in that session and submit it or the student will be locked out and will have to contact the instructor for access again.

A "practice course" is available to help students learn about the features of Blackboard (Figure 6.7). Students may access the practice course by going to their university's web site and logging in. An example of a practice course may be found at http://www.courses.maine.edu. Students may log in as either of the following students:

Username: James.Sawyer   or   Margaret.Jones
Password: student   student

From this site, students will be able to practice entering various links and have a chance to learn how to maneuver around the practice course before the actual course begins (Figure 6.6).

A visit to "faculty information" yields a screen (Figure 6.8) in which the instructor's name appears along with his or her e-mail address, work phone number, office location, and other information. There also may be a photo of the instructor, as well as any introductory comments he or she wishes to post.

Students will find all resources needed for the course under "Course Documents" (Figure 6.9), including course activities, web pages, word processing documents, and other course materials. Technical assistance is available by contacting a campus help

Figure 6.7. Blackboard Practice Course Login

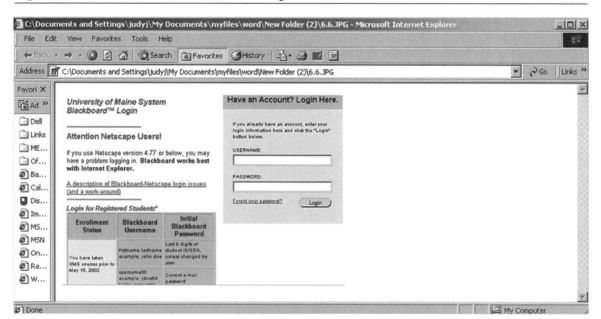

Reprinted with permission from the University of Maine, University College and Blackboard Inc. Web sites: http://www.courses.maine.edu and http://www.blackboard.com

desk or e-mailing the technical support person designated by the campus.

The "Academic Web Resources" link provides direct access to Blackboard's academic web resource, where students and instructors can find academic resources and content. Since it is context-sensitive to the course discipline, material is more relevant and effective for the purposes of the instructor and students. For example, accounting course academic web resources would link to news and information sources that are relevant to accounting. There is access to news, web links, reference works, and search engines that enhance one's ability to locate relevant information quickly.

Blackboard also provides systems administrators with complete access to all features, giving them customization and additional functionality. They can manage all portal functions and customization, course and organizational creation and management, institution and system tools, e-commerce features, user management, and institutional options from one location.

A COMPARISON OF FIVE COURSEWARE PRODUCTS

A comparison of WebCT, Blackboard, FirstClass, QuestionMark, and Prometheus is presented in

Figure 6.8. Faculty Information Screen

Reprinted with permission from the University of Maine System. Web site: www.courses.maine.edu

Figure 6.9. Course Documents for a Web Course

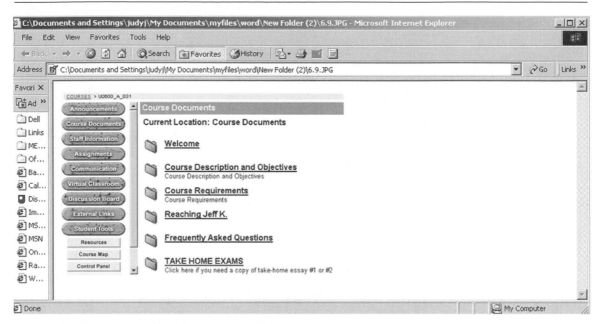

Reprinted with permission from the University of Maine System. Web site: www.courses.maine.edu

Figure 6.10, using the Landon online comparative tool. The online tool compares all possible applications of delivery software packages. While Figure 6.10 displays many of the applications available for comparison, the online tool includes many more applications. The reader may want to investigate other software and/or other applications by visiting the web site, www.edutools.info, which has more than 50 applications to choose from. It is a great way to get a sense of what courseware systems will work best for an instructor's institution and courses.

Figure 6.10. Sample Comparison of Five Online Delivery Software Packages

Applications	WebCT	Blackboard	FirstClass	QuestionMark	Prometheus
Accessibility	•	•	•		•
Bookmarks	•	•	•	•	
Multimedia	•	•	•	•	•
Security	•	•	•	•	•
E-mail	•	•	•		•
Newsgroups	•	•	•		•
Chat	•	•	•		•
Voice Chat	•	•			•
Whiteboard	•	•			•
Application Sharing	•	•			
Virtual Space		•	•		
Group Browsing		•			•
Self-Assessing	•	•	•	•	•
Progress Tracking	•	•	•	•	•
Searching	•	•	•		•
Motivation Building	•	•	•		•
Study Skill Building	•	•			
Course Planning	•	•	•		•
Course Managing		•	•	•	•
Course Customizing		•	•	•	•
Course Monitoring	•	•	•	•	•
Instructional Designing	•	•			•
Presenting Information	•	•	•	•	•
Testing	•	•	•	•	•
Marking Online	•	•	•	•	•
Managing Records	•	•	•	•	•
Analyzing and Tracking		•		•	
Curriculum Managing		•			•
Building Knowledge	•	•	•	•	•
Team Building	•	•	•		•
Building Motivation		•			•
Installation	•	•	•	•	•
Authorization	•	•	•	•	•

Applications	WebCT	Blackboard	FirstClass	QuestionMark	Prometheus
Registering	•	•	•	•	•
Online Fees Handling		•			
Server Security	•	•	•	•	•
Resource Monitoring	•	•	•		
Remote Access	•	•	•	•	
Crash Recovery	•	•	•	•	
Student Support	•	•	•		•
Instructor Support	•	•	•	•	•
Apple Server			•		
Unix Server	•	•	•		•
Technical Support	•	•	•	•	•
Number of Courses	•	•			•
Number of Students	•	•		•	•
Number of Connections	•	•			•
Number of Instructors	•	•		•	•
Other Limitations	•	•	•		•
Options	•	•	•	•	•
Exit Considerations					•

(Adapted with permission from Bruce Landon, Ph.D., et al. from www.edutools.info)

CHAPTER 7

Case Studies in Distance Education

Courses that once used a classroom lecture model have been changed into courses that offer short lectures with interactive texts, video, access to experts around the world, and an active learning and problem-solving approach.

Today the World Wide Web is the most popular medium used in teaching (Hazari & Schnorr, 1999). Consider the benefits of interacting with the web environment. Web interactivity can help engage students in active application of knowledge, principles, and values, and provide them with meaningful feedback. Web interactivity can foster greater participation by users.

Four case studies are presented in this chapter. These case studies are real-life illustrations of how distance education is working. Case Study 1 details a web-based introductory counseling course taught by Dr. Miriam Luebke at Concordia University, St. Paul, Minnesota. Dr. Luebke's course uses a module format. Case Study 2 describes a course, law and the Internet, taught over the Internet by Dr. Patrick Wiseman, a law professor at the Georgia State University College of Law. Unlike most other professors, Dr. Wiseman designs all his own software for his online courses. Case Study 3 looks at a program rather than a course. The program, the Associate Fellowship in Integrative Medicine, resides at the University of Arizona, Tucson. Dr. Andrew Weil founded the program and Sue South directs it. The development and implementation of the program are presented. And, in Case Study 4, an interactive television course is described. The course is taught by a 25-year veteran of distance education, Dr. Jon Schlenker, who teaches at the University of Maine at Augusta.

CASE STUDY 1*
Course: Introduction to Counseling
Medium: Web-based/Internet
Instructor: Miriam Luebke, Psy.D., Associate Dean for Assessment, Counseling, and Academic Support
Institution: Concordia University, St. Paul, Minnesota

OVERVIEW AND DESCRIPTION OF INTRODUCTION TO COUNSELING

It is summer and Dr. Luebke is preparing her course, Introduction to Counseling, for the fall semester. She has taught this course a number of times in the past, but this time things will be different. She will be teaching the course using distance education technologies. The distance education courses at Concordia are set up in a cohort fashion. That is, students complete degrees within their major in a cohort, which is, according to the *Dictionary of Statistics and Methodology*, "a group of individuals having a statistical factor (usually age [or class membership]) in common" (Vogt, 1993, p. 38). At Concordia, a cohort is formed when there is a sufficient number of students to form a group, usually about 16. More than 16 students have registered for Dr. Luebke's course. She sends all registered students letters to notify them that they will be required to attend a 5-day orientation on campus. The orientation consists of training in computer technology, including practice using the bulletin boards, discussion forums, chat methodology, and other technical as-

---

*Text for this case study taken from an interview with Dr. Miriam Luebke, December 2000.

pects of the course. Students will meet their instructor and participate in activities that familiarize them with classmates. They will make a connection not only with the faculty and other students, but also with the institution itself. They will receive Concordia tee-shirts and mugs, and will be introduced to the university community. Dr. Luebke asks students to communicate to her any goals they have with respect to what they wish to achieve through taking this course and also how they see the course taking shape to meet their needs.

At the orientation, faculty who will be teaching distance education courses meet with students to give them a preview of the types of things they will be asked to do in the course (e. g., participation in chats and bulletin board activities). The distance education courses are 6 weeks in length, and are taught in an accelerated way, in a fixed order. Students take only one course at a time, 5 days a week for 6 weeks, then move to the next 6-week course. They do this together, as a cohort, throughout the entire program.

Approximately 2 weeks before the start of the course, Dr. Luebke e-mails the course syllabus to her students and provides them with an opportunity to ask questions they may have come up with since the orientation. Because the courses are designed to meet the needs of students who are professionals in the field, Dr. Luebke plans her course according to feedback she has received from students prior to the orientation. The input students provide her with either confirms what she has planned or may suggest an area of emphasis she has not anticipated. Students appreciate this opportunity to provide input on the content of the course and find that they are better served by the program because they have had an opportunity to provide input from the start.

Paying close attention to adult learner theory, Dr. Luebke feels that adult learners have a sense of their goals and the relevancy of their education to their working life (i.e., counseling practice) and to their prior knowledge. She designs her course accordingly. In fact, at Concordia, instructors are given lots of resources to help inform their course development and design of syllabi to incorporate many aspects of adult learning theory. One such resource, a web site in the School of Human Services, provides a wealth of information for faculty on everything from what an instructor needs to know to teach on the Web, to

tools and tips for teaching, technology guides, and resources on distance education.

Another resource is a template for a course syllabus. Using the template (see Figure 7.1), faculty can make their syllabi uniform and include all components that the program requires.

Dr. Luebke's course comprises weekly activities that include a chat that lasts 45 minutes to 1 hour, approximately six lectures, about 12 bulletin boards, a variety of readings including those from textbooks and other print materials, and assignments and papers. All students are required to participate. The weekly chat can be done in a number of ways, such as in small groups working on group projects, or, in the case of the counseling course, students might practice counseling techniques in small groups while the instructor observes. This tends to be rather awkward and is not a technique that is used very often. Students actually practice their counseling skills on the Web using synchronous chats. In reality, students are reading what other students are typing (i.e., they are listening with their eyes), and responding by typing. Dr. Luebke is quick to point out, however, that the course is aimed at teaching counselors basic human relation skills from which any educator would benefit. In addition to the chat, students participate in bulletin board activities/discussion forums. For example, using a bulletin board, students talk about their listening skills, how they have applied them, and what they see resulting from use of these skills.

Students participate in the chats and bulletin boards using computers that are located in their homes or offices, or at a central location where students may access the Internet using publicly available computers. It is typical for two or three questions to be posted on the bulletin board every week by the instructor, and students have a deadline as to when they are required to respond. Students' responses to the questions and to each other become a threaded discussion, although an asynchronous one. This sets the stage for a more thoughtful, reflective, and in-depth discussion. Unlike the face-to-face classroom where students do not have the time to reflect or think about their responses before answering, web-based format allows for well-thought-out responses and discussion. Also, in a classroom, more extroverted students tend to dominate the discussion, whereas in distance education courses (with the bulletin board), all students are required to

FIGURE 7.1. Suggested Course Syllabus Outline

TITLE OF COURSE AND COURSE NUMBER COHORT

Institutions may want to include their mission statement here.

INSTRUCTOR

Instructor's Name

Institution Name and Department
Phone Numbers
Email Address
Hours of Availability
Web: http://www.cshs.csp.edu
School of Human Services 651-641-8897

Communication

Assignments graded _____ often.
E-mail checked every _____ days.
Bulletin boards checked every _____ days.
Assignment turn-around time _____ days/week.
Instructor's office hours _____ days/time.

CATALOG COURSE DESCRIPTION

Insert the Catalog Course Description

INSTRUCTIONAL GOALS AND OBJECTIVES

List Goals and Objectives

STUDENT GOALS AND OBJECTIVES

The module is grounded in principles and practices of adult learning. The instructional model is to be collaborative, making use of student experiences to enrich and enliven class discussion. Knowledge will be constructed in the dialog between experience, reflection, and theory. Part of the class process will be a deliberate effort to incorporate student goals and objectives into the module. These include:

1.
2.
3.

CHAT ROOM EXPERIENCE

Insert times of the chat; describe any rules of the chat; Identify any code words or short cuts; some examples are listed below. Please double-check the chat times of your particular cohort, as each cohort is different.

1. Optional Chit Chat from 6:45 to 7:00

2. Cohort Chat from 7:00 to 7:20

3. Small Group Chat from 7:20 to 7:40

4. Closure from 7:40 to 7:45

5. Class will start with instructor asking if everyone is ready. Each student will respond with "*" (asterisk) to indicate readiness. The "*" (asterisk) will continue to be used as a readiness and question transition indicator.

6. Questions for each chat will be posted at the end of the lecture section of the instructor bulletin board.

7. Small Group Chat Time will be to focus on small group assignments rather than a weekly topic.

8. To close each week, the instructor will start a round robin sentence completion. The closure will have two sentences that relate to the topic and will allow students to respond with short-quick answers.

COURSE OUTLINE

Learning Activities for Week 1 (Insert dates)

This first week begins on the day after the final class of the previous module, and ends on the day of the first chat.

Read: What will they read this week? Web Lectures? Handouts? Texts?

Bulletin Board: What are the bulletin board questions they should read this week? Usually two or three a week is normal.

Chat Room: What will the topic of the chat room be?

Assignment: List each assignment due this week, and which day of the week it is due.

Learning Activities for Week 2 (Insert dates)

This week begins on the day after the first chat, and ends on the day of the second chat.

Read: What will they read this week? Web Lectures? Handouts? Texts?

Bulletin Board: What are the bulletin board questions they should read this week? Usually two or three a week is normal.

Chat Room: What will the topic of the chat room be?

Assignment: List each assignment due this week, and which day of the week it is due.

Learning Activities for Week 3 through 5

(The above format is repeated until Week 6.)

Learning Activities for Week 6 (Insert dates)

This week begins on the day after the fifth chat, and ends on the day of the sixth chat.

Read: What will they read this week? Web Lectures? Handouts? Texts?

Bulletin Board: What are the bulletin board questions they should read this week? Usually two or three a week is normal.

Chat Room: What will the topic of the chat room be?

Assignment: List each assignment due this week, and which day of the week it is due.

ASSIGNMENTS AND BASIS FOR STUDENT GRADING

List each assignment, with a very clear explanation of your expectations. Identify its due date. If you are grading on a point system, list the point value. List, with extreme clarity, how they can get the grade they want. Students should feel no ambiguity about your expectations. Identify the course objective(s) that are met by each assignment change.

IN-PROGRESS POLICY

Students who are unable to finish all of the required coursework for a course may request an In-progress (I) for the module. After discussion with the Instructor, students must fill out a REQUEST FOR IN-PROGRESS GRADE form before the last day of the course they are requesting the "I" grade for. A copy of this form can be downloaded from your cohort's homepage (on-campus students may get the form from the instructor). You should negotiate with your instructor a date that your coursework will be completed by. Include this date on your REQUEST FOR IN-PROGRESS GRADE form. This form is now considered a contract with the Instructor and Concordia University for the completion of your work. If you are unable to complete the work by the contracted date, it is your responsibility to contact the instructor and resubmit the request for an extension. If you are unable to finish the work by the contracted date and have not requested an extension, you will receive a grade for the module based on the work that you have completed.

REQUIRED TEXT

Insert the required textbook(s) for this course. Please use the APA format. Example:

Ollhoff, J., & Ollhoff, L. (1995). *School-age care from the perspective of social role theory.* Minneapolis, MN: Tundra Communications.

RECOMMENDED READING

Insert the recommended reading(s) for this course, including Web sites, sources of information, etc. This section can function as the bibliography of your teaching.

INSTRUCTIONAL PHILOSOPHY

Insert your educational philosophy.

KEYWORDS

Insert words that are useful for library database and Internet searching in your subject matter.

PRIMARY SOURCES OF INFORMATION IN THE FIELD

List the primary journals that inform your particular discipline. Identify the major thinkers, the organizations that are doing the best research, etc. Identify where the learners should go if they need the best, most recent, most cutting edge information in the field.

(Copyright © 1998 by the School of Human Services, Concordia University. Reprinted with permission.)

participate and have time to think about how they will respond, rather than responding off the cuff. By contrast, in the traditional classroom, one person may answer all the questions, and the instructor does not have any immediate way of knowing whether the other students are learning or what they are thinking. The tools of the Internet courses, such as discussion forums and bulletin boards, allow faculty to check who has participated in the discussion and whether students are doing the work. It becomes very clear if they haven't read the material. Due to the accelerated nature of this course, students must keep up on their readings and assignments or they will quickly fall behind. Where traditional college courses span a semester, students in this course focus on one course at a time during each 6-week period.

Once the course has begun, students log in at a designated time and participate in the 45-minute to hour-long online synchronous chat. Before the formal chat, students are given time to chitchat, allowing them to reconnect, ask each other how things are going and what is going on in their lives, and have other social-type interaction. Dr. Luebke may begin the discussion with a comment about what the focus of the discussion will be. That might include a case study students have been asked to review ahead of time or specific questions about which she has asked them to think. Generally, Dr. Luebke finds that students appreciate the structured chat topics. After the chat and during the week, students access lectures posted on the Web or, depending on the course, faculty may e-mail lectures to students. Usually each lecture consists of about two to three pages that provide the students with background information, references to other readings, and case studies they are required to read. Faculty also may ask students to read chapters from the textbook and journal articles. Students are assigned papers in which they are asked to incorporate what they have learned in the course into their own practices, or apply the principles of the readings to what they are doing at the worksite. Students are asked to reflect on these activities and respond to the reflection assignments outlined in the syllabus. Approximately halfway through the course, Dr. Luebke asks students to e-mail her their reflections on the following experiences:

1. where the concepts and new ideas they've encountered so far have helped them to grow intellectually
2. where they have applied counseling or listening skills at home or work
3. where they have been disengaged from the learning so far
4. in what specific areas they are growing and why

This activity allows the students to take stock of where they are and to assess how the learning fits with their goals for the course. While this activity allows valuable reflection for the students, it also provides the instructor with information about where students are struggling and how she might address the problem areas. Dr. Luebke refers to this as "critical incident." Defined as looking back on one's learning and reflecting on process and what has been learned, this activity is required three or four times during a 6-week course. In addition, the syllabus assigns various reflection exercises for students.

The culminating activity for the 6-week course is a portfolio, which includes a Course Synthesis Matrix (Appendix K) and assignments on which the students have been working during the 6 weeks. Once the portfolio is complete, the student and Dr. Luebke meet to discuss its contents, and the student is assigned a final grade.

Faculty teaching distance education courses are encouraged to use the course syllabus template so that all courses will have uniform syllabi. This minimizes confusion students may face, ensures that all required components of courses are covered, and makes it easier for faculty who are teaching multiple courses to set up their course requirements and activities. The template (see Figure 7.1) is found on the faculty resources web site.

Dr. Luebke's syllabus is fashioned using the syllabus template. An excerpt from her syllabus demonstrates how typical weekly activities are assigned (Figure 7.2).

PORTFOLIO EVALUATION

At the conclusion of each 6-week course, student portfolios are evaluated by faculty in collaboration with the individual students. An example of a format used by one faculty member (Ollhoff, 1998) at the institution is provided in Appendix L.

The course in which this is used is SAC495, Topics in School-Age Care. The portfolio is worth one-

Figure 7.2. Excerpts from SAC450 Syllabus

LEARNING ACTIVITIES FOR WEEK 1: AUGUST 9–AUGUST 15

Read: Nicholas, Chapters 1 through 9 and Epilogue

Lecture 1: Knowing Where Our "Buttons" Are

Bulletin Board #1: List what you understand to be Nicholas's communication concepts and barriers to effective listening. (If you make this list as you read the book, it will help you to organize the information, and will make writing the Bulletin Board easy.)

Bulletin Board #2: Discuss an interaction you had with a child or youth where you were dissatisfied with the outcome. Use Nicholas's concepts about listening to explore what might have gone wrong. What would you do differently next time?

E-mail Reflection 1: Student Goals

Chat Room: Strategies for more effective listening with children and youth

half of the student's total grade. The other half of the grade is based on a review by the student of whether each course objective was met and the evidence provided by the student to back up the claim. Using a 3-point rubric (1 = doesn't meet, 2 = meets, 3 = exceeds), an evaluation is conducted by the student and faculty. Once these two evaluations have been completed, the student is awarded the appropriate grade.

THE FACULTY WEB SITE

The School of Human Services at Concordia has created a "Faculty Center web site" that contains links to various information and resources for faculty (Figure 7.3). The site includes a tremendous amount of information, including what all instructors need to know to teach a distance education course, how to write a syllabus, tips and tools for teaching, technology guides, information about students in the cohorts and faculty teaching in the school, and resources on distance education. To visit

the web site, each faculty needs a password, issued by Concordia.

Samples of what may be found at various links on the web site are presented here. The first, "Principles for Teaching Excellence" (Appendix M), outlines "Seven Principles to Guide the Development and Direction of the Adult Education Programs. Each principle is expanded, with implications and ideas for teaching practice" (Ollhoff & Ollhoff, 1997, p. 1). Although these principles and other resources found at the Faculty Center may be relevant to traditionally taught courses, the web site and information contained there are designed specifically to be used by distance education instructors.

Another example of a link within the Faculty Center is a section entitled "Compliments and Complaints from Students." The top five compliments listed are:

1. Faculty communicated frequently and fully.
2. The responses were timely.
3. The instructor kept me informed and answered my questions in a timely manner.
4. The syllabus was clear.
5. Faculty were willing to be flexible on assignments.

The top five complaints are:

1. The instructor did not respond enough.
2. The instructor did not respond soon enough.
3. The chats were unfocused and unplanned.
4. The syllabus was unclear.
5. The instructor did not give enough feedback on student progress in the course.

Comments explaining each of the compliments and complaints accompany these two lists.

Communication is the key here. When it comes to distance education courses, faculty do not have the luxury of being able to see the student; thus, they cannot pick up on facial cues or body language. Because of this, everything needs to be communicated clearly in writing. Feedback is a must! And the feedback must be frequent. This is the only link students have to the faculty about their learning. The syllabus must be written in a way so that all students understand exactly what is expected and when. It is important to have a student or colleague who is not

Figure 7.3. Concordia University School of Human Services—Faculty Center

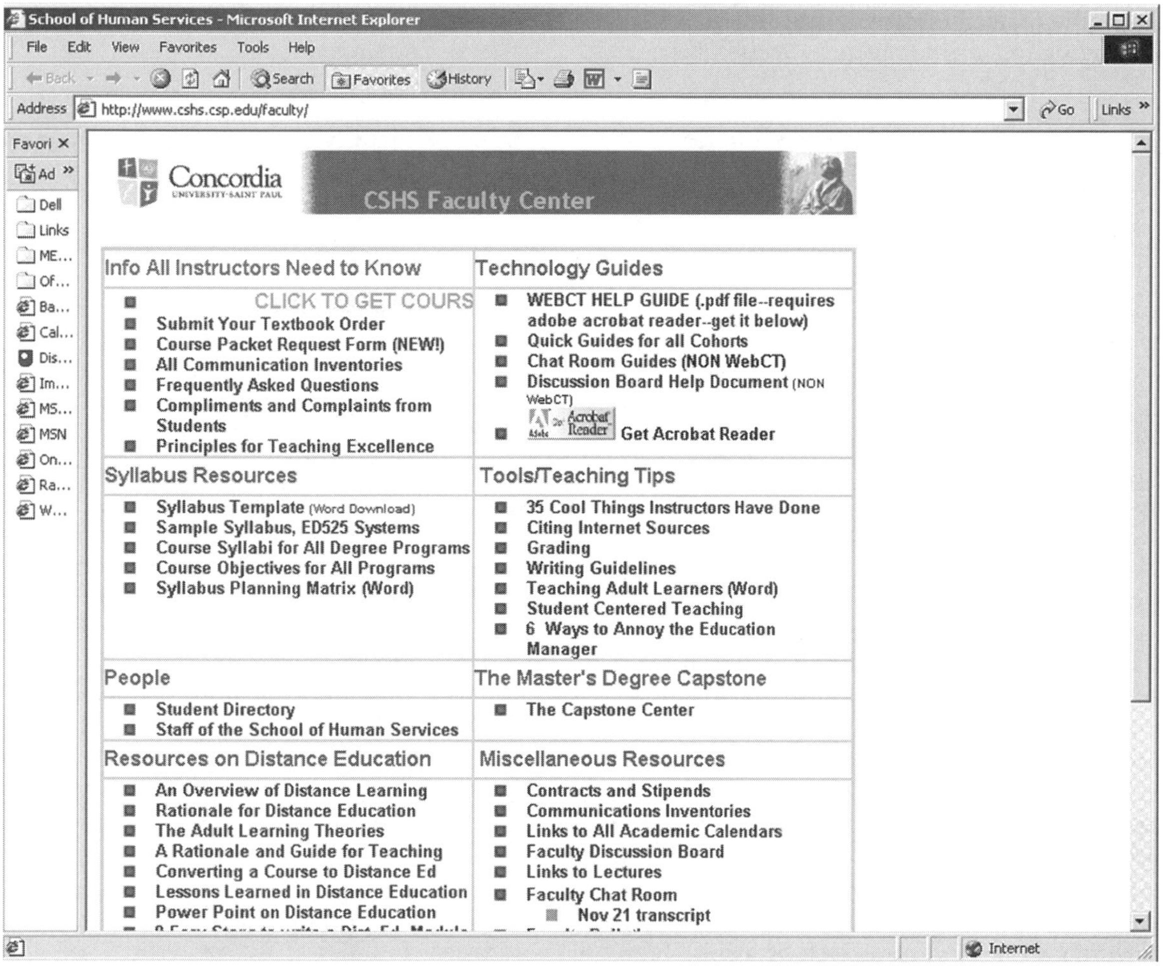

Reprinted with permission from Jim and Laurie Ollhoff. Web site: www.cshs.csp.edu

in the course read the syllabus and provide feedback about its clarity. Flexibility is also important, especially with adult students. Many adult students are working professionals and may have valuable suggestions about assignments. It is not always necessary to incorporate their suggestions into the course, but it is important to be open to them.

Communication with students doesn't always mean giving feedback on an assignment immediately. However, because distance education students often wonder whether their assignments have reached the instructor, it is important for faculty to

acknowledge receipt of materials students have sent. A short e-mail saying, "Got your assignment on counseling the child," or "Assignment on counseling the child has been received. Thank you," will provide the student with comfort and reassurance that his or her work has reached the instructor. Concordia suggests that near the end of the course, the instructor send a note to each student with an indication of how the student is doing grade-wise. This will allow the student to confirm that he or she agrees with the instructor's assessment. "It's not difficult to conduct a good class. If you communicate frequently and fully, if your syllabus is clear, and if you remember that you are dealing with adult students, always rich in experience and often shallow in confidence, you can have a successful class."

WHY THIS PROFESSOR LIKES TEACHING THIS WAY

Dr. Luebke describes herself as having an introverted, reserved style. She prefers one-on-one communication with her students. She also likes writing and the thoughtful process that goes along with that. Through the writing process and the back and forth writing with her students, she can see students' development in the words they write on the screen. Although she was a little nervous about the chat rooms and whether she would be able to participate quickly and follow the threaded discussions, she found that it was quite easy to do once she got the hang of it.

At Concordia, faculty retreats are set up twice a year so that faculty who are teaching in the distance education programs have an opportunity to sit down with other faculty and look at program goals, outcomes, and feedback from students, and share ideas about what worked well for them. Faculty also have opportunities to look at assessment as a topic and discuss what they have learned from their own assessments and what improvements may be made. This process provides a climate of continual improvement within the programs as well as a collegiality among faculty.

Dr. Luebke also senses a kind of excitement about learning within the distance education courses. Faculty and students are engaged with each other and with the materials, more so than in the traditional course. She feels that many faculty are skeptical about the extent to which faculty and students can become engaged over the Internet, but, as she stated in a December 2000 interview:

One only has to look at how many teenagers are in chat rooms every night for hours and hours. They are definitely engaged and connected with fellow human beings. I think we underestimate the power of words on the page to connect people. I have seen very powerful

learning take place without the face-to-face. By using the Internet as a communication tool and pulling it into a learning situation, the possibilities are unlimited.

WHAT ARE THE CHALLENGES AND WHAT ARE THE HIGHS?

The most positive part of teaching this type of course over the Internet for this faculty member is that she can see student learning right there on the screen. She can see how a class discussion evolves and arrives at a place where students are "getting it." There is a record of the learning. Second, she likes the opportunity for thoughtful and reflective discussions that the asynchronous format affords participants. Rather than blurting out answers to questions, which occurs mainly in a face-to-face situation, students have time to really think about what they want to say. And, as has been pointed out before, all students are involved, rather than just the outspoken ones.

Getting to know each student in the timeframe of the course is one of the challenges. Dr. Luebke finds that she has to make a special effort to engage all students so that this may be accomplished. Another challenge is keeping up with all the communication. Because of the demands of a course such as this, she is constantly responding to e-mails and writing comments on student work.

LESSONS LEARNED

Dr. Luebke shares the lessons she has learned from her experience teaching an Internet course. She has found that:

1. Planning is essential to the success of a course. You can't wing it in the distance mode. Students like to and need to know what the course will entail well ahead of time. Everything must be prepared before the start of the course. Projects, assignments, lectures, bulletin boards, reflections—everything—must be laid out before the course starts. Ideally this would happen in the traditional face-to-face course as well, but often it doesn't.

2. Good communication is a must. Faculty and students need to know how this will occur. Whether modeling good etiquette for e-mail or setting up guidelines and rules about when communication will be expected, everyone must have the same information and adhere to it as much as possible.

3. Know what expectations you have for students so you can clearly convey them to all who enroll in the course. For example, an expectation for the counseling course is that students use good writing and editing. Distance, especially Internet, courses help to build better writing skills. By practicing and seeing how others write, students often improve their own skills. The written word is different from the spoken word. In writing, individuals must be thoughtful and reflective about how they put things down, and that communication stands alone. There are no facial cues, verbal intonations, or body language to help interpret the communication.

4. Do everything possible to make students feel connected. The orientation program provides the foundation for connection. But when a student starts to fall behind or does not respond to assignments, it is important to pursue the student until you make contact and find out what is going on. Do not let students disappear without knowing why.

5. Stay up to date. As students can fall behind, so can faculty. It is important to be a faithful participant of the course in all aspects. Modeling this behavior is positive for students.

CASE STUDY 2*
Course: Law and the Internet
Medium: Web-based/Internet
Instructor: Patrick Wiseman, Ph.D., J.D., Professor of Law
Institution: Georgia State University College of Law, Atlanta, Georgia

OVERVIEW AND DESCRIPTION OF LAW AND THE INTERNET

Professor Wiseman has been teaching in the Georgia State University College of Law for over 15 years. For the past 6 years, he has taught a course entitled Law and the Internet. This 14-week, 3-credit-hour course has different content every semester and uses a constructivist model. That is, students direct and design the classes and content each semester. It is also similar to a seminar course (often used in other disciplines, especially philosophy and graduate education) in which students construct the content to some extent. Although this model is not typical of curriculum in law schools, Dr. Wiseman finds that it has great potential, especially in a course such as this.

Law and the Internet (see Figure 7.4) was conceived when Professor Wiseman, in his fascination with the Internet, decided that teaching a course using this tool and about this tool, would be an exciting and innovative way to get students to actively engage in the learning process and explore from a legal standpoint the current issues surrounding use of the Internet. The medium and the content were a natural combination.

Instructor preparation for the course is minimal. That is, Dr. Wiseman does not prepare lectures or class notes ahead of time because he does not know what the content of the course will be. Here is what happens.

During the first class of the semester, students are assigned the task of doing some preliminary research on the Internet to identify current issues directly linked to the Internet itself that they think are im-

*Text for this case study taken from an interview with Dr. Patrick Wiseman. Screen shots copyrighted by Dr. Wiseman are printed with permission. Web site: www.gsulaw.gsu.edu/pwiseman/home_pages/Law_Internet.

Figure 7.4. Welcome to Law and the Internet

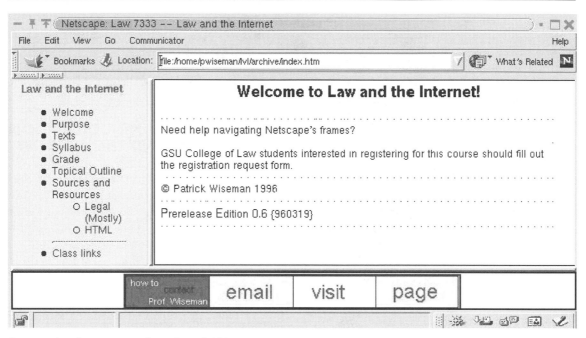

Reprinted with permission from Patrick Wiseman.

portant to address and that they would be interested in talking about during the semester. Because of the recent advent of the Internet and the nature of the law, many legal issues surrounding use of the Internet emerge everyday. Dr. Wiseman finds that this first assignment allows students to identify topics that are not only interesting and timely, but are challenging the law at its finest. Topics that have been used in the recent past include the 2001 Napster case, where two college students developed "music-sharing software" that enabled anyone with Internet access to download, at no cost to them, song recordings from produced and "for sale" CDs rather than buying the CDs or tapes at a retail store (see Alexander, Villaneuva, & Werner, 2001). Another topic that was explored during the summer of 2001 was the trademark disputes over domain names, where entrepreneurs use the names of famous or successful companies as their own to enhance the probability of their own success (see Isenberg, 2000). Still another topic explored during the course was Internet

adoptions, which was in the press during the summer of 2001. The exploration of this topic was spurred by the incident where British twins were put up for adoption over the Internet and subsequently "adopted" by two different families (see Dutrow & Wade, 2001). All cases mentioned here were happening during the period in which the course was being conducted.

Once topics have been identified, students participate in a synchronous online chat (Figure 7.5) during the second class session. During this time, the identified issues are thrown out and participants begin discussing the topics, not in a substantive way, but rather to rank those that are of most interest to them and to decide which topics they will spend time on during the semester. Once the topics have been chosen, Dr. Wiseman provides students with a schedule (Figure 7.6), and they tell him which of the topics they are going to be responsible for and how they will fit into the schedule. In the meantime, all students begin researching their own topics and doing

Figure 7.5. Chat Session

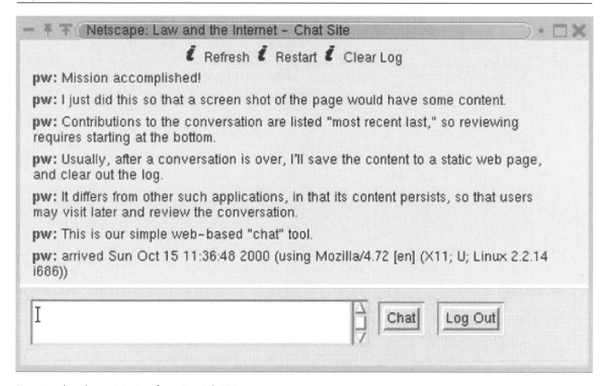

Reprinted with permission from Patrick Wiseman.

preliminary work on what will be their designated week's presentation. In addition, students complete assignments as laid out in the syllabus.

Each week, a different group of two or three students provides the substantive content for the topic at hand. This forms the basis for the weekly discussion. First the topic is researched, prepared, and loaded on the Internet. (See Appendix N for an example. The entire text is 26 single-spaced typed pages; therefore, only the introduction is presented for illustrative purposes.) The class then meets asynchronously to view the text the students have prepared. Based on this information, a discussion by the entire class ensues. This process continues throughout the rest of the semester, with a different group taking responsibility each week for one of the topics that the entire group decided on in the first class of the semester.

Evaluation of student performance is based on the professor's impression of the quality of student work throughout the course. A student's class participation in all forums, the forum statement (substantive contribution and responsibility for a topic), and a final paper and/or examination (Figure 7.7) form the basis of the grade each student is assigned. An underlying question in the evaluation of student work is, "Is the student merely expressing his opinion on a topic or is she bringing new legal information to bear?" In other words, are students behaving like lawyers or pundits? The goal, of course, is that they will behave like lawyers.

Students provide feedback to Professor Wiseman about the course throughout the semester using an online feedback form called "Continual Evaluation" (Figure 7.8). Using this feedback, he is able to adjust course assignments, if appropriate.

Additionally, at the end of the semester students complete an online evaluation of the course (Figure 7.9).

Figure 7.6. Fall 2000 Class Schedule

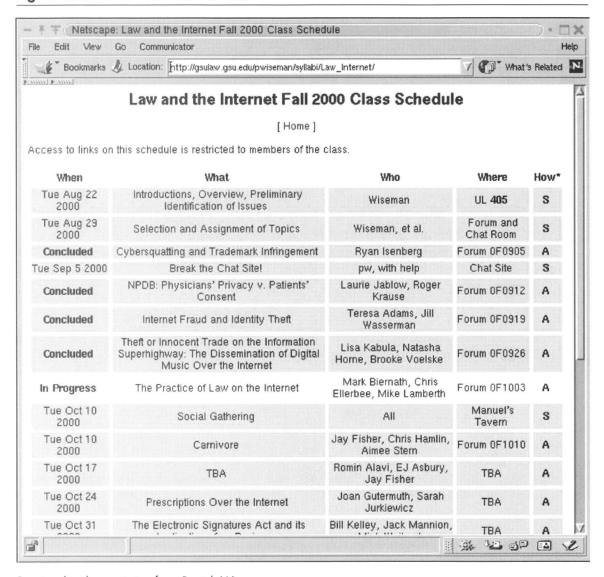

Reprinted with permission from Patrick Wiseman.

HOW DOES THIS COURSE DIFFER FROM FACE-TO-FACE COURSES DR. WISEMAN TEACHES?

1. The constructivist aspect is not always adhered to. There are courses Dr. Wiseman teaches in which he wouldn't even attempt a constructivist model. One such course is the first-year property course.

He feels that in the property course, there is a certain amount of subject matter that needs to be covered from the beginning of the semester to the end. And the information is pretty standard fare, unlike in the Law and the Internet course, where the information and topics are ever changing.

2. The exchange is different. In Law and the Internet, the professor does not participate much at all

Figure 7.7. Legislation Examination

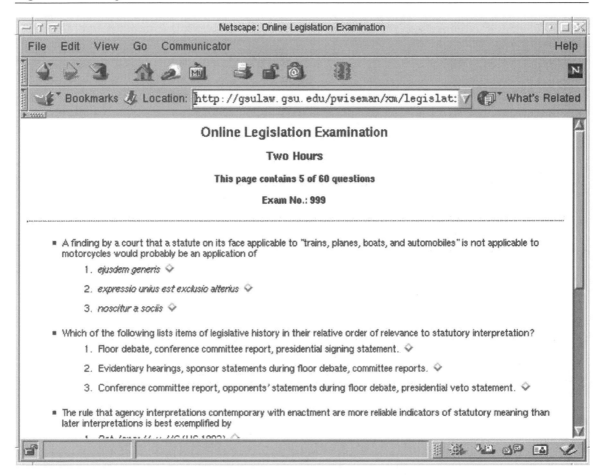

Reprinted with permission from Patrick Wiseman.

in the substantive exchange. The only time he might engage in the discussion is when he has a reaction to what is being said in the discussion by students, but this happens very infrequently. He deliberately keeps out of the discussion, for the most part, because sometimes students perceive the professor's opinion or remarks as the "right way to think about an issue," and Professor Wiseman wants to avoid that happening. Another time he might intervene is if the discussion has "gone off the rails in terms of the law." In this event, he will tell the students that they need to double-check their information. In his other courses, which are face-to-face, he is very much involved in the presentation and discussion of the material. He considers himself the "expert" in the face-to-face courses, and a "learner" in the online course.

3. Students have control in the online course with respect to content. The professor has control over content in the face-to-face courses.

4. The course evolves, rather than being preconceived.

5. Professor Wiseman does all his own programming for the course; from the web site to the links, including "under the hood" administration programs (see Figure 7.10) for his own use, he is his own instructional designer.

Figure 7.8. Online Feedback Form

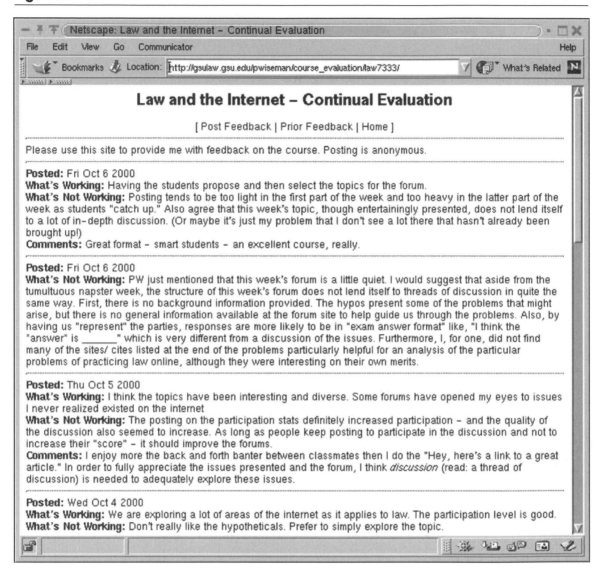

Reprinted with permission from Patrick Wiseman.

HOW ARE THE COURSES THE SAME?

1. All courses, whether face-to-face or distance, taught by Dr. Wiseman have distance education components—an online discussion forum and an online syllabus.
2. He uses a conversational style in all his courses.

Professor Wiseman's experience has made him feel as though he would like to incorporate into his face-to-face courses what he has learned in teaching the online courses. Some of the excitement he has experienced in the Law and the Internet course he has not experienced in his face-to-face courses. In the face-to-face courses, he finds that he has a tendency to convey too much information. In retrospect, he doesn't like that style of teaching and does not feel like he was engaging students with the materials as he should have been. In the Internet course, he finds that students are totally engaged in the material. They

Figure 7.9. End-of-Course Evaluation for Law and the Internet

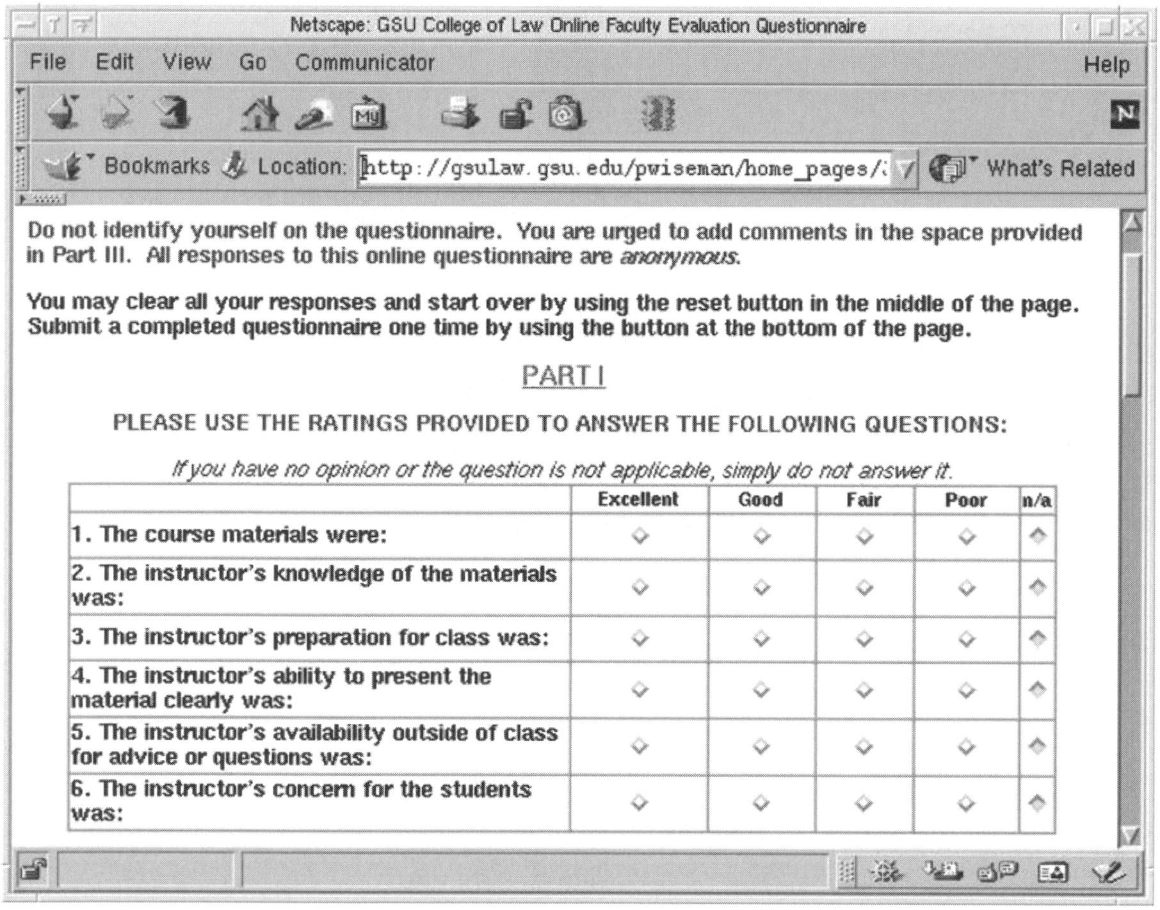

Do not identify yourself on the questionnaire. You are urged to add comments in the space provided in Part III. All responses to this online questionnaire are *anonymous.*

You may clear all your responses and start over by using the reset button in the middle of the page. Submit a completed questionnaire one time by using the button at the bottom of the page.

PART I

PLEASE USE THE RATINGS PROVIDED TO ANSWER THE FOLLOWING QUESTIONS:

If you have no opinion or the question is not applicable, simply do not answer it.

	Excellent	Good	Fair	Poor	n/a
1. The course materials were:	◇	◇	◇	◇	◆
2. The instructor's knowledge of the materials was:	◇	◇	◇	◇	◆
3. The instructor's preparation for class was:	◇	◇	◇	◇	◆
4. The instructor's ability to present the material clearly was:	◇	◇	◇	◇	◆
5. The instructor's availability outside of class for advice or questions was:	◇	◇	◇	◇	◆
6. The instructor's concern for the students was:	◇	◇	◇	◇	◆

Reprinted with permission from Patrick Wiseman.

are doing it all. With the experience he has had with the Internet course, he has made a deliberate attempt to change his teaching style in the face-to-face courses to try to engage students in the learning by making classes more conversational.

WHAT ARE THE CHALLENGES AND WHAT ARE THE HIGHS?

Challenges faced by Professor Wiseman include getting students to engage the material using e-mail. Early on, students were not very technically proficient, so they needed instruction about how to use the technology and how to write html. Now, he says, students are totally inept; they write their paper in Word and save it to html, which creates problems in the end product.

The "highs" of teaching a course using technology and distance education are substantial. First, as a by-product of the online course, students learned skills as well as content (except how to write html). That is, they learned how to use the Internet, e-mail, and other technology skills that will be useful to them in the practice of law. This was not a purpose, or an intention of the professor; rather it was an unintentional positive outcome of the course. Second, using the Internet allows the professor to convey the latest and most current and timely information to students almost as quickly as it becomes available. The professor can instantly post news hot off the press to the web site for students to read. Even when the professor uses

Figure 7.10. Under the Hood Course Administration

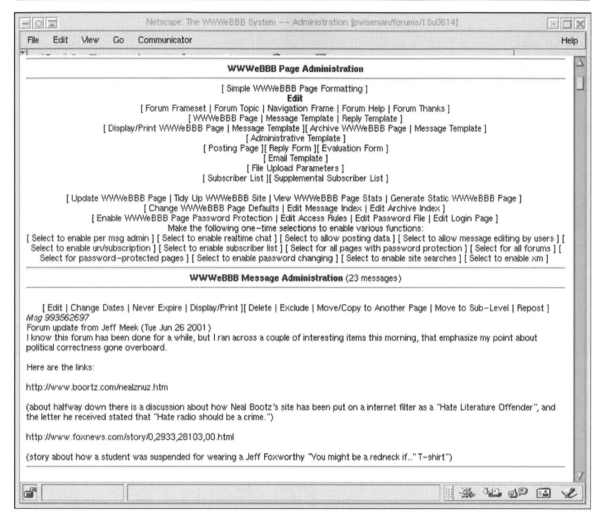

Reprinted with permission from Patrick Wiseman.

a textbook (which in the case of law sometimes is essentially outdated before it hits the market), he can supplement it online.

Of his experience, he says:

It is more fun and more work than any of the other courses I teach. It is more fun because it is obvious that the students are having fun with the course; they are engaged in the material and are excited by it. It is more work because I have an enormous amount of material that I have to grade. I am not as good at time man-

agement as I expect my students to be. What I should do is assign a number to each person's contributions during a forum so that at the end of the semester I would have 10 to 12 scores for each student that would help me to arrive at a grade for the student. I can also go back and look at the forum participation statistics [Figure 7.11] that are built into the software. This pulls up the student name, the number of contributions, and links to their contributions so I can review each of their contributions. (Interview, July 2000)

Figure 7.11. Forum Participants Statistics

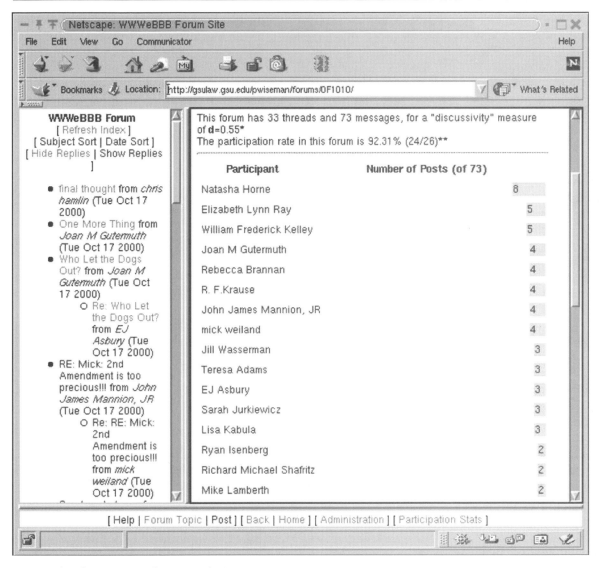

Reprinted with permission from Patrick Wiseman.

LESSONS LEARNED

Professor Wiseman offers these lessons to others who want to teach distance education courses.

1. Simplify. Simple is better, but don't oversimplify. Don't overdo graphics. Many graphics make the material look visually appealing and interesting, but use of these slows down the process of down-loading material. In other words, don't let the technology get in the way of the pedagogy.

2. Use the right tools. For example, for "brainstorming" topics, use synchronous chat tools. For delivering materials, use an asynchronous mode. Working on a hypothetical case in a small group requires synchronous tools. Make sure the pedagogy is driving the technology, not vice versa.

3. Don't teach. The teacher is the manager of the

course. Make the students do the substantive work. Use of a constructive model in courses allows students the experience of not only learning, but also researching, synthesizing, and making decisions about what is important. Exercise professorial restraint. When you give students control of content, keep comments to a minimum.

4. Take risks. Try things that you have never tried before. Don't be afraid to look or even be stupid. Be willing to lose control. And, above all, don't panic!

5. Do reinvent. Don't use available computer applications and live within the constraints of packaged course tools. Rather, be willing to push the limits. Don't reinvent the wheel; you may not be able to improve on it, but be open to your own creativity.

6. Build community. Provide ways for students to get to know each other, either by an offline face-to-face meeting or an online "a little about you face book," where students are able to see pictures of each other and learn something about other students in the course. The face book also may have links to e-mail addresses. Reflect on the process of community publicly with students and use the chats and forums to give continual feedback to students, while encouraging them to do the same with each other. Have students evaluate one another's work on a continual basis. List contributions from each student and hold all students to community standards (i.e., respect for one another's comments and responsibility for their own contributions). Above all, publicly credit students for their efforts at and contributions to the community effort.

7. Accommodate diversity. Accommodate all students and make sure all web sites are accessible to all students. Also accommodate technological diversity; use plain text, not html, for everything synchronous, including e-mail; minimize web page bandwidth; minimize graphics; and use standard ASCII character sets where possible.

8. Automate. As much as possible, automate group feedback. Show passage of time on the class schedule by using a color code scheme (see Figure 7.6 for an example in black and white). Allow students to retrieve grades and evaluations. Generate e-mail distribution lists and face books from class rolls and various databases. However, don't try to automate everything. For example, giving individual students qualitative feedback is important. And, grading student work should not be done in an automated way. Remember, technology enables pedagogy innovation.

9. Reflect. Ask what works and keep doing it. Ask what doesn't work and stop doing it. Create feedback forms that can be used often, something short and simple. What works may be measurable. For example, to demonstrate the correlation between participation and grades, you may choose to use a scatter plot.

CASE STUDY 3*
Program: Associate Fellowship in
    Integrative Medicine
Medium: Distance learning technolo-
    gies (Web, e-mail, online discussions,
    audiotapes, videotapes) and three
    separate residential weeks in Tucson,
    Arizona
Director: Sue South, M.A.
Institution: University of Arizona, Tucson
Program Founder: Andrew Weil, M.D.,
    Director of the Program in Integrative
    Medicine of the College of Medicine

OVERVIEW AND DESCRIPTION OF THE ASSOCIATE FELLOWSHIP IN INTEGRATIVE MEDICINE

The Program in Integrative Medicine of the College of Medicine, University of Arizona, which is a residential fellowship, began in 1996. The program, directed by Andrew Weil, M.D., allows four physicians to take part in a full-time, 2-year commitment to study integrative medicine in Tucson. The program is "the first effort to change medical education to include information on alternative therapies, mind–body interactions, healing, and other subjects not currently emphasized in the training of physicians" (Horrigan, 2001, p. 97). A few years after the program began, other physicians, who were not in a position to "reside and study" in Tucson for 2 years, began inquiring about the feasibility of delivering the program using distance education technologies. A needs assessment was administered before the start of the program. More than 200 physicians responded to a survey in which questions about their interest in an integrative medicine program were asked. Additionally, they were asked what kind of structure they would prefer, what topics they would like covered, how much experience they had had using the Web, and what they would be willing to pay for such a program. Upon analysis of the responses, it was determined that there was an audience for a distance education program in integrative medicine. Program staff responded favorably and obtained a small grant with which to fund the distance version, called the Associate Fellowship in Integrative Medicine. In August 2000, the first cohort of physicians began the program using distance education technologies, studying and participating from their homes or offices at times that were most convenient for them.

The Associate Fellowship in Integrative Medicine, founded by Dr. Weil and directed by Sue South, M.A., is a 2-year program designed for physicians and nurse practitioners who wish to incorporate the philosophies and techniques of integrative medicine into their medical practice. The Associate Fellowship emphasizes clinical applications, case studies, and collaboration to provide a broad conceptual and practical education in integrative medicine. The Associate Fellows learn the philosophical basis or foundations of integrative medicine as well as elements that represent the practical application of integrative medicine. Foundations and clinical courses together prepare the health care practitioner for transition into an integrative medicine practice. Included in the foundations courses are:

1. **Healing Oriented Medicine** focuses on the nature of the body's healing system; case studies of spontaneous healing; the placebo response as a therapeutic ally; lifestyle medicine; healing versus curing; and strategies for protecting, enhancing, and activating the healing system.
2. **Philosophy of Science** addresses the philosophical heritage and current structure of sciences; the impact of major discoveries on the prevailing paradigms of science and the philosophical setting in which they operate; and the strengths and limitations of the current scientific method and paradigm, specifically as applied to medicine.
3. **Art of Medicine** reflects on the doctor as a facilitator of healing; effective communication and the art of suggestion; relationship-centered care; the role of intuition; techniques for motivating behavior change; and matching therapeutic approaches with individual patients.

---

*Text and illustrations for this case study taken from an interview with Sue South, M.A., director of the Associate Fellowship Program in Integrative Medicine; *An Overview of Associate Fellowship* the Arizona Board of Regents, 2000; and the Program in Integrative Medicine web site, http://www.integrativemedicine.arizona.edu, and reprinted with permission.

4. **Medicine and Culture** teaches the origins and development of conventional medicine as well as other major systems of healing; culture-specific diseases; cultural definitions of health and illness; cultural influences on medical thinking; the role of ceremony and ritual; and anthropological perspectives.

5. **Spirituality and Medicine** discusses the spiritual dimension of human life and its relevance to health, illness, and healing; the distinction between spirituality and religion; the importance of taking a spiritual history; the relationship of spirituality and medical outcomes; and spiritual healing techniques.

6. **Ethics** introduces and discusses the ethical issues associated with being a health care professional in an active integrative medicine practice and includes ethical aspects of the doctor–patient relationship, development of effective treatment plans, and administrative issues.

The clinical elements of the program include:

1. **Nutritional Medicine** in which contributions of diet to health and disease are explored, including specific information on the benefits and risks of common foods and dietary patterns; the therapeutic role of vitamins, minerals, and other nutritional supplements; and nutritional therapies for specific diseases.

2. **Botanical Medicine** reviews the preparations, uses, benefits, and risks of medicinal plants, and their possible interactions with pharmaceutical drugs, and identifies a basic repertory of botanical remedies with known safety and efficacy.

3. **Mind–Body Medicine** addresses the scientific basis of mind–body interactions; a critical review of existing therapies; the role of the mind in health and illness; the identification of diseases with prominent mind–body components; and how to assess the moods and belief systems of patients. Medical hypnosis and guided imagery are components of the onsite weeks.

The supporting elements of the program are as follows:

1. **Research Education** helps Associate Fellows master critical thinking and appraisal of research, and

how to find and assess existing research, and evaluate its validity and significance.

2. **Integrative Medicine and Law** helps students understand the legal implications and issues associated with a practice in integrative medicine.

3. **Medicine, Leadership, and Society** provides the basis for examining the administrative aspects of practicing integrative medicine, including strategic planning and business operations, communication and interpersonal skills, networking and collaboration opportunities, and community-building strategies.

Other topics covered in the program include Homeopathy, Chinese Medicine, Manual Medicine, and Energy Medicine. (More information about the program is available at http://www.integrativemedicine. arizona.edu.)

A module format is used to deliver content. Some of the modules take a week, and others may span up to a 4-week period. The curriculum is presented through various methods, including the Web, e-mail, online discussions, articles, books, audio- and videotapes, and some residential time. There are approximately 50 physicians in each cohort. Physicians from around the world participate in the program online. In addition to coursework, physicians have an opportunity to design treatment plans using an integrative approach for "virtual patients," while receiving "over-the-shoulder" consultations from experienced practitioners. Facilitated by program faculty, Associate Fellows also engage in online conferences regarding particular patients, in which they discuss their own diagnosis and treatment plan for the case and receive input from fellow students. Associate Fellows participate in interactive exercises designed to help them learn efficient and targeted ways of thinking about integrative medicine. There are special-interest groups in which small groups of fellows discuss topics of interest with other participants with similar interests, subspecialties, and/or clinical situations. Fellows are expected to reflect on their learning, perceptions, and reactions throughout the 2-year experience. This may take the form of journal entries that may be shared with other members of the class. Group projects and collaboration are essential to the fellowship learning experience, and Associate Fellows are encouraged to give professional presentations in their own geographic area as part of the learning experience.

Associate Fellows gather three times during the 2 years for 1-week sessions in Tucson, Arizona. During the three 1-week sessions, physicians participate in hands-on activities, watch demonstrations, and meet with program faculty and other physicians in their cohort. The residence weeks occur at the beginning of the 2 years, at the halfway mark, and at the end of the program. Although coming together as a group encourages community building, activities throughout the curriculum are built in to ensure this connection. Community building is an essential part of the program and provides a safe place where physicians can discuss professional as well as personal challenges. Activities that encourage participating physicians to examine themselves as people and as physicians are an integral part of the learning experience. One example of this self-examination process is a nutrition self-assessment in which each individual looks at his or her own nutritional habits and receives advice from fellow classmates on how diets may be changed and improved for health. This involves self-disclosure and confidentiality and is done over the Web. Once this activity has been completed, each doctor is asked to conduct the assessment on a family member and then on a patient.

A locally developed software program provides the vehicle through which student physicians dialog with each other. The dialog is synchronous in that it is online for a week to 2 weeks, but the dialog is asynchronous in that physicians can see what others have written on a particular topic and participate any time during the 1- to 2-week timeframe. Since there are between 40 and 50 physicians, a totally synchronous dialog would be cumbersome, to say the least.

Associate Fellows are expected to possess some technical skills upon entry to the program. With the exception of the three residential weeks in Tucson, the Associate Fellowship is a distance learning program. Computers play a major role in communication, learning, and community building, with most contact between the program staff and the Associate Fellows, and among Associate Fellows, occurring through e-mail and the Web.

The presentation of instructional material on the Web is a sophisticated process and requires certain hardware and software specifications. It is highly

recommended that students have access to the Internet via DSL, cable modem, wireless, ISDN, or other comparable method that is faster than 100 Kbps. Additionally, certain Internet service providers (ISPs) have not proven to be effective with the program's materials. Students are advised which ISPs are most effective. With respect to skills, students must have a working knowledge of a Macintosh or Windows operating system, basic knowledge of a word processor and typing skills, regular use of e-mail, regular use of the World Wide Web, and the ability to download documents from the Web. Each participant must have access to a Macintosh or Windows PC with at least 300 MHz processor, a minimum of 64 MB of RAM, printer, CD-ROM drive, backup system, and internal or external speakers (sound blaster card for Windows machines). Software requirements include Mac OS or Windows version 1995, 1998, or more recent (e.g., 2000 or XP), a word processor such as Microsoft Word, either Netscape Navigator 4.7 or Internet Explorer 5.0 or higher, and an e-mail package. Students are responsible for getting their own technical support, which is not offered by the fellowship program.

To compare residential with distance programs, the residential fellowship program, which takes only four physicians at a time, differs from the distance Associate Fellowship program in the following ways. Aside from the full-time, residential commitment, the residential fellowship program trains physicians to be leaders in the field of integrative medicine. Upon completion of the program, these individuals will take on a leadership role such as a directorship, a research role, or an academic role. Physicians in the residential program are trained to start their own clinics or educational programs in integrative medicine, whether in a teaching capacity, a director capacity, or as a researcher. By contrast, the distance Associate Fellowship is a clinical program. These physicians are in active medical practices while they are engaged in the fellowship, and the philosophies, skills, and knowledge they gain as a result of the program are integrated into their practices as they learn. That is, while they are engaged in the learning process, they are asked to use the newly acquired ways of practicing medicine with their patients. It is a progressive kind of training. Many patients are served and at the same time educated in alternative medicine. According to Director South, each physician serves about 2,000 patients in his or her practice; thus, integrative medicine reaches tens of thousands of people during each 2-year training period.

The Associate Fellowship is not a degree-granting program. Rather, Associate Fellows receive a certificate of completion. The program is not accredited because no accrediting agency exists that could endorse the program; however, the University of Arizona Program in Integrative Medicine would support the establishment of an accrediting organization for a comprehensive education in integrative medicine.

Evaluation of the program includes an assessment of physicians' learning, the administrative components of the program, and the structure of courses and program elements. There is an online module evaluation (Appendix O) that physicians complete at the conclusion of each module. It asks how well the module met their needs, how satisfied they were with the module, and whether it met the objectives that were outlined for it.

Modules are divided into half- to 1-hour segments to make them manageable for a practicing physician. Thus, a physician can sit down at the computer for half an hour and complete a reading or exercise whenever that time is available, rather than having to block out long periods of time to attend to an assignment. Although students may progress at their own pace to some extent, they are required to complete weekly assignments of about 8 to 10 hours of work each week. Assignments include readings, online assignments, dialog, conducting research, completing a report, doing a site visit or field trip, or engaging in an interview with another physician. As this university has shown, it is important to structure important aspects of every distance education course (e.g., assignments and evaluation) to maximize use of the technology, while maintaining the quality of the learning.

There are currently 83 modules of varying lengths (i.e., 1 week to several weeks), and more are being developed, with an anticipated total of 150 to 200 modules. The structure of the program is the same for every participant. There are no electives. There are more than 3,200 web pages currently up. Once all modules have been developed, more than twice that number of web pages will be online (Figure 7.12).

SAMPLE ASSIGNMENT

Physicians were asked to visit an alternative medical practitioner such as an acupuncturist or massage therapist, conduct an interview, and assess the space in which the alternative practitioner works. The second part of the assignment was to do an inventory of the physical and social environment of their own practice, that is, to look at their own waiting room (e.g., the colors, what they see and smell, what the lighting is like, what is on the floor and walls, what they hear, and how old the magazines are). After the interview and their inventory process, they were asked to compare their own work environment (Figure 7.13) with that of the alternative medical practitioner (Figure 7.14). They also were asked to write about what things they would want to change about their own office environment.

Use of pictures in an online course is helpful to both faculty and students in clarifying the point being made. Faculty can use pictures in the sample assignment, as in Figures 7.13 and 7.14, to illustrate what they are looking for in the assignment. Effective instructors use the technology at hand to their benefit.

WHAT ARE THE CHALLENGES AND WHAT ARE THE HIGHS?

The two major challenges for program faculty and staff are (1) playing catch-up while trying to deliver quality education on the Web, and (2) working within a traditional university setting. With respect to the first, the staff operates only a couple of months ahead of the students' schedule and assignments. This creates pressure for the developers of modules and staff in general. It also makes it more challenging to keep the instructional quality at a high level and to keep the instruction progressing at a certain pace.

There are 12 staff people who are responsible for the development and delivery of the entire program, including the three residential weeks. There are web

Figure 7.12. Associate Fellowship in Integrative Medicine

Emphasis on Evidence

Alll content is closely tied to the medical literature. LIterature citations link to Medline abstracts when available.

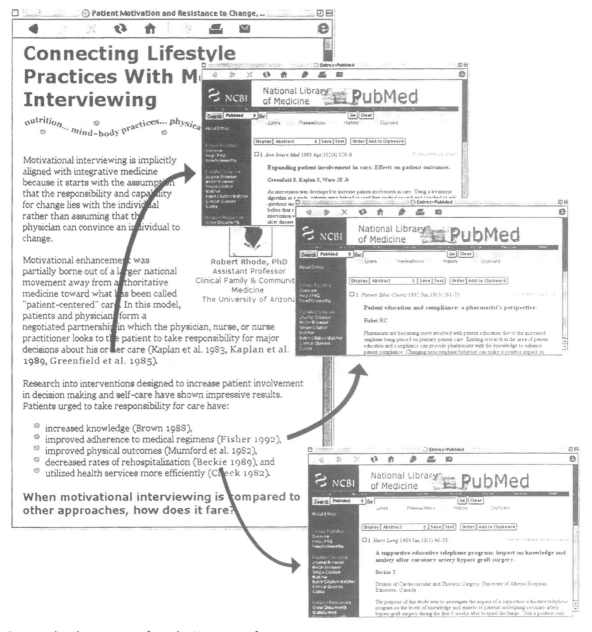

Reprinted with permission from the University of Arizona.

Figure 7.13. Traditional Treatment/Examination Room

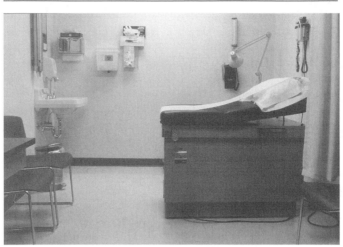

Reprinted with permission from the University of Arizona.

developers, instructional designers, and some faculty who serve as staff. There are also program coordinators who register students, manage the logistics of the residential weeks, and act as communication liaisons, making sure students receive all printed material every month and keeping the schedule and program on track. There is a programmer who does all the back-end programming and who is responsible for making sure the network stays up and working, and that all online materials go into the correct database. Director South, in her capacity, makes sure that everyone has what they need, and oversees all the activities involved in the delivery of the program. A physician who graduated from the program serves as the medi-

Figure 7.14. Alternative Examination Room

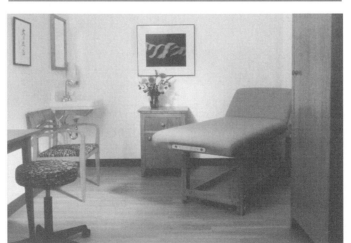

Reprinted with permission from the University of Arizona.

cal editor, writes curriculum, and looks at the clinical relevancy of the material as well as every piece of curriculum that goes up on the Web. He checks content, format, and the delivery of materials. Dr. Andrew Weil participates in a limited way by lecturing during the residential weeks and providing advice to physicians online when appropriate. A top priority for the program staff is to keep everything at a high level of quality and to maintain that quality over time.

The second major challenge is working within a university environment, specifically, the bureaucracy and policies. The Associate Fellowship is funded by tuition and is a revenue-generating program. Universities are not necessarily equipped to handle revenue-generating programs. This further supports the notion that new ways of delivering education using technology need new educational structures in which to reside, rather than trying to fit these new ways into traditional institutional structures.

According to Sue South, the "highs" have been the people. The physicians who are enrolled in this program are very caring and committed to finding the best medical care for their patients. This commitment and care is demonstrated in physicians' assignments and web dialog among themselves. Another positive has been the realization of what a very small team of professionals has been able to create in terms of a high-quality educational program using distance education technologies. The faculty and staff realize that you can't just take a face-to-face lecture, put it on the Web, and expect it to be successful. It takes planning and techniques that are applicable to this kind of delivery mode to make a successful course. Unlike many distance education programs that have very high attrition rates, the Associate Fellowship program has not lost anyone to attrition. Sue South attributes the program's 100% retention rate to the care taken by faculty and staff to plan the content well and deliver it using teaching techniques that work. One such technique has been to address the needs of the audience for short learning segments by creating modules that may be completed in short periods of time. To maintain the high quality of instruction and learning, staff members are always looking at the research on other distance education programs and considering what works and what does not. They use ideas gleaned from the research about what is effective or successful and search for ways to improve upon what they are doing.

LESSONS LEARNED

In the short period of time that the Associate Fellowship program has existed, staff and faculty have learned important lessons.

1. You can't just take something on paper and slap it onto the Web. You have to make the learning engaging, interactive, and action oriented. The material must be relevant to the lives and practices of those physicians involved in the program. This must be done in ways that motivate students and keep them engaged, such as monitoring progress and participation, and encouraging community.
2. People are hungry for integrative medicine, and the only feasible way for them to get it is through the Web. It is imperative to find ways to deliver excellent instruction over the Web and to respond to individual needs and learning styles.
3. Community is essential for learning at a distance. Distance education can be such an impersonal environment in which to learn that it is important to attach the message to the messenger by using language in each module that sounds like the faculty member is speaking. It should be a very conversational tone so students feel the sense of belonging to a community of learners. In addition to the conversational tone, graphics such as pictures of the instructor are used, and faculty offer personal experiences as examples.

FEEDBACK FROM STUDENTS

Students are encouraged to use online feedback mechanisms for commenting on various aspects of the program (see the online module evaluation form in Appendix O). Additionally, students are asked about their assignments frequently. Questions include, "Is the dialog helpful?" "How clear and understandable are the printed materials you receive every month?" "What is your assessment of the small-group projects?" "What methods used in the program help you learn best?"

Comments and feedback received from students include the following: "I am definitely enjoying the Associate Fellowship. It is a joy and a privilege to be able to communicate with others of like mind."

"Your web site is awesome. I show it off to friends."
"I am really enjoying the material—this fellowship
has rekindled such a wonderful spirit for medicine."
"Your web site diffuses anxiety about the technological aspect of the Associate Fellowship." "The staff
has wonderful energy and a commitment to the program." "There is unbelievable dedication and responsiveness on the part of the staff."

As mentioned earlier, there is an attempt to accommodate the different learning styles of the physicians. Learning styles are assessed early in the
program, and results are used when making decisions
about how to deliver content. For example, several
physicians were intimidated by the amount of written dialog on the course web page, and they would
read it but would not contribute any comments of
their own. By monitoring the dialog, program staff
members were able to pick up on this pattern and
contact these physicians individually to find out how
they could be better accommodated.

WHO ARE THE STUDENTS AND WHERE DO THEY LIVE?

Students participate from all over the world. Over
20 states in the United States are represented, and
between two and four international students have
been enrolled in the program. Many medical special-
ties are represented, but most physicians are inter-
nists. The average age of the students is 44 years, and
most are well established in their own medical practices. Those who come to the program come with a
desire to change their practice and learn more effective ways to treat their patients. Many are frustrated
with the strict allopathic medical model and want to
be more holistic in the ways they educate and help
their patients, using resources from a variety of
schools of thought. This program teaches them how
to do that and provides them with a network of other
physicians who think as they do, who value their way
of thinking, and who share and support their ideas
and opinions.

CASE STUDY 4*
Course: Introduction to Sociology
Medium: Interactive television (ITV)
Instructor: Jon A. Schlenker, Ph.D.
Institution: University of Maine at
    Augusta (UMA), Augusta, Maine

OVERVIEW AND DESCRIPTION OF INTRODUCTION TO SOCIOLOGY

A long-time veteran of ITV teaching, Dr. Schlenker
now teaches nearly all of his courses using this medium. A look back at his career reveals more than
30 years, 25 of which he has been using ITV. Back
in the late 1970s, the University of Maine at Augusta
(UMA) received a small Title III grant, which funded
a mini-ITV system that hooked up UMA's system
with five hospitals in central Maine. Dr. Schlenker
was one of the first professors to teach a course
using the system. His first course was Social Geron-
tology. The system, which was very antiquated, only
lasted a couple of years. Subsequently, UMA purchased over a million dollars worth of equipment,
and the Community College of Maine (CCM) was
established. The system connected Augusta and
Lewiston and was headed by Dr. George Connick.
(See Chapter 2 for more information about the evolution of the Maine system, including the CCM.) A
call was put out to all faculty to submit proposals
for courses they wished to teach over the multisite
system. Dr. Schlenker submitted a proposal and was
asked to teach Cultural Anthropology. The first year
constituted a pilot of the two-site, two-way video and
audio interactive system. This pilot was evaluated by
the author and deemed a success. This was the beginning of the current distance education network at
Maine and a long career in ITV teaching for Professor Schlenker.

Dr. Schlenker is responsible for eight different
courses, which he teachers at various times during a
2-year timeframe. They include Introduction to College Experience, Social Problems, Introduction to
Sociology, Sociology of Deviance, Social Gerontol-
ogy, Introduction to Anthropology, Cultural Anthro-

---

*Text for this case study taken from an interview with Jon Schlenker, Ph.D. Photographs by Cynthia Hook, Associate Director of
Marketing and Publications, University of Maine at Augusta.

pology, and an Honors course, Critical Thinking and Writing. In addition to his ITV courses, he teaches one face-to-face course a year, most recently, Sociology of Minorities. Dr. Schlenker currently teaches three or four ITV courses each semester. He taught two full-loads (four ITV courses) in the spring of 2000. (Each ITV course counts as two traditional face-to-face courses.) A choice perhaps, but he comments, "It has to be done. There is no one else who can teach the courses that need to be offered during the spring semester."

When asked how ITV teaching differs from face-to-face, Dr. Schlenker responds that teaching an ITV course (Figure 7.15) forces him to be more organized and better prepared. For example, exams and assignments must be planned well in advance of the actual date they will occur. In the case of exams, they must be turned in to those in charge of logistics (e.g., delivering exams and other materials to sites) at least 2 weeks before the exam date. Or, while in the traditional classroom graphics may be put up on a black- or whiteboard on the spot, in ITV teaching they must be prepared ahead of time. This allows the technician who assists Professor Schlenker to be ready to show them when appropriate. Dr. Schlenker also uses course booklets that contain the syllabus outlining assignments, course policies, class schedule, evaluation procedures, and phone-bridge sched-

ules. A faculty profile is offered, and all supplemental materials, including a bibliography of related readings, are included. The course booklet also contains the graphics that will be used as part of the class presentations. The Introduction to Sociology course booklet is custom published by McGraw-Hill. Students purchase the course booklet along with the required text for the course.

Another difference between ITV and face-to-face teaching is the effort one must make to encourage interaction. In the ITV classroom, Dr. Schlenker uses 16 different modes of interaction to get students involved. During the first class period, he does a "call around" where students are instructed to call in from their respective sites. Cordless phones in all remote sites are used to dial in to the broadcast site classroom where Dr. Schlenker is. The call around establishes a connection between the students and faculty, and among students. During the second class, he has students participate in an exercise that encourages interaction. In his Introduction to Sociology course during the Fall 2001 semester, he contrived a list of 20 statements, all of which were false but could be construed as true. Using the statements, the class discussed the sociological research that demonstrates why the statements are false. Another exercise is the "postcard assignment." Each student sends 10 postcards to Dr. Schlenker during the semester in which

Figure 7.15. Origination Classroom

Photo by Cynthia Hook. Reprinted with permission from the University of Maine at Augusta.

they react to one of four questions. The assignment is graded and worth 4% of students' final grade. Questions on the postcard assignment include:

1. What is at least one thing you heard today in class that you did not know before?
2. Is there anything discussed in today's class that you have doubts about?
3. What is at least one question that came to mind during today's class?
4. Did you learn anything today that you could apply to your everyday life?

Even if students do not call in by telephone to interact, this assignment forces them to interact with the professor and with the material. Professor Schlenker assigns activities that require students to use multilink phone-bridges (10 lines) to review before an exam, or to discuss questions about their term papers, and the like. Phone-bridge assignments may be conducted in class or outside of class. For example, sites where only one student is present may be linked to other sites with one or two students using the phone-bridge, for a total of 10 to 15 students. These students form a small discussion group and may complete an in-class assignment in which groupwork is used. Dr. Schlenker uses some online components in

his ITV courses as well. For example, computer conferencing is used so students can interact among themselves. The major interaction mode used is the "call in" component of every class period. These interaction techniques allow students in remote sites (Figure 7.16) to feel like they are part of the class discussion rather than outsiders looking in on a class. It also allows them to become familiar with fellow classmates around the state. When the caller calls in on the telephone line, a banner flashes across the classroom monitor enabling the professor to see the site from which the call is coming.

Dr. Schlenker feels that student interaction in his ITV classes far surpasses that which occurs in his traditional face-to-face classrooms. He attributes this to the efforts made and the attention paid to encouraging interaction in the ITV classroom. In traditional classes, just because students are face-to-face with the instructor and with other students, it is erroneously concluded that more interaction occurs. In fact, many students in face-to-face situations never utter a word the entire semester.

Dr. Schlenker has incorporated his distance techniques into his face-to-face classes because they make the learning more efficient and the courses better. Dr. Schlenker states that "ITV teaching has made me a better teacher." He feels more energized and en-

Figure 7.16. Remote Classroom

Photo by Cynthia Hook. Reprinted with permission from the University of Maine at Augusta.

thusiastic about his teaching as a result of his experiences with ITV.

WHAT ARE THE CHALLENGES AND WHAT ARE THE HIGHS?

When asked to describe challenges of ITV teaching, Dr. Schlenker has to think hard. He actually feels that he has had an advantage over new faculty in that he was one of the first to teach ITV courses and has "grown up" with the system. As the system developed, he developed as well. So, while others, new to the nature of a distance education system, may experience new challenges, Dr. Schlenker does not encounter new challenges very often. In fact, he was instrumental in helping the development along by making suggestions and trying out new techniques for content delivery. He has worked as a consultant to technology staff when new products are introduced. They usually come to Dr. Schlenker and other veteran distance education faculty who are willing to try the new products out and provide feedback on them. "In the beginning, it was technology driving instruction. Now it is instruction driving the technologies," he states.

Dr. Schlenker has worked closely with instructional designers and technicians to develop ways in which to deliver education. And, he continues to rely on their expertise in the technical realm while he concentrates on his teaching.

Dr. Schlenker's major concern is the workload. At times it can be overwhelming. One semester runs into another because students who have not completed assignments on time in one semester finish them up in the next semester. Course preparation is a continuous activity for the professor as well. Tying things up at the end of one semester runs into preparing other things for the next.

The highs, on the other hand, include the energy Professor Schlenker feels when teaching over ITV. He likes the variety that ITV offers. Every class is different. Every semester is different. He says he always has to be "up." Some of his interaction exercises give him interesting feedback about his teaching and allow him to make adjustments when needed. Although Professor Schlenker has a "camera presence," and teaching ITV comes naturally, many professors without a camera presence tend to adapt to teaching over ITV, and after a short period of time become quite comfortable with this environment.

Dr. Schlenker has great enthusiasm for his teaching, which is reflected in the positive feedback from students. His thorough preparation and distribution of course materials before the course begins gives students a head start. Students say they like having all course materials at the start of the course and that this encourages them to be more organized in the way they approach the assignments.

With respect to student satisfaction with ITV courses, Dr. Schlenker finds that the more distant the student, the higher the satisfaction. Some students who are taking the course from the origination site, Augusta, feel resentful that they have to be in an ITV course. But students who live in the northern part of the state or on one of the islands, are most appreciative of the opportunity to access college courses and programs via ITV. This finding has been consistent since the earliest evaluation studies conducted by the author. Humorously, Dr. Schlenker comments that "students up in Jackman love to go to the site in their pajamas with a cup of coffee and a bag of donuts and sit there and get credit for the course."

Dr. Schlenker has always remained positive about his ITV teaching and attributes his success to his attitude. He has done numerous presentations around the United States on ITV teaching. And he has conducted workshops for new professors who are interested in teaching using this technology.

HOW HAS ITV IMPROVED OVER THE YEARS?

Many improvements have been made in the ITV classroom since the 1970s. For example, the professor must look into the camera lens at the rear of the classroom to give the impression to remote site students that he is looking at them. Early classrooms had a camera only at the back of the classroom, and it was hard to remember to look at the camera. In today's classroom, the rear camera is mounted on a television monitor at the back of the room (Figure 7.17), positioned so the professor can see what is being displayed for students to see on other monitors around the classroom and those in remote sites. It is more natural for the professor to look at the monitor than to look at a camera.

Figure 7.17. Monitor in Origination Classroom

Photo by Cynthia Hook. Reprinted with permission from the
University of Maine at Augusta.

Another improvement from the early days is that a technician actually participates in the instruction. That is, the technician, who sits in a control room (Figure 7.18) during the class, is responsible for controlling when graphics appear on the monitors to coincide with various lecture points made by Dr. Schlenker. The technician also monitors call ins from students and alerts the professor when a student is on the line. The viewed aesthetics are much more pleasing to students as well. Instead of seeing the professor against a blackboard or a white space, students see him or her superimposed against a coastal scene, or a photo of New England's fall foliage, or, as shown in Figure 7.19, against a snowy winter scene. Dr. Schlenker likes to use photos from his own collection as a more pleasing background to his presence.

Figure 7.18. Control Room

Photo by Cynthia Hook. Reprinted with permission from the
University of Maine at Augusta.

Figure 7.19. A Professor Shown Against a Snowy Winter Scene

Photo by Cynthia Hook. Reprinted with permission from the University of Maine at Augusta.

Another improvement has been the mechanisms used to alert the professor that someone from a remote site has a question. Dr. Schlenker used to have to wait for students in remote sites to call in to ask questions and participate. At times, he would be onto a new topic by the time a call got through. New technologies have helped to alleviate this problem in part by flashing a note on the monitor that a caller from a particular site is on the line.

LESSONS LEARNED

With 25 years experience, Dr. Schlenker has many lessons to share. They include:

1. His strong feeling that faculty should have experience teaching their course in a face-to-face classroom before embarking on an ITV teaching experience. The curriculum should be in place and the instructor should have a sense of how he or she will deliver the content. The instructor should have an idea of what he or she wants to accomplish and what the assignments will be. Dr. Schlenker does not feel that ITV is a good place to stumble. It takes time before courses are perfected and modified, and experimentation should be done in a live classroom rather than on camera. Additionally, curricula and support materials must be prepared ahead of time in collaboration with an instructional designer, and instruction must be coordinated with graphics display by the technician.

2. Teamwork is essential for the success of the course. Instructors must learn how to work with both the instructional designer and the technician as a team. By doing this, faculty give up some ownership of ideas. For example, Dr. Schlenker often comes up with an idea about how to present a concept and may make a sketch. He gives this to the instructional designer, who may expand, alter, enhance, or even change the sketch altogether. For some faculty this may be difficult to accept, but Dr. Schlenker has worked this way for so long that he feels like he is part of a team whose task it is to come up with the best way to convey material to students.

3. If possible, work with the same technician, who has a similar personality and work ethic to your own. Working with the same technician makes the class run more smoothly, and when the work ethics and personalities of the instructor and the technician are similar, it makes the class function more effectively. Further, the technician gets to know how the professor works and often can anticipate possible problems ahead of time.

4. Always preview the slides and graphics that will be used in a class to make sure the layering is in the correct order and that each slide will appear in the proper sequence. Over time, the technician becomes familiar with the instructor's way of teaching and can anticipate how the instructor will proceed. It also becomes second nature for the technician to "read" the instructor's body signals and anticipate what the instructor will say or do next. The technician also may act as timekeeper. When discussions get off course and time is passing, the technician may flash up a graphic that says something to the effect of "time to move on."

5. Make a daily schedule or lesson plan and try to stick to it. Knowing where you should be at a given time is important and being there is even more important.

6. Something should happen every minute on the monitor. This keeps the student's attention and interest. Some faculty use photography as a background so students will not be looking at the professor against a blank background. It gives an aesthetic value to the shot of the professor at the podium (see Figure 7.19).

7. When discussions occur in the origination classroom, the faculty should always repeat important points to ensure that everyone, both remote and classroom students, will know what has been said.

WHO ARE THE STUDENTS AND WHERE DO THEY LIVE?

There are 100 remote sites around the state of Maine so students live everywhere. The largest number of students Dr. Schlenker has had in one class is 390! Although this class was very large, most of Dr. Schlenker's courses have somewhere between 45 and 250 students. The introductory courses tend to be on the high end, and specialized, upper-level courses tend to be smaller. He has a teaching assistant who helps him with tasks related to the course.

Students range in age from high school age (Figure 7.20) to advanced age. They may be degree stu-

Figure 7.20. High School Students Taking a Course at a Remote Site

Photo by Cynthia Hook. Reprinted with permission from the University of Maine at Augusta.

dents or specials who are taking the course out of interest. The ITV courses reach prisoners using tape delay, a school for the deaf, some businesses, and Winter Harbor Naval Air Station, in addition to students in the 100 remote sites.

Students complete course evaluations each semester. Dr. Schlenker has developed his own form, which focuses on the teaching and learning rather than the technology, and the institution administers its standardized form, which has some questions related to the medium of instruction.

SPECIAL ADVANTAGES OF ITV

Dr. Schlenker feels disadvantaged in his face-to-face courses. He does not have his graphics, he doesn't have his technician, and he is all by himself. Writing on the chalkboard to demonstrate something does not measure up to the sophisticated slides and pictures that can be displayed using technology. And having a team of experts with which to collaborate provides many options for a faculty member. Dr. Schlenker prefers the team to his lone presence in the classroom.

For the student, advantages include easy access, flexibility, little or no travel time, and an ability to view videotapes when a class has been missed or the student wishes to review. ITV is a good distance option for students who do not own a computer or are not technically adept to take an Internet course.

Maine has one of the most highly developed ITV systems in the country, with more than 14,000 students participating. Faculty who at one time protested the use of ITV are now involved, and students give high marks to the courses delivered using this medium.

CHAPTER 8

From Design to Delivery

The new student, defined as 25 years of age or older and employed full-time, was originally the target audience for distance education. During the 1980s and 1990s, many adult students began returning to college and were demanding more flexibility and accommodations with respect to institutional scheduling to fit their own work and personal schedules. However, as distance education became more visible and available at so many institutions, traditional-age students also opted for the flexibility and convenience distance education offered. In the 1980s, institutions of higher learning began feeling the effects of declining enrollments and increasing competition among colleges and universities for students fresh from high school. Today, we find that "more than half [of distance education students] are women. As a group, distance learners are highly motivated. Their course-completion rate exceeds that of students enrolled in traditional on-campus courses. The successful distance learner is by definition a committed student" (*Peterson's Guide*, 2001, p. 4). Plans to design and develop distance education options for all students, young and old alike, have sprung up across the nation and around the world.

Much research has been conducted that examines the stages of distance education from design to delivery. While the articles related to what is involved in creating and delivering courses using distance education technologies are beyond the scope of this book, a sample of research has been selected for review in this section. The articles reviewed here were selected because they cover a cross-section of issues— breadth rather than depth—and because they are applicable to issues that currently are being faced in distance education.

WHAT DO WE KNOW FROM THOSE WHO HAVE TRIED IT?

Equipment

In the mid-1990s, Grambling State University, which is an historically Black university in rural southern Louisiana, "found itself facing changing demographics, a more global economy, and an advancing information age" (Lowery & Barnes, 1996, p. 91). To prepare itself for the 21st century, Grambling needed to take immediate initiatives. After much deliberation, the administration determined that distance education seemed to be a conceivable solution to many of the challenges it faced. Having resolved to move forward with distance education, Grambling administrators were faced with choosing technologies that would best serve the university's needs and determining how such technologies would be financed. Crucial to the success of a distance education enterprise were technological and support staff, policies and procedures, instructor and staff training, program identification procedures, marketing processes, and instructional design and development systems.

To attain the technology, the political clout, and the fiscal resources necessary to move forward, several partnerships were formed. Among them were a partnership with the Black College Satellite Network, a large federal grant awarded under the Title III program, and an arrangement with Digital Equipment Corporation. There was also an arrangement with Grambling's Student Body Organization, a partnership with a wireless cable company, the acquisition of special hardware and distance learning software, and, finally, alliances with the regional electric utility company and neighboring university. Grambling also acquired a fully outfitted TV studio that put them in an optimal position for the delivery of distance education.

However, as Lowery and Barnes (1996) posit, success of distance education not only involves equipment and programs, but also depends on "adopting policies, procedures and processes for effective operation, and on mainstreaming distance programs into existing university structures" (p. 93). Grambling's distance education programs included third-party programs produced by independent vendors, university-produced academic credit programs, and workshops. Other success factors included an effective communication process, techniques that increased learner–instructor interactions, and an adequate evaluation process.

Programs

Yet another success factor for Grambling's distance education endeavor appeared to be related to its ability to capitalize on academic assets. This included identifying programs and vertical markets, selecting and training instructors, formulating marketing and implementation plans, choosing appropriate media for delivery to identified audiences, and designing quality instruction for delivery over various combinations of media (Lowery & Barnes, 1996). After considerable measures had been taken to assess the needs of the university campus-wide, the most appropriate, cost-effective delivery medium was chosen. Lowery and Barnes conclude that with the willingness to do things differently, a commitment to determine needs relative to distance learning, and execution of a well-planned approach to accomplish the task, any institution can duplicate what Grambling University has achieved.

Student Audience

Also of critical importance in the plan is defining the expected student audience. It is important to study the characteristics and lifestyles of the target audience in order to facilitate decisions such as the choice of media, programming, and scheduling. For example, if the target audience comprises students who have access to personal computers and the Internet, but who live far from any college campus, it may be most feasible for the students to take a course over the Internet. If, on the other hand, the students spend an extended amount of time traveling in a car, as traveling salespersons might, the use of audiotapes might make sense. Or, if the students to whom courses will be delivered have little time or are not very technology literate, use of the Internet might be limited to e-mails and other simple administrative processes.

Cost and Budgeting

Boettcher (1998) examines another aspect of developing distance education options—that of cost. She emphasizes that "there is no simple answer to the question of how much it will cost in time and money to develop a distance learning program" (p. 56). It depends not only on who you are as an institution and what you want to offer, but on the institutional goals, the research options, and arriving at a realistic cost expectation. For every distinct vision of distance learning, there is a distinct design and, likewise, distinct costs. One strategy for budgeting for a distance education program is to create a budget for each phase of the program: one for the initial development phase, one for the marketing and delivery phase, and one for the ongoing maintenance phase. This type of budgeting is difficult to carry out in traditional academic structures because "when a faculty member is tasked with the responsibility of teaching a course, that faculty member is responsible for all of the phases of the course, . . . [from design to delivery,] including testing, assessment, and student interaction" (Boettcher, 1998, p. 56). Phase budgeting lowers cost by taking the highly paid research faculty out of the delivery phase of the program. It is also important to develop a business plan when designing a budget for distance learning programs. The business plan includes funding needs for all phases of course delivery, including design, development, and all dissemination phases. Additionally, a business plan addresses other questions related to the infrastructure, marketing, recruiting, admissions concerns, counseling processes, assessment, and library and technical support resources. Ultimately, the business plan outlines the budgeting as well as the decision-making processes.

Prior to budgeting, the goals of the distance education program must be clarified. How many times does the institution want to deliver a program? How will materials be delivered within the institution? The issue of licensing of curriculum materials, which may allow other institutions to deliver the program or courses, must be solved. Questions regarding whether the course will be taught by the faculty member who designed it or someone else, and how many staff will be needed to facilitate student interaction and course delivery, also must be answered.

To aid in calculating cost, Boettcher recommends considering two questions: how much instructional time makes up a three-credit course, and how long does it take to build an hour of learning materials? By estimating the number of hours, one can calculate the costs using salary figures of those involved in the course delivery. She estimates that it takes approximately 18 hours for a faculty member to create 1 hour of instruction on the Web. Assuming some start-up time (i.e., becoming familiar with the system and technology used in a course), moving a course to the Web could take as much as 1,000 hours. This figure has some shock value for deans and administrators; however, as faculty become more adept with the web environment, the number of hours required to complete such a task will decrease. Other strategies for building materials to be delivered in a distance education course include using course templates, adopting materials for the Web, and collaboration and partnerships with other faculty.

Building Community

The issue of building community in a virtual environment deserves attention as well. Everhart (1999) discusses the benefits of linking a communications center to the university's database. He speculated that by the year 2000, there would be approximately 20 million new learners in the United States, 25% of whom would be traditional undergraduate students, ages 18 to 22. Mature, lifelong learners who require continuing education would make up the other 75%.

Geographic restrictions no longer exist as a barrier to individuals seeking a college education, since students can choose a higher education institution from an array of providers. Although such barriers have fallen, Everhart (1999) alleges that "the feeling of remoteness is the biggest barrier to distance learning" (p. 12). Therefore, providing access and a sense of community to distance learners is essential.

Before the recent introduction of software that supports communication between students and the instructor, and among students, communication was another barrier to distance learning. However, virtual communication tools have been developed and continue to proliferate. For example, bandwidth has increased and is likely to continue to increase. Interactive multimedia networking and the use of video are becoming faster and more prevalent, and Internet access continues to expand. To establish a virtual community, one in which students and faculty alike are more connected and can develop a better relationship, it is important to link administrative and curricular software applications using a home page. With respect to higher education, the home page provides students with access to campus resources, a vehicle for interaction with faculty and other students, and a means by which to take exams and receive course materials. Personalized home pages reinforce an interactive, personal kind of learning environment, as well as cultivating relationships between faculty, students, and administrators. With such integrative software, a university can leverage its existing information technology and hardware investments; permit dissemination of information in a personalized and individualized way to students, faculty, and administrators; and, finally, better serve the expectations of today's consumers of education.

Everhart (1999) maintains that since the choice of a particular college or university has one of the most significant impacts on students' lives, "higher education is possibly the most likely market to build . . . relationship[s] with its constituents" (p. 16). Establishing a virtual community is a mutually beneficial endeavor as well as a practical reality for education today.

Use of Time and Allocation of Resources

According to Van Dusen (1998), higher education faces a variety of problem areas and modern technology is a way to address them. Problem areas include spiraling tuition and fees, the priority given to research and scholarly activities over teaching and advising, curricula that are out of step with workplace realities, and a lack of attention given to the needs of nontraditional and adult learners who work full-time and have families.

Technology may be the "magic bullet" with which to make headway toward a solution. Investments in technology have proven to be cost effective. Instructional technology has forced individuals to think about teaching and learning in new ways. But, a significant overhaul is necessary in order to make the academy more accessible, affordable, and effective using technology. Van Dusen (1998) suggests that what needs to change is "the way we use time, how we allocate resources, the role of faculty and other staff, and the mission of our institutions" (p. 59).

Institutions need to reconsider two historical components of institutional structure: the use of time and the allocation of resources. With respect to the structural component, there needs to be more funding for technology in the academy. Faculty need training in how to use the technology in their teaching, and the infrastructure needs to be bolstered. As the issue of access has become more important, so too have instructional technology and distance education.

With declining enrollments at traditional higher education institutions, affordability is at issue. To address the concerns of affordability, institutions need to explore the elements of cost that can be controlled, such as improved scheduling of classes and better allocation of resources. Not only have administrative expenditures been declining, but institutions are hiring more nontenured, part-time faculty. While this may reduce costs, "there are serious implications for both the professoriate and for students seeking a quality education" (Van Dusen, 1998, p. 63). Institutions are addressing the issue of affordability in an inadequate manner.

Institutional Effectiveness

Higher education stakeholders have different opinions on what institutional effectiveness actually means. In the traditional classroom, multimedia technology has allowed students to relate mutually "with a process from diverse angles such that their understanding becomes multi-dimensional. [In the virtual classroom, however,] time and institutional resources are dramatically restructured" (Van Dusen, 1998, p. 64). While studies have concluded that there are no significant differences between learning delivered by technology and learning delivered in person, Van

Dusen asserts that the research is inadequate and that technology-based learning needs further study to determine its effectiveness.

Some uses of technology, such as electronic registration and course scheduling, have proven cost effective, but "applying technology to the classroom to reduce costs is really putting the cart before the horse" (Van Dusen, 1998, p. 66). Instead, he suggests that economic benefits may be yielded if higher education institutions focus on how technology enhances learning. An investment in faculty development and support services for success is critical in delivering quality education using distance education technologies.

Institutions across the country have wrestled with the questions of what technology is best and how institutions can ensure that both students and faculty are ready to use it. At St. Cloud University in Minnesota, as at so many other institutions, the introduction of technology has posed many challenges. Thoms (1999) discusses the pervasive entrance of the computer into classrooms and the need for teachers to learn guidelines and a different set of skills with which to create classroom materials. She emphasizes that such media need to be used effectively. This "requires a systematic approach to course design, materials design and development, equipment, delivery, remote site origination, computer interaction with ITV, and computer-delivered presentations" (Thoms, 1999, p. 60). Critical to successful teaching at a distance is the ability of faculty to make adjustments to their teaching style. This includes an understanding of related ethical issues of critical concern to faculty and administration. Responsibility for preparing instructors to use technology in their teaching falls on the shoulders of both the administration and the faculty.

Thoms has proposed a number of guidelines relative to designing ITV courses and their criteria for educational materials. These include guidelines with regard to visual literacy, such as using color and a consistent background; the use of transparencies, such as keeping the font size large and including graphics; and computer-delivered presentations, such as keeping text to a minimum and performing a test run. When these guidelines are followed, not only is the instructor forced to be well prepared and organized, but the overall effectiveness of the course is enhanced. Preparation and organization are two key elements in successful online and ITV delivery. But as important as these are, they do not replace the need for the instructor to have mastery of the content of the course, to have excellent skills in using the technology, and to be open to seeking assistance when it is needed.

INSTRUCTIONAL DESIGNERS

Instructional designers have become an integral part of a course design team in distance learning. Not only are they helpful to faculty, but they have been trained specifically for their job through degree programs. They are familiar with most technologies available to faculty and can recommend effective ways to integrate technology into a distance education course. Unlike many traditional courses, distance education courses emerge as polished productions with all the bells and whistles that make them interesting to and engaging for the student.

MODELS FOR DEVELOPING AN ONLINE COURSE

There are different models at different institutions when it comes to instructional design. Among them are faculty-designed, instructional technology-developed arrangements (Rosenblum, 2000), partnerships between institutions and technology companies, faculty using courseware, and listservs.

Faculty-Designed, Instructional Technology-Developed

In this approach, instructional designers collaborate with the instructor to customize the online delivery to meet the objectives of the course. All materials to be used in the delivery of the course are given to the instructional designer by the faculty member (e.g., content outlines, images to be used in the presentation, text documents, and any audio selections), and the instructional designer readies everything for course delivery. In preparation for the course, an instructor is encouraged to talk with other instructors who have had experience using some of the tools he or she wishes to use. Many times, experienced faculty can shed some light on the pros and

cons of using various online discussion methodologies in courses, as well as which examination/quiz format to use. Faculty also can gain insight about teaching a course online by actually taking one themselves. Short of taking a course, faculty are encouraged to take advantage of workshops on their campuses in which techniques for teaching online are offered.

Partnerships

Some institutions have partnerships with technology providers. For example, the Institute for Academic Technology (IAT) was developed as a partnership between the University of North Carolina at Chapel Hill and IBM (Conway, 1996). The vision for IAT was to create a place where faculty and administrators could gather to help develop new technologies and to learn how to use them effectively. Instructors and administrators from all over the country were welcomed, and training and demonstrations were provided at no cost to participants. The philosophy of IAT was one of advocacy for faculty and the transfer of information. Distance education and classroom design became the primary goals of IAT, "a conceptual continuum running from place-bound classrooms to any time, any place virtual learning environments" (Conway, 1996, p. 28).

Eventually IAT became a place where educators' problems were discussed and strategies to solve the problems were developed. IAT staff became experts not only in integrating technology into various curricula, but also in recognizing possible obstacles. They "help[ed] institutions create meaningful change by integrating technological form with pedagogical function" (Conway, 1996, p. 28). The combined endeavors of IAT and IBM have helped faculty use technology to enhance course content and improve teaching. They also have provided information and assistance that create exciting and effective learning experiences for distance education students.

Faculty-Designed, Faculty-Developed Using Courseware

Another approach to preparing an online course when instructional designers are not available is the faculty-designed, faculty-developed approach (Rosenblum, 2000). Software tools like WebCT allow faculty to easily adapt their courses to the web environment. Briefly, Blackboard and WebCT are web course management tools that provide a framework for the instructor, using templates for syllabi, discussion areas, and online quizzes. (See Chapter 6 for more information about these course management software packages.)

Campus technology staff can suggest courseware packages and provide instruction in how to use them to set up a course. Often institutions contract for site licenses to use course management software packages, and faculty may select from among these. When selecting a courseware package, the instructor should keep in mind the needs of potential students and his or her own teaching style. Once a package has been chosen, faculty should become acquainted with all its features. Many instructors find it helpful to browse other online courses or to talk with experienced faculty about their online courses for ideas or insights. Using this framework, professors can build personalized courses to fit the needs of their own teaching methods and the needs of their students.

Listservs

There are also listservs that support online teaching, too many to list here, but a few of the better ones include one at the University of Connecticut, the Professional Organizational Development Support of Faculty Using Computing Technology in Higher Education. Another, created by Stephen Ehrmann's TLT Group, is a support resource used by many institutions as they develop and deliver distance education courses (see www.tltgroup.org for more information). Additionally, the University of Maryland's University College provides online help for faculty teaching online courses (see www.umuc.edu).

However one proceeds, it is of utmost importance to have support, both administrative and technological. If the institution's administration does not support online teaching, both philosophically and financially, it will not be successful. It would not be feasible for most faculty to deliver a course from their own web page, since a working knowledge of HTML language would be required. Online courses use features such as file transfer capability, discussion boards, and other resources that make the virtual classroom interesting. Technology support for faculty is critical as well. Faculty need support not only to learn about the features used in online courses, but throughout the course to ensure a smooth delivery.

When planning an online environment, it is important not to lose sight of the goals and objectives of the course. Careful planning on how to verify the identity of students enrolled in the course and what kind of examination procedure to use is important. Once course policies have been determined, students should be apprised of them at the beginning of the course. A syllabus, course schedule, and any other materials necessary to the course should be posted on the web site. Materials in which students are given information about the school's computer system and instructions about how to maneuver through an online course are very important to students' success. These should be made readily available to all students enrolled in the courses offered by the institution. A personal welcome to students in the course using an audio or video clip by the faculty member may make students see the instructor as "real" rather than some virtual ghost.

Other things to think about include whether the course will be asynchronous or have a real-time component, what kinds of learning activities will be required, what kind of student participation will be expected, and what to do in the event of temporary technology failure. It is also important for faculty to use techniques to encourage active communication and participation, to provide timely feedback to students, and to have mechanisms in place for getting feedback from students about how well the instructor is doing. And, faculty should always be open to and ready for new and better technologies with which to teach. Institutions must provide professional development and training to keep faculty current on the technology they employ.

CHAPTER 9

The Course: What Are the Ingredients?

Educational delivery is changing to fit a new breed of students. Students who are computer literate, who carry palm pilots and check their e-mail on cell phones are the people entering our institutions today. Children who have grown up with home PCs and chat rooms, who play sophisticated electronic games every day, and who have always had computers in their school classrooms are now college age. Looking back over the past century, institutions have made little progress in meeting the needs and desires of changing populations. In fact, today's institutions of higher education are very similar to the model of the 19th century; however, students are dramatically different from those who attended the early university. Daniel Gilman of the University of California in 1872 declared that "the university is the most comprehensive term that can be applied to indicate a foundation for the promotion and diffusion of knowledge . . . to train young men as scholars for all the callings of life" (Lucas, 1994, p. 144). Young men, he says? Well, today, men *and* women of all ages—young, middle, and old—are enjoying the benefits of a university education. However, the university model students prefer today is closer to that present during the time of Socrates in the 5th century, when a student and his teaching master would meet in a garden or at a temple or at some other noncampus location at a time when both desired to conduce in the learning process. So it is with distance education: People participate in the learning experience somewhere away from an institution's physical campus at a time convenient for them. Technology-based education is more compatible with today's students' thinking, needs, and orientation. "Getting online now is a way [for educational institutions] to be prepared for the future of higher education" (Serwatka, 1999, p. 74). And, designing distance education courses and instruction that will afford students a respectable and satisfying education is critical to moving higher education into the 21st century.

DESIGN CONSIDERATIONS

When designing distance learning programs and courses, the first thing an institution should consider is the student audience. That is, what are the characteristics of the target population? Education must be designed to cater to this group. Today's students are demanding courses that are convenient, focused, applicable to their career choices, and available to them in a variety of formats. More and more they are calling for an education they can manage on their own terms, completing assignments and coursework in their own time. They are well versed in the latest technologies and expect their professors to be skilled and experienced in the same. They count on institutions to offer educational options that allow them to use their technological expertise. Choice of technologies must be matched to the needs of the students. "In planning the media for distance learning programs, the three most important things are lifestyle, lifestyle, lifestyle," states Boettcher (1998, p. 57). Everhart (1999) points out that more than 44% of students enrolled in American institutions of higher education today are mature, lifelong learners who require continuing education. Although technology is not the animal it used to be, it is not yet the animal it is going to be. However, planning courses that use technologies will need to evolve as the technology does.

Other considerations for course and program development include the level of administrative support for distance learning, technical support systems available to faculty and students involved in distance learning, and the institution's infrastructure.

It is also critical to the success of distance education programs to have policies and procedures in place that ensure effective operation, including marketing processes, instructional design and development systems, and instructor and facilitator training (Lowery & Barnes, 1996).

THE ONLINE COURSE

Online courses may not be for everybody, but students who are interested need a way to assess whether this mode of learning will suit their needs, their lifestyle, and their learning preferences. Institutions easily can make an online self-assessment available to any student thinking about taking a distance learning course. This may be as simple as the one used by Oregon (see Appendix E) or one used by the University of Maine System (Appendix P). After determining whether online courses would satisfy their needs, students can assess their computer skills using an instrument like the one found in Appendix Q.

Students also may be referred to the FAQ (frequently asked questions) section of the school's distance learning web site (see Figure 9.1). Here they will find questions other students have asked about

Figure 9.1. University of Maine System University College Frequently Asked Questions

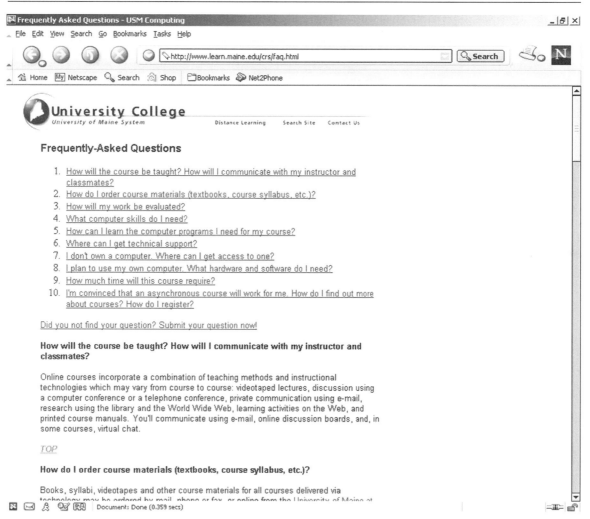

Reprinted with permission from the University of Maine System. Web site: www.learn.maine.edu

distance learning as well as answers to them. "A Guide to Online Courses" at the University of Maine web site (Appendix R) presents comments by faculty and students about a variety of topics.

Once students have decided that online is the way to go, an interactive online orientation is a must before the start of the semester. Many courseware vendors include online orientations as part of their offerings. The orientation should provide information about the distance learning technologies, the culture of distance learning, and how the course works. Technologies may include demonstrations on how to download and install a tutorial CD-ROM and video player software, if they will be used during the course. Students should be shown how to run a PowerPoint presentation on the Internet, and how to send and receive attachments. The orientation is designed to help students learn to maneuver through the course and become comfortable using the software used to deliver it.

In planning the course, a professor and a team of designers and technical experts must consider ways to maximize the learning and teaching process while using the tools offered through technology. The course should be designed to interface with the medium. Traditional face-to-face course materials may not fit with the technology. Thus, the instructor and the team of experts will need to figure out the best way to deliver the content of the course using the most appropriate technology tools.

The Syllabus: What Structure?

When creating a syllabus, faculty should take into consideration students' lives and schedules. Faculty must communicate expectations about student participation (frequency, type, quality, and its weight in the grading process) in simple, straightforward language and provide a clearly written schedule of weekly assignments and test or paper due dates. Faculty should keep a schedule of activities for themselves: when to interact with students and respond to questions, when to grade assignments, and when to give feedback on performance. Students should have explicit information about how to contact the professor (i.e., phone numbers and e-mail address), when they can expect a response, and where they may get help if they need it. Pro-

viding links where students may access tutorials on technical issues—including a telephone number, toll free if possible—and where students may call to get technical assistance or course support will help them feel more secure in taking the course.

It is a good idea to include discussion questions with weekly assignments on the syllabus so students will be aware of what they are expected to discuss online. This allows them to prepare ahead of time and keep the questions in mind as they complete readings and other assignments. Faculty should offer several different topics for discussion and let students select those in which they will participate.

Variety is key when deciding the kinds of activities students will be required to complete. For example, it is a good idea to intersperse activities such as small-group discussions or project planning with lecture and peer critique of papers. Another good rule of thumb is to require all students to hand in at least one hardcopy of a paper or essay. This establishes another connection between the student, the faculty, and the course. Handing in papers is what students are used to and, even though the course and assignments may be completed virtually, it is important for the instructor to send the message to students that the end products of a virtual course and a traditional face-to-face course are the same.

When assigning projects, readings, and discussions, faculty should set reasonable due dates. Students have a life outside of the class and with that life come many responsibilities. This does not mean that standards should be compromised; rather, it means that in distance courses faculty should have no more or no fewer expectations of students than they do in face-to-face courses.

Interaction

Interaction among the participants in the teaching–learning process is essential to good instruction. Necessary to the success of interaction are addressing group dynamics, encouraging student involvement in course activities, providing visuals, and carefully planning how these will be accomplished. Selecting courses that are cognitive rather than psychomotor, courses designed to facilitate interaction and provide feedback, and a highly organized team of people to deliver the instruction are a few of the key recommendations for successful distance education courses (Martin, Foshee, Moskal, & Bramble, 1996).

Communication is the foundation of successful distance learning courses. It must be ongoing, regular, continuous, and easy. Navigating through the course is accomplished through ongoing communication—between faculty and students and among students. Unlike face-to-face courses where students can show up and sit through the class period, in online courses there is no "showing up." They cannot sit passively. They must interact! Student presence is virtual/invisible. Faculty and instructional designers must structure the course in a way that supersedes this invisibility. Assignments and class activities that require students to interact must be a regular part of the course. Peer critique of assignments, chat rooms, online discussions, small-group projects, and study groups all have interactive components.

It is important to communicate to students that when they do not understand something in the course, it is *imperative* to their success that they communicate their confusion or questions clearly and in a timely manner to the professor. This must be stressed over and over again throughout the course. Body language, such as a confused look on a student's face, does not work over the Internet—yet, although progress is being made in this area too (see Lin-Liu, 2002). As important as letting a professor know that something is not clear, is for students to express enthusiasm, understanding, and excitement about what is happening in the course. When students are not participating, it is up to the instructor to follow up to find out why. An e-mail or phone call to the student will allow the professor to find out if the student is having problems with the course. This kind of follow-up also will let students know that the professor is aware of their presence or absence, even though the class is not face-to-face.

Communication can be easy with the broad range of pedagogical options available to instructors. Design teams and faculty must plan the structure and delivery of a course so that communication among participants is a routine part of every class session. This is key to the success of the course. And, participation should count as part of the grade. It is on the shoulders of interaction that successful learning rests.

Instructors must communicate online in the same way they would talk in person, interjecting their own personality into their writings. But, comments and writings must be very explicit and clear. Prompt feedback makes students feel less isolated and more connected. It also motivates students to participate regularly. Instructors also must be good managers and well versed in effective teaching techniques. Faculty will find themselves acting in a facilitator role rather than a talking head. By design, online learning is interactive, and asynchronous communication provides students and faculty with choices about how, when, and with what tools they will interact with others in the course.

Creating Community

Faculty must work to create a sense of community within the class. Students like the connection they feel to others and to the materials in an online course. When a professor shows interest in discussions by commenting on students' ideas and insights, students feel valued and encouraged to participate more. Sometimes faculty and students feel closer because of the frequency of their online interaction. Bulletin boards, forums, chat rooms, and e-mail afford all participants, students and professor alike, many opportunities to interact with each other. Conference features allow all communications to become part of a permanent record for the course. Students and faculty may read or review all communications at any time during the semester. Messages may be posted during the timeframe allotted for the topic or conference, and all messages are available to members of the course.

Feedback

A continual feedback mechanism should be in place so students can register thoughts and comments about what is working and what would make the course better. Students are more likely to provide feedback if it can be done anonymously. It is up to the professor to monitor all feedback and take action when appropriate. In addition to improving the quality and success in web-based courses, student feedback has a significant impact on the learning process as a whole. "Mechanisms must be incorporated [into] web-based environments to evaluate the medium, content, format design, and structure so timely intervention can occur if a problem is identified" (Hazari & Schnorr, 1999, p. 32).

One method for collecting assessment and feedback data is by employing an online feedback form. This form provides the faculty member with feedback about the course in a timely manner. Referred to as a type of informal assessment, online feedback forms have many advantages over asking students to e-mail feedback. For example, forms can be integrated on web pages, they are easy to complete, they are focused, they do not depend on browser-specific commands, and they provide a similar structure, as do other course web materials with regard to the context of the course. The online feedback form enables students to discuss what they learned, consequently providing the instructor with useful information regarding concepts that still need reinforcement. Ultimately, the instructor "is given the extraordinary opportunity to modify the course on an ongoing basis, or to maintain the flow of class as it is currently being presented" (Hazari & Schnorr, 1999, p. 34).

Hazari and Schnorr (1999) link this web-based informal assessment technique to a cognitive behavior modification technique "designed to help students develop goal setting behavior, planning, and self-monitoring" (p. 36). Throughout a course, students are given the opportunity to master concepts by having this new means of regulating and monitoring their own learning as they respond to the questions and receive ongoing feedback. Instructors can scaffold students' learning in a nonthreatening manner by observing how they respond to questions as well as by soliciting an ongoing dialog.

Student motivation is increased by the use of such a web-based assessment technique, because students feel that the instructor is interested in their feedback and, ultimately, their success. And, to achieve greater success in web environments intended to promote teaching and learning, faculty are empowered by using technologies to facilitate their own teaching using the feedback they receive from their students.

An end-of-course evaluation provides students with the opportunity to talk about the technology, the course (syllabus, materials, assignments, and other features), the workload, online interaction and course organization, and other elements of the course.

Presenting Course Materials

Technology offers faculty many choices in how they present class materials. In an ITV course and online, visuals enhance the presentation of text and content and make the subject matter more interesting and engaging for students. Interactive courseware offers many possibilities for the teacher, including video, graphics, animation, and interactive elements. And, it is essential that instructors know how to effectively use these tools. Thibodeau (1997), an interactive courseware development specialist, offers tips for using video and graphics, and discusses considerations for faculty when designing text elements. Key considerations relative to video include:

- using long, medium, and close-up shots to establish visual introduction;
- using zoom-in to focus the learner's attention on a specific object;
- focusing on an object long enough to allow it to "register" with the learner when introducing something new;
- making sure there is no distracting movement in the video and that the area of focus is well lighted;
- using video formats such as a "walkthrough," a "talking head," a "show and tell," or a "talk show";
- using the first-person method to help personalize the content of the video;
- using audio and video together to reinforce learning and to make sure the visual ties directly to the accompanying audio;
- showing future events or the consequences of inappropriate performance prior to instruction; and
- using video rather than still photos if the content requires movement. (Thibodeau, 1997, p. 84)

Considerations involving graphics include:

- using graphics or animation when a realistic presentation may overburden the audience with too much detail;
- using graphics to reduce the amount of nonapplicable details and to highlight key information;
- avoiding the use of biases or stereotypes in graphics or animations (gender, ethnicity, religion, etc.); and
- using humor cautiously. (Thibodeau, 1997, pp. 84–85)

Considerations when designing text elements include:

- limiting the amount of text on the screen;
- positioning text appropriately;
- formatting the screen appropriately by converting sentences containing serial items to lists, reserving italics for titles or headings, and providing a generous amount of white space to separate blocks of information; and
- verifying the appropriateness of colors used for text under simulated presentation conditions. (Thibodeau, 1997, p. 85)

With respect to interactivity design considerations, the following are offered:

- break the content down into small units and build in questions with positive and negative feedback;
- move from content to practice to summary to keep the learner from becoming bored and to help facilitate learning;
- provide an opportunity for interaction every three to five screens;
- base questions upon previously acquired knowledge and allow students opportunities to utilize what they have learned rather than just memorizing and reciting answers; and
- present information through active exploration, such as problem solving or learning through discovery. (Thibodeau, 1997, p. 85)

Tracking Student Participation

Online learning courseware allows for the tracking of student progress and encourages continual feedback by students and faculty. Additionally, assessments that are embedded in the assignments allow teachers to monitor student performance.

When using e-mail, one of the primary communication vehicles in online courses, it is advisable to develop a mechanism for identifying which course a student is in. Requiring all students to use the course identifier (e.g., PSY 101) as the subject line of an e-mail will assist the professor in distinguishing e-mail from different courses. Questions should be cataloged into topics so individual responses will not have to be created each time the same questions are asked. The bulletin board can be used for posting questions and answers so all students can access them. Faculty must be clear in their communication with students and make sure the students know assignment due dates, examination dates, and where and when the professor may be reached.

The professor must monitor online discussions but keep participation to a minimum. Times when he or she might become involved are when the discussion is off track or when he or she wants to reinforce a good point made by a participant.

Feedback to individual students is important, and the professor should model good writing, using a conversational tone and complete sentences with proper grammar. Humor or self-disclosure, where appropriate, will humanize the professor. Communication with students should be brief and to the point. If too much text is on the screen or if too many screens are used to make a point, students may lose interest. Being involved in the weekly class activities is a good way to monitor student participation and performance as well.

Structuring Online Discussions

Online discussions among students have some advantages over face-to-face contact. Asynchronous meetings eliminate any potential time and space conflicts among participants. Participation occurs anytime and anywhere.

Electronic discussion groups are an effective communication and learning tool. In comparison to traditional forms of classroom discussion, they underscore such benefits as convenience, depth of commitment, and exam preparation.

The flexibility of electronic discussion groups can accommodate the needs of all students, from impulsive learners to reflective learners, and everyone in between. Electronic discussion groups also foster a sense of community by helping students to create relationships beyond the scope of the environment of classroom discussion, offering advice or help to one another.

Because participants of the discussion groups must write their thoughts, they tend to think before they express their ideas. Students gain valuable writing skills in the course of their class interactions and assignments. Electronic discussion groups further support convenient interaction according to the time schedule of the student and teacher. Faculty use electronic discussion groups for a variety of reasons, such as:

- to facilitate overall discussion;
- to encourage group interaction on problems;
- to stimulate class discussion and build class community;
- to facilitate after-hours student academic interaction and encourage shy [students];
- to encourage ESL students to become more fluent in English and more comfortable using the computer;
- to provide a forum for discussion of current topics in the field that students can use at their own time and convenience. (Karayan & Crowe, 1997, p. 70)

Students also find benefits in using electronic discussion groups. Some students feel that with this mode they are more likely to ask a teacher a question, participate in course activities outside of their normal workday, and think before answering a question.

It is important to assign tasks students must do to prepare for the online discussion. As mentioned earlier, including discussion questions in the syllabus allows students to think about what they will be expected to discuss. Many students must be taught how to discuss topics as a professional in their field. The instructor can do this by modeling appropriate ways or providing students with places they can find such discussions. Various discussion formats may be demonstrated by having students engage in a debate, a review of a peer's work, a critique of an essay, a spontaneous open discussion, or a case study analysis. Students may be asked to summarize their learning as a result of the online discussion. "People typically find that they are drawn into the subject matter of the class much more deeply than in a traditional course because of the discussions they get involved in" (Kearsley, 1997).

Providing timely, concise feedback on assignments, including discussion groups, encourages students to do their best. Positive comments about what students did well are always welcomed. Gently probing students who have not responded or who have given superficial comments may assist them in digging deeper to come up with something of substance. While sensitivity to different learning and interaction styles is important, the instructor also must be aware of cultural and language skill differences among students. Courtesy to all students is essential for the health of the interaction.

Assessment

Students must be able to get a sense of how they are doing in the course. Self-assessment tools designed by the instructor should be available for online use. Quizzes, exams, peer critique groups, question and answer sessions, and feedback forums are techniques that can be used throughout the course. Software packages assist instructors in creating online quizzes. For example, WebCT (http://www.webct.com) has a quiz creation module. Online quizzes provide students with instant feedback on their learning. Online assessments help students evaluate their knowledge gain and competence in a topic.

A variety of activities that keep the students engaged in the learning process should be developed as part of assessment. Creating "get acquainted" exercises for the first session will allow students to begin to know their virtual classmates. Some faculty find that a face book (i. e., an online collection of pictures of students, with names and e-mail addresses) is valued by students; others find that anonymity works just as well. It is also important to keep online content presentations interesting for students. Use of graphics, video, and audio enhances a class lecture. Using these tools is a major advantage over face-to-face courses; however, a "text-only" version should be available so students can download text easily and quickly. Students should be encouraged to print out hardcopies of course information such as the syllabus and contact/help information. They also should be encouraged to use the course web site regularly. This is where students will find updates, course changes, notices, and other important information posted.

Faculty should always monitor student progress and performance and give students personal attention. Both may be easier to do online than face-to-face because of the multitude of online interactive tools available, such as chat rooms for small-group work and threaded discussions (bulletin boards) for large groups. If using a courseware such as WebCT or Blackboard, there should be a link on the course web site to a student help section where students may find tutorials for using the courseware.

Students, too, need to be able to provide the professor with feedback on the course. There should be anonymous online class feedback forms where students may write their comments and offer suggestions for a better course. Additionally, students should be invited to contact the professor by phone or in person if they so desire. Students should always know when and where the instructor may be reached and what his or her virtual office hours are as well.

These, then, are the necessary ingredients for a successful course. Those who are well prepared and include the elements discussed here will avoid unnecessary frustration when it comes time to deliver a course.

CHEATING: ARE THERE IMPOSTORS AMONG US?

As in any life situation, there will always be individuals who attempt to cheat in their educational endeavors. This phenomenon may begin in early years and extend through higher education and beyond. Cheating may occur in distance learning, and does, just as it occurs in traditional face-to-face learning. Skeptics as well as proponents of distance learning, however, want assurances that the work submitted by a student is indeed the work of that student and not of someone else.

Some contend that cheating in online courses is more difficult to detect than in courses where student and faculty see each other on a regular basis. But this author contends that cheating in online courses requires more energy and more planning, and may well be more *easily* detected by the instructor. Consider the following:

- Most online learning is labor intensive and requires daily attention by the student. In the online class, the cheater must ensure that the impostor is attending to the class activities on a daily basis. In face-to-face classes, students attend class once or twice a week, pass in assignments, and take tests or complete papers. Here the cheater may use another's paper or ask someone else to complete an assignment. If the test is given in class, there are ways to cheat as well.

- In online courses, student to student contact is more frequent, and during the course of a semester a familiarity is developed with others in the class. This happens as a by-product of the structure of the online course and in required discussions (i.e., bulletin boards, forums, chat rooms, and e-mails). In face-to-face classes, especially in large lecture courses, a familiarity with other students is not as common. Discussions are sometimes

nonexistent, and unless students form their own study groups they are less likely to develop relationships with other students in the class.

- In well-taught online courses, feedback to students by the professor is a regular activity. Likewise, feedback to the professor by the student is often a critical part of the course structure. Through this feedback the professor gets to know the distant student, sometimes more intimately than face-to-face students. The professor also establishes a relationship with the student and gets to know his or her communication patterns, allowing the professor to discern atypical responses and assignment completion by that student. In traditional classes, although face-to-face with the student, the professor may never have any significant communication with the student aside from the assignments completed or an occasional "hello" as the student enters the classroom.

- Activities embedded in the online class, such as self-assessments, peer critique groups, quizzes, feedback forums, and the like, all require a great deal of energy and attention by the student who is taking the course. And, although face-to-face courses may have similar activities, the online student (as well as the face-to-face student) must participate frequently. Finding an impostor who is willing to pay such attention to course activities for the cheater may be difficult.

While it is certainly a possibility that a student might get an impostor to do all these things, it would, no doubt, require as much if not more effort than taking the class him- or herself. Aside from the care and monitoring successful cheating demands, students who engage in this sort of activity are cheating themselves most. In addition to losing an opportunity to learn, students face the potential consequences of such an activity and the probability of disciplinary action by the institution, if caught.

Is there any guarantee of the authenticity of the learner in any learning situation? Probably not. But there are ways to short-circuit attempts at cheating, whether online or in the face-to-face classroom.

1. Have a "get-to-know-you" session at the beginning of the course using a synchronous chat session and spontaneous questions and conversation.

2. Put together a face book (see Case Study 2 in Chapter 7).
3. At the beginning of the first class, ask students to outline in an e-mail to you, their own learning goals for the course. Likewise, at the end of the course, ask them to assess how well they met their goals, citing assignments and other class activities as evidence (see Case Study 1 in Chapter 7).
4. Maintain frequent contact with each student via e-mail.
5. Monitor student forums and/or chats with an eye for irregularities in communication patterns.
6. Assign peer groups and require that they assess one another's work.
7. Establish a trust policy and outline consequences for cheating. Prominently display this policy in the syllabus.

While these efforts may not guarantee anything, they will at least make cheating a difficult task for the student.

CHAPTER 10

Student Support Services

Key to the success of any educational enterprise is a wide array of student support services. Institutions usually have a Student Services Division where recruitment, advising, registration, orientation, placement, prior learning assessment, and financial aid are housed. These services are a given in the traditional higher education institution. In the early 1990s, when distance education was becoming more prevalent, special support services for distance education students often were overlooked. Institutions made little effort to offer services electronically. In fact, most institutions that were developing and delivering instruction either online or using ITV continued to use on-campus services for their off-campus and distance students. It quickly became clear that, while some services applied to both the campus-based student and the distance learner, changes were needed in the way these services were offered that were specific to distance education students' needs. Today, institutions are doing a much better job at serving students who choose distance learning as an option. Most institutions that offer distance courses and programs have at least some student support services designed to assist students enrolled in the courses and programs.

Researchers and educators concur that student support services are a must for students learning at a distance. Many have written about what services should be available, but not all give advice on how to provide them. Distance learning providers agree that students need technical support services and administrative services (e.g., electronic application and registration services). More and more, institutions are converting to 24/7 arrangements for technical support. Institutions such as Mercer University, NYUonline, Jones International University, the University of Maryland's University College, Kentucky

Commonwealth Virtual University, and others provide round the clock technical support for their students. Many use vendors and others provide the support on their own (Young, 2000b).

Those in the distance learning world feel that students need electronic access to course catalogs, library, bookstore, and advising. But there are many questions about how to provide these services in a coordinated and effective way. Some institutions have been more successful than others in putting their student support services online. For example, the University of Wisconsin has implemented an integrated approach to student support services. They use a "Learner Relationship Management System (LRMS), a data warehouse that tracks all student contact with the institution . . . to help coordinate the efforts of support staff in various offices" (Kelly, 2001, p. 5). The institution provides services to online programs, including advising (both general and educational), technical support, registration services, course tracking, administrative services (like registration and payment options), a bookstore, and learner tracking. The university prides itself on responding to students' questions and needs within 24 hours, and claims a one-stop approach to services.

Grossmont College District in El Cajon, California (www.grossmont.gcccd.cc.ca.us/grosmontonlin/online.htm), provides a listing of equipment and software needed by students taking online courses, interactive self-assessments for successful online learners, information about how to set up an e-mail account and how to start a class, and tutorials for online learners (Saba, 1999b).

UCLA Extension student services (www.OnlineLearning.net/OnlineLearningExplained) provides "contextual learner assistance" (Saba, 1999b, p. 3). There is a personalized welcome by the Director of

Information Technology, and the web site takes the student through a series of steps from the big picture to common questions and concerns and explanations, to the popular "Is Online Learning for Me?" survey.

Coastline Community College in Fountain Valley, California, uses web casts and live video so students can participate in face-to-face counseling sessions with on-campus counselors. Even better than a telephone call, counselors find that it is a positive experience for both the student and the counselor. Coastline also is experimenting with providing career planning on the Internet. It already provides students with online registration forms and online course schedules. Other live video services include orientation sessions and information on library services. Staff there feel that live video puts a human face in the picture and makes the session more personal (Carnevale, 2000c).

The University of Maine System University College (www.learn.maine.edu) provides a variety of online student support services, including library services, bookstore services, services for students with disabilities, technical support, financial aid, application for admission, registration, and quick guides for help with software used by the university.

"Some college officials foresee a day when virtual universities will offer all their services—from registration to book sales—around the clock" (Young, 2000b, p. A49). Others see commencement as an event that will be provided online, such as the one that was conducted in March 2000 at Britain's Open University (Walker, 2000).

In 1997, the Western Cooperative for Educational Telecommunications (WCET or the Cooperative) developed a guide in which they identified specific support services that distant learners need and developed guidelines for basic good practice in delivering these services using the Internet. The "Guide to Developing Online Student Services" was on their web page for a year—from October 2000 to September 2001. The decision to take the Guide off the web site after a year was made because it included examples of particular services from various institutions' web sites and they felt that it would be impossible to ensure that these examples would remain current for more than a year. The methodology used to create the Guide may be found on WCET's web site, www.wiche.edu, and is not re-

peated here. The project was supported by a grant from the U.S. Department of Education's Fund for the Improvement of Postsecondary Education. A successor project, "Beyond the Administrative Core: Creating Web-based Student Services for Online Learners," is currently underway and is expected to be disseminated some time in 2003.

The Guide is incorporated into the author's descriptions of student services important to distance learning students. Student support services that will be addressed here are divided into three categories: administrative services, services for students taking courses, and special services. Within the three categories the following services will be presented.

ADMINISTRATIVE SERVICES:

- Information for prospective students
- Recruitment
- A comprehensive electronic information system or web site
- Application for admission
- Financial aid
- Placement testing
- Registration
- Orientation services
- Academic advising

SERVICES FOR STUDENTS TAKING COURSES:

- The course web site
- Course syllabus
- Faculty office hours
- Grades
- Examination procedures
- Technical support services
- Library services
- Bookstore services
- Services to promote a sense of community

SPECIAL SERVICES:

- Career services
- Services for students with disabilities
- Personal counseling
- Instructional support and tutoring

The chapter will conclude with some tips for designing web-based student services, also developed by WCET.

ADMINISTRATIVE SERVICES

• **Information for Prospective Students.** If an institution has provided an entry point on its Internet or web site for "prospective students," this section probably will be the first place a new user will visit. It is therefore very important to create an accurate and positive impression of the institution and its distance learning offerings. Information placed on the web site for these students serves several purposes. First, it helps an individual make an informed decision about whether the institution's online learning opportunities are likely to meet his or her needs and helps the individual gauge the likelihood of success in the program. Second, this section of the institution's web page gives the college or university a perfect opportunity for marketing its online or distance learning offerings. It becomes, in part, a portal to the entire institution.

It is important to make online learning opportunities highly visible and clearly organized on the institution's web page. Too often, colleges and universities hide their online programs several layers deep in the institution's web site. The Internet enables an institution to highlight opportunities for learning via technology. Institutions should try to give a real sense of the institution and its distance learning offerings by taking advantage of the Internet and related technologies to convey the special characteristics of the institution and its online or distance learning program.

It is important also to offer prospective students the opportunity to assess their personal readiness for an online course or program. At a minimum, this section should contain a list of questions that students can ask themselves to determine their likelihood of success in an online course. There are a number of self-assessment tools designed to help prospective students determine their readiness for online learning. These assessments don't provide assurance of success, of course, and many are fairly superficial. However, they do offer some additional information about the traits that tend to make one a successful online learner. In addition, some assessments also include at least a general set of questions designed to assess a user's level of technical proficiency (see also Appendices E, P, and Q).

Information and/or tools should be provided for assessing hardware and software capabilities. Prospective students should be guided through steps necessary to determine whether they currently have adequate hardware and software capability to take an online course from the institution. Specifications, including hardware and software, Internet service provider, e-mail, and browser, such be listed and defined. If possible, a way should be included for students to test these capabilities through the institution's web site.

There should be a link to frequently asked questions (FAQs) about cost, transferability, timing, and equipment related to the online and other distance learning offerings. It makes sense to anticipate the kinds of questions a student might ask and to collect the answers all in one place. There also should be a link to a person the student can call or e-mail who can provide additional information about distance programs. Contact information should be displayed prominently, perhaps immediately after the FAQ section.

• **Recruitment.** When we think of recruitment, things like visits to high schools by college recruitment officers, television and newspaper advertising campaigns, college view books, brochures, and word of mouth may come to mind. When distance education courses and programs are found in the context of a traditional institution, we do not often think of separate recruitment efforts to attract students to these courses and programs. While recruitment offices are found in nearly every kind of institution, few are found that are identified as "distance education" recruiting offices. There may be specific efforts to inform students about a particular program being delivered this way, but recruitment in distance education as an activity has not yet been a major focus. That may be different for institutions that deliver all courses and programs using distance education exclusively; however, a look at the web sites of these institutions or a call to the administrative offices of the college or university reveals that "recruitment" per se is not a separate entity. When recruitment efforts are made by higher education institutions, and students come, they may find that some of the courses they are interested in taking are delivered using distance education technologies. On the other hand, when students are looking specifically for an institution that delivers some of its courses or programs using distance education, it is the student, not the institution, who is making the effort. Students seeking increased access to programs not available in their local institution, or convenience, or flexibility, may search for distance education opportunities. Something institutions may consider adding to their web site is a link to a site and chat room that are dedicated to distance learning topics. Prospective students can go there to learn more about distance learning opportunities and chat with students who have had experience in these courses as well as faculty who teach them. Another good information source for prospective students is the "frequently asked questions" link located on the distance education component of the institution's web site.

• **A Comprehensive Electronic Information System or Web Site**. A place is needed where students may get information about distance education courses as well as support services, and other information that might have an impact on the learning experience. Questions that should be answered include:

1. How does this institution define distance learning?
2. What courses are offered this semester (when, where, and how are they being delivered)?
3. What degree and certificate programs are available and what qualifications do I need to enroll?
4. What courseware does the institution support and where can I learn how to use it?
5. Where do I find an application for admission?
6. Is there an online bookstore where I may purchase books? An online library where I may obtain resources?
7. What support services are available to students?
8. How do I get help when needed?

Students must have easy access to answers to these and other questions they may have before enrolling in courses. At the UMS University College web site, www.learn.maine.edu, a link, "getting started," takes students to a page that explains some of the things they need to know about distance education. There is a link to "frequently asked questions" (Figure 10.1), as well as a "Guide to Online Learning" (Appendix S) where comments by faculty and students about distance learning are found. Links to the two self-assessments, "Are 'Online' Courses for You?" (Appendix P) and "Computer Skills Survey" (Appendix Q), are located here as well. Students may use these to assess their skills and their fit, and also

to determine whether their computer is equipped for the technical requirements of the course. They also may find information on this web page about the availability of computers owned by the institution for use by students in a nearby remote location. A link to course listings where students will find information about their particular course choice (such as requirements for the course and what courseware is used) is also on the web site.

Many institutions offer assessments similar to those at Maine, which may be completed by students online to help them determine whether distance education is a viable option for them given their own characteristics and preferences, and whether they have the equipment and technical skills required to successfully complete a course. The online assessments are completed by the student and submitted, and immediate feedback is provided. Once the student considers the feedback, he or she may decide to take the course. With that decision made, the student may move to the next step, application for admission.

• **Application for Admission**. Once a student decides to enroll in a course or program, the admissions process is usually the first step taken in becoming associated with an institution. To make this section of the web site practical, the institution should ensure that the process itself controls the site architecture, so that a student is guided clearly through the necessary steps. Online application services are becoming more mainstream in this age of technology, not only for distance education students but for students desiring admission to traditional universities as well. Applications may differ from one program to another, but a good web site has links directing students to the appropriate application. For example, at the University of Maine System, each of the seven campuses has its own application. A visit to the UMS University College (distance learning) web site, www.learn.maine.edu, displays a link to "apply online." When students click on that link, they are connected to a web page with instructions on how to apply to one or more of the seven UM campuses. Another click allows a student to create an online e-mail account to use in the application process, or if the student has already established an e-mail account, there is a prompt that allows the student to log in and begin the application process. A menu leads the student through the application and allows him or her to fill in all information

Figure 10.1. University College Frequently Asked Questions

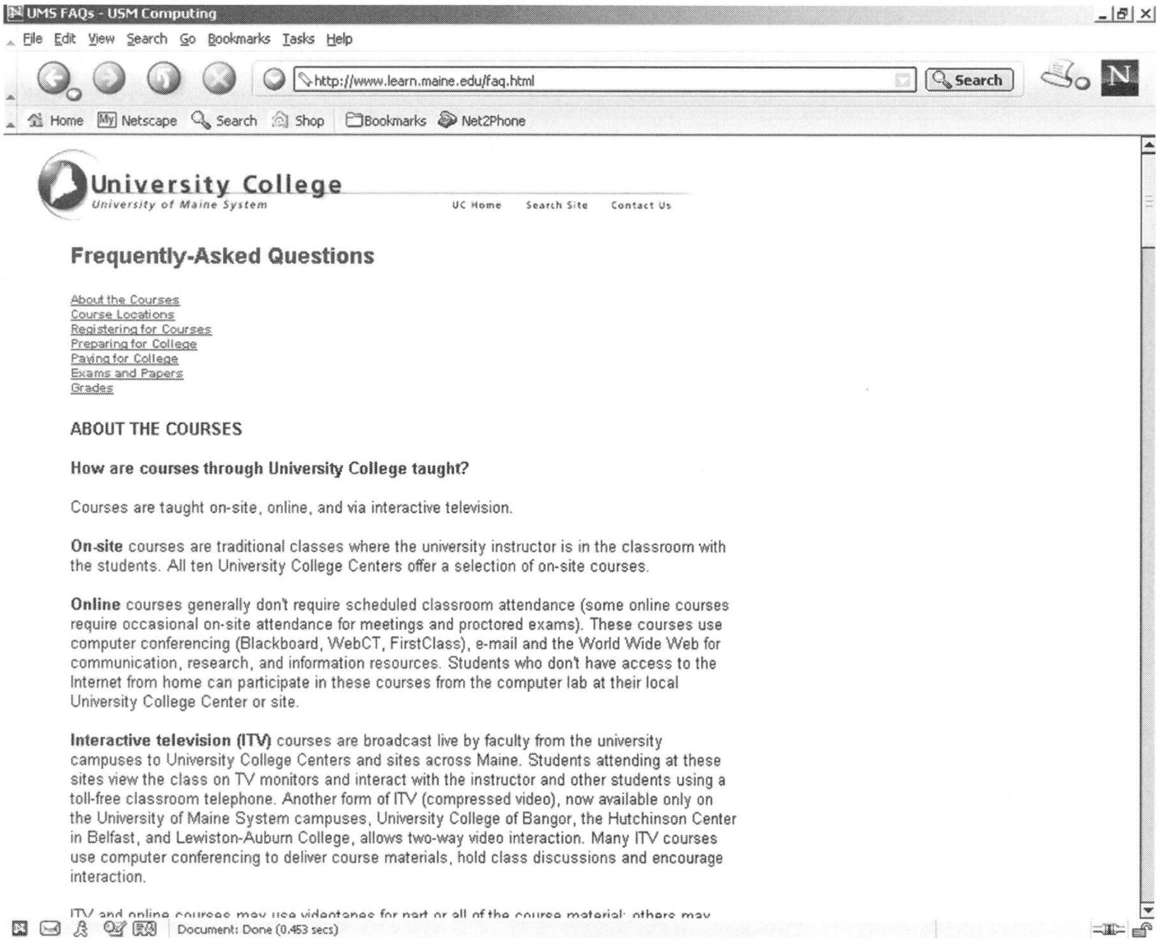
UMS FAQs - USM Computing

File Edit View Search Go Bookmarks Tasks Help

http://www.learn.maine.edu/faq.html

Home My Netscape Search Shop Bookmarks Net2Phone

University College

University of Maine System

UC Home Search Site Contact Us

Frequently-Asked Questions

About the Courses
Course Locations
Registering for Courses
Preparing for College
Paying for College
Exams and Papers
Grades

ABOUT THE COURSES

How are courses through University College taught?

Courses are taught on-site, online, and via interactive television.

On-site courses are traditional classes where the university instructor is in the classroom with the students. All ten University College Centers offer a selection of on-site courses.

Online courses generally don't require scheduled classroom attendance (some online courses require occasional on-site attendance for meetings and proctored exams). These courses use computer conferencing (Blackboard, WebCT, FirstClass), e-mail and the World Wide Web for communication, research, and information resources. Students who don't have access to the Internet from home can participate in these courses from the computer lab at their local University College Center or site.

Interactive television (ITV) courses are broadcast live by faculty from the university campuses to University College Centers and sites across Maine. Students attending at these sites view the class on TV monitors and interact with the instructor and other students using a toll-free classroom telephone. Another form of ITV (compressed video), now available only on the University of Maine System campuses, University College of Bangor, the Hutchinson Center in Belfast, and Lewiston-Auburn College, allows two-way video interaction. Many ITV courses use computer conferencing to deliver course materials, hold class discussions and encourage interaction.

Document: Done (0.453 secs)

Reprinted with permission from the University of Maine System. Web site: www.learn.maine.edu

that ordinarily would be asked for in a paper form of the application. In addition, there are links to a checklist, to forms that can be downloaded, or for changes the student wishes to make to an application that has already been submitted.

The admissions process gives an early impression of the institution. By making it possible for students to apply online without difficulty, the institution serves their needs as well as its own. If the admissions process is confusing or complicated, students may go elsewhere to take courses. So, the admissions process first should be clearly detailed, including admissions requirements. The online application should be easy to find, and a link to it clearly displayed on the web site. The form should be simple to complete online, and deadlines for application must be in plain sight. Additionally, there must be several payment options, and students should be provided with a way to reopen their application once it has been submitted as well as ways to track the application process.

- **Financial Aid.** For many students, financial aid has a critical role in the educational choices they make. It may affect which institution a student chooses to attend, the credit load, and even whether the individual can pursue higher education. Learning about financial aid can be a daunting experience for any student. Because of its great importance to students and its complex nature, financial aid information and services should be easy to find, accurate, and straightforward. If students are given the necessary online resources, they should be able to understand, apply for, and receive financial aid without ever visiting the campus. Information should be presented to give the student a basic knowledge of financial aid, including how to find out about what kinds are available, along with links to the sites where these are found. Tuition and fees should be prominently displayed. Policies and procedures that may affect a student's financial aid and registration decisions should be defined. Forms such as the Free Application for Federal Student Aid (FAFSA) and the federal student code for the institution should be provided. Students should be able to download forms if they cannot be completed online, and there should be links to related sites like FastWeb and collegeNet. For example, in Maine, students may apply to the Finance Authority of Maine (FAME) and the Maine Education Services (MES) Foundation for financial aid. Links to both FAME and MES are provided at the University College's web site. There are also links to all seven UM campus financial aid offices.

• **Placement Testing.** Students new to the institution may need to be tested to determine their appropriate placement in courses such as mathematics and writing. Computerized testing has become prevalent in many institutions, and students who need to take placement tests can often do so online, or at an off-campus center or remote site. At UMS University College, placement testing is free to all students and is done on the computer at an outreach center or off-campus site. Students must make an appointment to take the test and can do so by calling a student services coordinator in their region. However an institution chooses to administer this testing, it should be as convenient as possible for students who do not have access to a university campus.

• **Registration.** Registration is perhaps the most used and most important online administrative service. It is a service that every student will use every time he or she enrolls in a course. Therefore, designing an effective online registration system deserves significant attention. As with online application, online registration is becoming very common in tra-

ditional institutions because of the available technologies. The registration process should be detailed and easy for students to use. Because some courses have prerequisites, students should be aware of these and other university policies, or registration in a course may be blocked. In light of this, it is important for students to have access, through links on the web site, to course descriptions in an online catalog, a student handbook, and contact information for assistance. Students also should be advised about other options for registering besides the online option. Some institutions have developed very effective automated telephone systems that students may use to register. Important to all students are clear and detailed information about each step in the registration process, policies related to registration, a link or reference to course descriptions by department, course availability, and downloadable forms.

• **Orientation Services.** Since many students have never taken a distance education course before, it is important to provide some kind of orientation for them. This may be done online, over ITV, or in person; however, most students who sign up for a distance learning course prefer to have an orientation delivered in the same way the course will be. Institutions should offer a clear description that gives the student a sense of what it will be like to take a course using these technologies. Access to other students' testimonies may be useful, and opportunities to speak with faculty who teach the course may be offered. A general chat session before the course starts will allow the student to begin to use some of the skills he or she will be required to use once the course begins. Included in the orientation should be a description of the knowledge and skills needed to participate in the course. Requirements for word processing, how to set up an e-mail account, how to use a web browser, and how to participate in forums, chats, or bulletin boards are all important for the student to know up front. Information about the course web site and how to use it should be included in the orientation. Students also should know how to move from link to link and how to contact the professor or a staff member for technical assistance when needed. The support services available to distance education students must be explained, and letting them know when and how to use the services will assist students in feeling more secure about this new experience. Orientation sessions are provided by UMS at specific times prior to the beginning of each semester and are delivered online and using ITV. The times, days, and how to access them are explained on the "getting started" link of the web site (see www.learn.maine. edu). Registration is required. If students cannot "attend" one of the sessions, orientation videotapes are available to them. Students may benefit from "tips for success in an online environment" in the orientation session. Online tours are often useful to new students, who need to know what will be expected of them in distance education courses (e.g., knowledge of computer system, software, word processor, e-mail, browser, and search engines). The institution should provide information about where they can learn these skills or should direct students to appropriate workshops or tutorials before they enroll in a course.

• **Academic Advising.** Nearly all students use this service at some time in the first year of study and throughout their educational experience. The registration process, placement, orientation, educational planning, and financial aid are all intertwined with academic advising. Students seek advising on all aspects of their education. Online students need academic advising as much as do campus-based students. Institutions must be positioned to provide this service electronically to students at a distance. Using the Internet, institutions can provide a range of academic advising services, from building a course schedule for the next term and over the long term, to informed educational planning. Although many other student services are provided online with ease, advising can be a little trickier. Usually immediate and ongoing interaction is needed between student and advisor, especially in planning a course of study and being advised on course scheduling. While much may be done electronically, it is in the best interest of students for the institution to provide times and places where they can meet personally with an advisor either face-to-face, over the telephone, or using a real-time teleconferencing session. In addition to the personal meeting, students may be referred to self-help guides for making educational decisions. Most important is that students have all the information needed to make informed decisions about their educational path and access to knowledgeable professionals who can offer the appropriate assistance.

SERVICES FOR STUDENTS TAKING COURSES

Once the administrative issues have been attended to, the student is ready to begin the course or program in which he or she has enrolled. Services to students during the course are as important as the support students receive prior to beginning the course. Additionally, there are "special services," which may not be used by all students but must be in place for those who need them. In this section, support services directly related to course taking will be addressed. The next section will present special services that may be used by only a few students.

• **The Course Web Site.** Aside from the general web site maintained by the institution, are web sites that address issues applicable to specific courses. For example, let's take a look at one University College course that was offered in Spring 2003. The course, ANTO 170 Popular Archaeology, was delivered using the courseware Blackboard, as indicated by the Blackboard icon to the left of the course listing (see Figure 10.2). There is also an "info" link next to the course listing where students may find general information about the course with a click of the mouse. A description of the course, the delivery method, course expectations and grading, cost, and required course materials are detailed here. In case students have other questions not covered in this brief description, they are directed to call University College Tele-Service Center at a toll-free telephone number. By clicking on the course name, students enter the course web site and either are able to log on as a registered user or may preview the course as a guest (Figure 10.3).

On the left side of the screen are a number of tools students can use to maneuver through the course, including announcements, a course calendar, tasks, grades, e-mail, user directory, address book, and personal information. There is also a search engine with which to search the Web. The rest of the screen is dedicated to current information such as "today's announcements," "today's calendar," and "today's tasks." The information found in these cells changes daily as the course progresses.

• **Course Syllabus.** A course syllabus should be found on the course web site, with a description of the course, usually from the university's catalog; an

Figure 10.2. University of Maine System University College Spring 2003 Course Web Sites

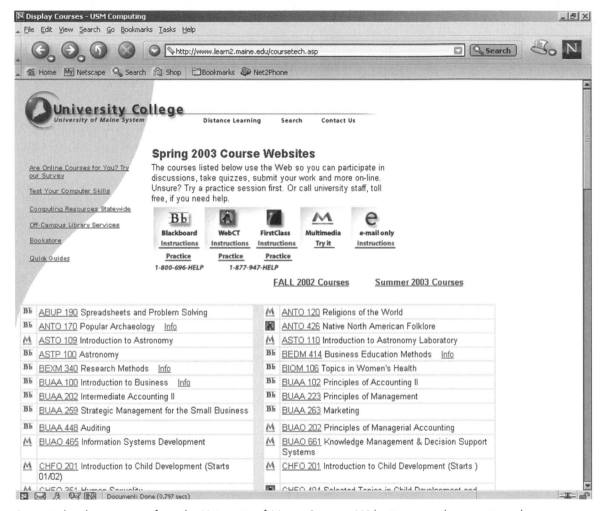

Reprinted with permission from the University of Maine System. Web site: www.learn.maine.edu

introduction to the professor; goals and objectives of the course; and a description of how the course will proceed. Required readings and assignments, and a calendar of due dates, must be clearly presented also. As much as possible, the syllabus should provide students with a week by week detailed account of what is expected in the course. This may include learning activities, readings, asynchronous and synchronous assignments, and how these will be graded. Information about late submission of assignments, or other course policies, should be clearly spelled out. Details about how to contact the instructor, such as when, where, and how, must be placed where every student will see them. The professor also may include a link to "frequently asked questions." This may save some time for both professor and student, and minimize the times faculty are asked the same question. (See Figure 7.1 for an excellent syllabus template.)

• **Faculty Office Hours.** Students taking distance education courses need to know when they can "meet" with faculty and how to contact them outside of regular office hours. Some faculty set particular times each week when they will be available for students. They may be available synchronously in a chat room or by e-mail, or they may have regular telephone office hours. Faculty office hours must be easy to find on the course web site. However professors decide to make themselves available, it important they do so regularly and faithfully.

• **Grades.** Institutions must provide online access to grades so students can easily browse their student records. At the UMS, a Distributed Student Information System makes it possible for students to check their grades on the Web. The system must be secure, yet accessible to students enrolled in the institution's courses.

• **Examination Procedures.** Some instructors face a dilemma when deciding how to test their students. Since the course is delivered electronically, shouldn't the test be also? This is a question to which there is no universal answer. It is based on the professor's preference. There are models of behavior related to examination procedures from which instructors may choose. For example, some instructors feel that "testing" per se is not a good indicator of how well the

Figure 10.3. Popular Archaeology Guest Access

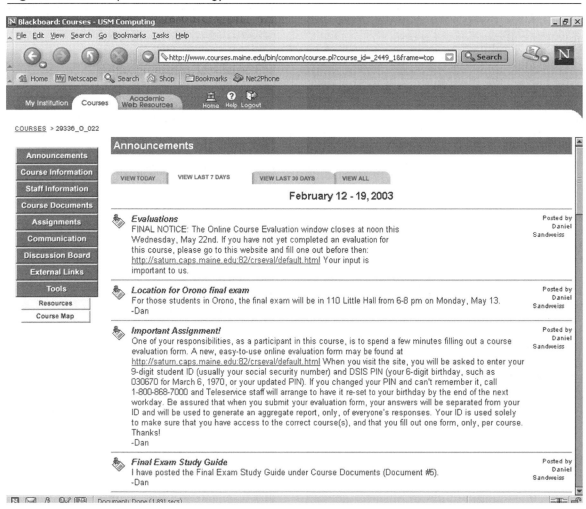

Reprinted with permission from the University of Maine System. Web site: www.learn.maine.edu

student has learned the course materials and chooses rather to assign papers or online activities like discussion boards, chats, and groupwork in lieu of tests. Others may feel that the test is an assessment technique they want to use. They may allow students to take tests online either individually or in groups. Some even allow their students to repeat the test as many times as they wish until they receive the grade they want. (This is a special arrangement where software such as QuestionMark is used and each time the test is repeated, students get different questions from an item bank.) Still another group of faculty require students to attend an in-person, proctored testing session several times during a semester. Whatever assessment method the instructor chooses, he or she must establish procedures before the start of the class and clearly state them up front. This gives the student more information with which to make an informed decision about whether to enroll in the course.

• **Technical Support Services.** It is important to make various forms of technical support available both to newly enrolled students and to continuing students. It is easy to assume that a student who enrolls in an online course or program is already comfortable using computers and knowledgeable about relevant communication tools. However, this is not always true. Nor, in many cases, do students know how to set up computer accounts. Much of this aspect of an institution's technical support is important to include in new student orientation services, as described earlier. In addition, continuing students will always require ongoing access to technical support. In the absence of an established technical support structure, faculty are likely to become the de facto providers of technical help to students, which is far from ideal. Most institutions that rely on technology for instruction are now recognizing the importance of establishing a systematic approach to providing students with technical support. There are two approaches to providing technical support—and both are necessary. First, it makes sense to prepare students to handle many of their own basic technical support issues by giving them the necessary information and means to do so. Second, regardless of how prepared an institution is and how informed its students are, there will always be some technical support issues that will require the rapid attention of a person on campus. A help desk

that offers answers to technical questions is often the most logical solution. It should be accessible at off-hours as well as regular business hours. Information on how to contact the help desk should be prominently featured on the institution's web site. Some institutions have turned to commercial vendors to provide technical support for their students. Some have found that using an external source for this service has enabled them to make good technical support available to students at less cost than providing the service themselves. Other schools have determined that they can do a better job on their own. Each institution should arrive at a determination as to which approach is better within its own context. Whatever the institution decides, it should provide site visitors with an overview of technical support services available from the institution and define them and any eligibility requirements (e.g., student must be enrolled in a course at the institution). And, network down times and maintenance times should be posted before they occur.

• **Library Services.** Library services for distance learners are somewhat different than those for campus-based students. Students who are on campus can physically go to the library and access resources needed to support their learning; however, students who are not on campus must find other ways to get these materials and resources. One of the downfalls of distance learning in the past has been the quality of this service. However, more universities are putting their libraries online, and off-campus students as well as campus-based students are able to use the library online (Figure 10.4). For coordination purposes, institutions are advised to appoint a librarian who will coordinate library services for distance learners. The name and contact information for this person should be placed in a prominent spot on the course web site as well as on the university's general distance education web page. Distance learning providers must outline information about what library resources and services are available to distance learners. They also must provide clear instructions on how to use the online library resources, with links to specific resources that may be needed. Again, a link to library FAQs saves the institution time and effort in responding to questions that have been asked before. Library services for off-campus or distance education students must include links to

Figure 10.4. University of Maine System University College Library Services

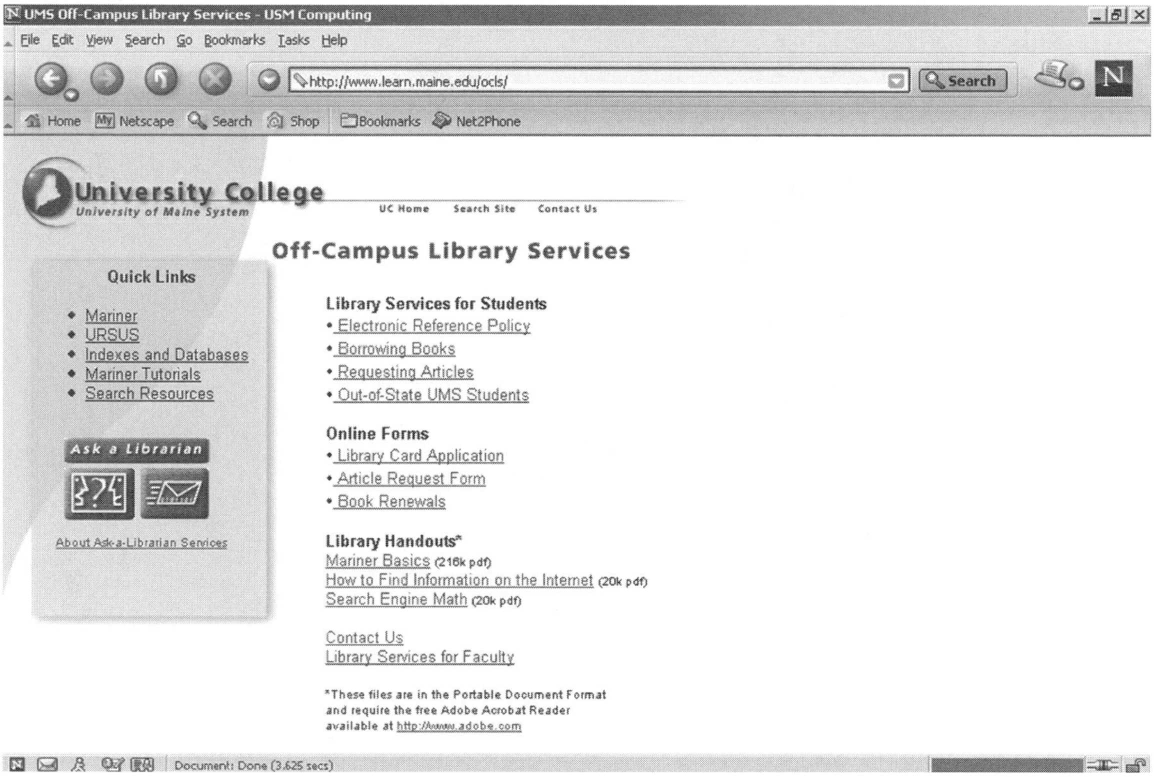

Reprinted with permission from the University of Maine System. Web site: www.learn.maine.edu

a librarian, library use policies, information for out-of-state students, search resources, technical help, and forms with which a student can obtain a library card, renew books, and request books and articles. Students should be able to request services electronically and have materials delivered where it is most convenient. Whenever possible, materials should be delivered directly to the student via electronic transmission, courier, fax, or postal mail. Online forms will make the request process easier and more convenient. Realizing that not everyone has had experience in a university's library, the institution should provide an online tutorial on how to use the library from a distance. Going beyond offering basic instruction in research to providing complete online tutorials that enable students to develop information competence (sometimes called "information literacy") will serve the student and institution in the long run. Libraries can work with instructors

to scan in materials for reserve. Students can then access these materials using the Internet. At UMS University College, off-campus library services are provided by Mariner (Figure 10.5). Here students may visit a variety of library collections, indexes, and databases; access tutorials; get course information; and go directly to a help desk for assistance.

• **Bookstore Services.** Online bookstore services should be organized in a purchase-friendly environment. The online offerings should be as similar as possible to those of on-campus bookstores. Available items should not be limited to texts; other supplies also should be available, including clothing, stickers, mugs, and other items with the school's insignia. Making it possible to purchase these items from a distance gives distance learners an opportunity to feel that they are part of the institution. Some institutions choose to contract with a vendor to provide book-

Figure 10.5. University of Maine System University College Online Library Resources

Reprinted with permission from the University of Maine System. Web site: www.learn.maine.edu

store services, while others provide these services themselves. To ready a bookstore site, the institution should create an online environment in which students can browse through textbooks, services, and merchandise. Any return or other policies should be prominently displayed. Provisions for several payment options should be made, and policies related to them should be clearly stated. Easy to use online order forms should be available, and information about ordering either online, by phone, or by fax should be provided. Students should be informed about turn-around time and should be asked for "ship to" information.

• **Services to Promote a Sense of Community.** In order to succeed, distance learners need to feel that they are not isolated either from the institution, the instructor, or other students. Institutions' experience and research demonstrate that students' retention, completion, and satisfaction depend heavily on achieving a sense of connection with the institution. The quality of an online student's experience is based on much more than the instructional content of courses and degree programs. Recognizing

this, many instructors of online and distributed courses establish regular means for faculty and students to communicate with one another on topics beyond the course material. This is also helpful in establishing a sense of connection between the student and the institution. Obviously, this need for a sense of community is stronger for some students that for others, whether they are on campus or miles away, but student-centered institutions are finding ways to create community for those who seek it. There are a variety of ways to provide this sense of connection. The institution might develop a student government, issue a newsletter, and use the web site for special announcements for distance learners. Chat rooms might be set up with topics of potential interest to off-campus learners, or a virtual community might be established using a MOO (see Chapter 6).

SPECIAL SERVICES

While the degree to which students will use the following services may vary depending on student population, characteristics, and needs, the following are, nonetheless, important services for institutions to provide to distant learners.

• **Career Services.** Online career services should provide resources to help students develop career plans as well as locate potential employment opportunities, both during their educational careers and beyond. A number of national resources are available to supplement those developed by an individual college or university. Individuals should be advised about services and resources that are available to current students, alumni, community members, and employers. A link to online career self-assessment instruments developed by individual institutions' counseling offices as well as private vendors, can help students in defining their interests, values, and skills, and in identifying possible career choices. Descriptions and lists of internships, service learning opportunities, cooperative education, part-time jobs, and volunteer opportunities will give the student a good start toward making career choices. Many institutions offer assistance in making connections with local businesses and/or organizations. Alumni networking is another popular way for current students to make connections with the job world. A display of these sources, career services events, internships, and other employment opportunities also will help students as they embark on a job search.

• **Services for Students with Disabilities.** Providing services for students with disabilities requires institutions to describe the specific services available to disabled students. Equally important, however, is the need to ensure that all web pages developed by the institution are accessible. To accomplish this, there must be a text-only version of all web pages. Ideally, they should conform to the *World Wide Web (W3C) Content Accessibility Guidelines* (see www.cast.org/bobby), which explain how to make web content accessible to people with disabilities. These guidelines emphasize the importance of providing text equivalents of nontext content such as images, prerecorded audio, and video. They provide three conformance levels. An institution's web page can be tested easily using *Bobby*, a free service based on W3C guidelines (www.cast.org/bobby). Although there are some important aspects of accessible web

page design that cannot yet be tested by *Bobby*, it is a useful first step to ensure accessible web page design. At a minimum, an institution's web page should provide a list of services available to students with disabilities, a glossary of terms, policies, and ADA/504 regulations. The web page should specify the disabilities that qualify and make clear what documentation is required to receive these services. Links to web sites that provide useful information for students with disabilities should be included, along with contact information for someone on campus who can assist these students with questions.

• **Personal Counseling.** Of all the student support services usually available to on-campus students, personal counseling may seem the least susceptible to being offered via the Web. Face-to-face interaction may seem essential to the very nature of the counseling process, and there are legitimate privacy concerns to address. E-mail therapy is not a substitute for formal mental health treatment, but, if privacy issues are made clear, it is still possible to provide some personal advice counseling over the Internet. In addition to—or instead of—providing one-on-one counseling at a distance, institutions can make available other kinds of valuable counseling services to students via the Web. These include self-help materials and various kinds of public forums in which issues of general concern to college students can be discussed in a shared context. Institutions also should list a contact person at the university for 24-hour crisis coverage, or, if one is not available at the university, toll-free numbers for crisis help, community hot lines, and other assistance. The issue of informed consent is important when counseling services are to be provided on the web. For this reason, the web page should make clear the degree to which confidentiality is (or is not) protected when students and counselors communicate via e-mail.

• **Instructional Support and Tutoring.** Institutions generally provide workshops on topics such as note taking, writing a research paper, study skills, and others. Online tutoring may be provided for students at a distance, but generally "workshops" on these topics are accessed by going to a campus and participating. Students may meet with a tutor online via e-mail or a live chat, or using asynchronous technologies such as threaded discussions or bulletin boards. Others may choose to meet by phone. Some institutions limit the subject areas for which online tutoring is provided (e.g., math, writing), but other institutions provide tutoring for a full array of subject areas. Online tutorials for nonsubject areas, including Internet access from home, e-mail, quick guides for understanding course management systems, library services, listservs, and special software, are usually available. Institutions can provide workshops online using a format much like any online tutorial. Workshops also can be provided using teleconferencing, but students should have the option of attending special workshops either on campus or at a remote site.

CONTINUUM OF GOOD PRACTICE

WCET presents a "continuum of good practice" in using the Web for student services, which can be summarized as follows:

1. Post information on courses, curriculum, and student services.
2. Create links to and from campus-based services and to external web-based resources.
3. Provide web-based applications for admission and web registration systems.
4. Develop systems that give students access via the web interface to their individual records, enabling them to initiate and handle routine transactions on their own. Password-protect access to authorized users.

   - At a minimum, these systems allow students to make changes to their address or password and to have read-only access to other parts of their records, such as grades.
   - The more advanced systems use highly interactive, self-help approaches. They are designed to give students, rather than central and departmental administrators, control over many decisions related to their academic careers. Students can determine, in a virtual environment, the impact of one decision on another. They can ask "what if" questions to help determine their academic progress. The best of these also address students' nonadministrative needs, including counseling and academic support.

5. Use campus portals to provide personalized interfaces for all users. Through a secure access point, portals offer students (as well as faculty and other users) customized access to a variety of information and tools, including self-directed student services. Some institutions are building their own portals, while others are working with commercial vendors.

SOME TIPS FOR DESIGNING WEB-BASED STUDENT SERVICES

A few final suggestions to keep in mind when designing a web page that features available student services are summarized here.

1. Feature online and distance learning opportunities prominently on your home page. Even if your institution's distance learning or online programs are located administratively under a separate division, such as Continuing or Distance Education, it is important to provide a link on the institution's home page. Many colleges and universities neglect to display these offerings prominently—although it is crucial to do so both from a marketing perspective and from the perspective of users seeking distance and online learning opportunities.
2. Be consistent in design throughout the site. Create guidelines to ensure that all parts of your site have the same look and feel. Follow existing recommendations for effective web site design, many of which are themselves available on the Web.
3. Remember to create links to and from other relevant pages throughout your institution's web site. Pasting a brochure on the Web or putting information online in the same form as it appears in print creates isolated pieces of information, rather than integration of services. Think of ways to integrate services by linking from one to another whenever it makes sense, and place the links where users will be sure to see them. It is important to recognize the ways in which services are intertwined and to facilitate related transactions. Ideally, for example, a student ought to be able to register, apply for financial aid, and pay tuition and fees as part of the same interaction.

4. Keep your focus on meeting students' needs. Although today's Internet tools make possible a variety of near-dazzling effects, remember to develop your site with your students' needs at the forefront of your design.

5. Provide quick access to "a real person" on every page. Ensure that students can contact and receive help from someone if they cannot answer all their questions through your online information and services. Provide contact information (phone numbers, fax numbers, and e-mail addresses). Make it a required policy to answer all queries within a limited timeframe that is clearly stated.

6. Use terms that students understand. Terms such as "matriculation" and "Bursar's Office," and financial aid terminology, are often confusing to students. Even if your institution uses these standard terms, try to find other language to help students navigate your site easily.

7. Link to external sites when they would be helpful. Investigate external resources that are already available via the Web and provide links to them when it is more effective to do so than to develop original material for your site. There are many excellent resources already available via the Internet; link to these rather than spending resources to duplicate what they provide.

8. Make services user-oriented and process-driven rather than provider-oriented. Consider the perspective of all potential users (e.g., prospective students, current students, faculty, staff, alumni, and site visitors) and provide entry points for each. In addition, provide direct access on the opening page to important functions and services.

9. Enable students to do as much business online as possible. Empower students to initiate and complete many transactions themselves.

10. Be sure that the web pages are accessible to users with disabilities. Follow the *World Wide Web (W3C) Content Accessibility Guidelines*.

PART IV

Quality That Counts

Measuring quality in higher education has deluded many faculty, staff, and even researchers for decades. Does an institution's financial endowment or faculty educational degree attainment, or the condition of its physical plant, indicate quality? Is quality measured by students' grades in courses? Is it measured by its participants' level of satisfaction? Or is quality measured by how many students return to the institution for more education? All of these factors may be indicators of quality but they also may be indicators of other attributes like student motivation and determination, or faculty–student interaction and communication, or even convenience factors, or the wealth of the institution's graduates, or the percentage of faculty with terminal degrees, or legislative support. Quality, defined simply as "essential character: nature; . . . an inherent or distinguishing attribute, . . . superiority of kind" (*Webster's II New College Dictionary*, 1999, p. 905), encompasses all the variables listed above. But when we speak of the quality of an institution or the quality of its programs and courses, what do we mean and how do we measure it? Quality may be difficult to define, but, as conventional wisdom suggests, we know it when we see it.

It seems that good or high quality in education connotes excellence, value, worth, and superiority. Quality, then, is measured in relation to something else. *U.S. News and World Report* annually publishes its list of the "best" schools in the United States. A look at the methodology reveals that the rankings of institutions are based on a number of variables. Among them are academic reputation, faculty–student ratio, institutional funding, student and faculty caliber, and retention and graduation rates. These variables are weighted, and calculations result in the best, the mediocre, and the worst.

In educational institutions we often hear that efforts are being instituted to "improve the quality of learning" or "to improve the quality of a program or course." Central to quality of learning is the subject being studied and the ways in which students are encouraged to think about that subject. If we ask students what would make the quality of their education better, we probably would get as many different responses as students who were asked. For one student, quality might mean improved knowledge, skills, attitudes, and competence in a particular discipline. For another, it might mean more individualized instruction taking into account his or her preferred way of learning, resulting in intellectual development. Learning and degree attainment that lead to a good job might be the indication of improved quality for another. Having more aesthetically pleasing classrooms might be the factor that makes the quality good for still another student, or being able to study with a famous professor might enhance the quality for others. According to Mayhew, Ford, and Hubbard (1990),

> First, quality is a receding horizon. There are no static, acceptable norms of performance. Second, in spite of theoretical considerations, if quality is to be improved, it must be defined with enough specificity so that its attributes are at least suggested, if not clearly delineated. Third, quality improvement is inexorably bound up with assessment and feedback. (p. 27)

The complexity of the question of quality forces us to explore many different factors. The sum total of all these factors equals the "quality," whether poor, adequate, or excellent.

Distance education offers academics opportunities to pursue the best quality for everyone. Technology introduces many options for students and faculty, encompassing everything from individual student learning styles, to convenience factors, to pace and place of study, to pedagogy that can be varied to fit the needs of the many students engaged in the learning process as well as those of the faculty teaching. Faculty can be innovative with many teaching tools at their disposal, and students can pick and choose courses from many institutions, how they take those courses, and when they engage in the learning process.

Good quality, it turns out, may be defined differently for different individuals. Regardless, a definition must be established, the quality of education must be assessed and evaluated regularly, and we must look at a variety of indicators to get a clear picture of the kind of educational experiences we are providing for our students.

Chapter 11 offers suggestions about how to assess and evaluate distance education. Chapter 12 discusses standards and accreditation issues, and presents a firsthand account of how policy makers view distance learning. In Chapter 13, the author provides a summary of distance learning from past to present, discusses important lessons learned, and presents her ideas and hopes for the future of distance learning.

CHAPTER 11

Assessment and Evaluation

Assessment and evaluation in instruction are important parts of any educational enterprise. They help enhance the teaching and learning experience. Assessment and evaluation provide measures of quality and allow for adjustments to be made along the way.

Many institutions offering distance education courses and programs have developed their own systems and instruments with which to assess and evaluate the quality and effectiveness of course delivery as well as student outcomes. Many have tried to use the same instruments that they use with their traditional courses and programs, but quickly find that the old tools are not applicable to the new ways of delivering education. For example, standard on many course evaluations is the question, "Was the classroom a comfortable environment for learning?" While this question might have some applicability to traditional learning, it will tell us little about the effectiveness of a distance education course. Likewise, having no questions about the technology leaves us wondering about an important component of the course.

What has become standard in many distance education programs is an assessment of a student's readiness for courses that use technology as the delivery mode of instruction. Institutions have adopted and/or modified a survey that was developed by Bob Loser, Jean Trabandit, Barbara Hathaway, and Teresa Donnell of Northern Virginia Community College's Extended Learning Institute, which helps students assess whether distance learning courses are for them (See Appendix P). Surveys are also available that assist students in determining whether they have the technical skills required to participate in and complete a distance learning course (see Appendix Q). Once these preassessments have been completed and analyzed, students may either enroll in the distance education course or choose other options such as enrolling in a traditional course or participating in a technology preparatory workshop for future distance education courses.

Assessments of student characteristics have revealed that successful distance learners possess specific attributes: a high level of motivation, ability to self-start and work independently, having knowledge and skills in the uses of technology, and being able to work without immediate feedback. Preference for an independent learning style is also desirable. However, this is not to say that students who do not possess these characteristics cannot develop them. Students who have preferred face-to-face classroom learning in the past have discovered some of the benefits of distance learning through experimentation. Benefits such as flexibility, convenience, and control of one's schedule and time often outweigh the benefits of being in the classroom with the professor and other students. Furthermore, with the use of sophisticated technologies, students even find the learning process more exciting than that of traditional ways, and assessment usually is built into the software for easy self-assessment and evaluation.

An inherent assessment in online courses is found in the writings of students. In e-mail, threaded discussions, and forums, students' written communication can be an indicator of growth and learning. Responses to queries and even the type of questions students ask can demonstrate a level of knowledge and skills not always seen in the classroom. Additionally, course management systems (e.g., WebCT and Blackboard) allow student work to be stored. The archive is available and retrievable with the click of a mouse. This allows the professor to see improvements in students' writing that have been made during the timeframe in which the course was given.

Another important indicator of course quality is its web site. Does the web site have links to all materials that are needed to complete the course? Does the site direct students to online help? Is there a syllabus that is clearly written and spells out all requirements? Are there sample assignments, projects, or products that students may view? What about the kind and number of interactive activities—will they give the students practice in exchanging information and encourage them in discourse? Is the web site easy to get around? Are clear links provided so that students can access needed documents and participate in activities in a timely fashion? Can students access the faculty, academic assistance if needed, and a technical support staff when trouble arises? Are pertinent e-mail addresses, telephone numbers, faculty office hours, and times at which technical help is available clearly spelled out on the course web site?

FLASHLIGHT PROGRAM

Although some institutions have their own ways of conducting assessments and evaluations, many have purchased site licenses to the "Flashlight Program." "Flashlight" (see Figure 11.1) is an international project with headquarters located in Washington, DC, at the Teaching, Learning and Technology (TLT) Roundtable. The program's direc-

Figure 11.1. The "Flashlight Program" Web Site

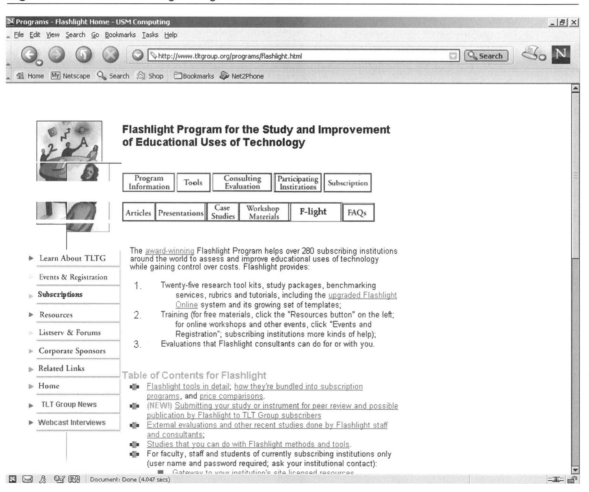

Reprinted with permission from the TLT Group. Web site: www.tltgroup.org

tor, Stephen C. Ehrmann, has written numerous articles describing Flashlight (many of his articles can be viewed on www.tltgroup.org), is vice president of the TLT Group, conducts workshops, and provides consultation to institutions.

The Flashlight Program allows practitioners and researchers to design their own assessment and evaluation instruments, using item banks, to look at the effectiveness, quality, and efficacy of their own distance education endeavors. Flashlight has developed a tool kit that institutions may use to evaluate and study their technology uses. Begun in 1993, Flashlight worked with five disparate institutions of higher education, among them the Education Network of Maine (ENM), to develop a model upon which Flashlight is based. The Flashlight Program continues to develop tools and resources for site-licensed institutions to access. Among the resources available are the Current Student Inventory (CSI) item bank, training workshops and consultation, and *The Flashlight Cost Analysis Handbook*. Currently being designed and piloted are study packages for (1) distance learning in nursing (e.g., uses of the Web and web course management systems like WebCT and Blackboard), (2) faculty use of software used for presentations (e.g., PowerPoint), (3) an item bank/tool kit for the study of faculty issues, and (4) an evaluation of student support services.

An online system, *Flashlight Online*, allows faculty to develop surveys online using more than 500 items from the CSI item bank and/or combining items from the item bank with those created locally. These personally developed surveys can be administered online and operate from servers at Washington State University. This allows institutions the luxury of surveying online without investing in their own equipment, software, or technical administrative services. This service is part of the site license for the Flashlight tools. More than 100 institutions currently subscribe. More about Flashlight can be found on www.tltgroup.org/programs/flashlight.html.

FLASHLIGHT AT THE EDUCATION NETWORK OF MAINE

During the pilot phase of the Flashlight Program, the ENM conducted a study of its students to look at interaction and communication in distance learning courses. The author combined her own locally developed items with items from the CSI item bank to develop an instrument (see Appendix T) with which to answer three research questions:

1. To what extent are students communicating with each other and with faculty?
2. How satisfied are students with the level of interaction and with the course?
3. Are there statistically significant differences in satisfaction level among students in the four audience locations and between various subgroups of students?

There were 23 distance education courses involved in the study, with a total of 1,955 students enrolled. Surveys were mailed to all students, and 780 of them returned usable surveys (40% return rate). The results of the study are not pertinent here, but for those who are interested, see Johnson, 1997a. The point here is that evaluations of distance courses may be conducted using locally developed instruments or ones created using Flashlight or, as was done at the EMN, instruments in which items from both sources are used, as shown in Appendix T.

SEVEN PRINCIPLES OF GOOD PRACTICE

Flashlight is closely tied to the "Seven Principles of Good Practice," developed by Arthur W. Chickering and Zelda Gamson in 1987. The article Chickering and Gamson wrote about the seven principles "concern[ed] what research had found about teaching–learning activities that produced improved outcomes" (Ehrmann, 2000, p. 38). The research has set the groundwork for education systems standards and the implementation of the seven principles of good practice—a foundation used by higher educational institutions everywhere. In 1996, Chickering and Ehrmann revised the article with a focus on technology. The article is a significant update because it focuses on technology in education. Chickering and Ehrmann understood the importance of integrating the Seven Principles of Good Practice into new and innovative technology-enhanced and -delivered education. Because of the significance of the early work by Chickering and

Gamson (1987), and the subsequent work by Chickering and Ehrmann (1996), portions of the latter article are reprinted here. The article may be found in its entirety at the Flashlight web site (www.tltgroup.org).

The article describes some of the most cost effective and appropriate ways to use computers, video, and telecommunication technologies to advance the Seven Principles, which are as follows (Chickering & Erhmann, 1996, article modified and reprinted with permission from AAHE, Chickering, and Ehrmann):

1. Good Practice Encourages Contacts Between Students and Faculty

Frequent student–faculty contact in and out of class is a most important factor in student motivation and involvement. Faculty concern helps students get through rough times and keep on working. Knowing a few faculty members well enhances students' intellectual commitment and encourages them to think about their own values and plans.

Communication technologies that increase access to faculty members, help them share useful resources, and provide for joint problem solving and shared learning can usefully augment face-to-face contact in and outside of class meetings. By putting in place a more "distant" source of information and guidance for students, such technologies can strengthen faculty interactions with all students, but especially with shy students who are reluctant to ask questions or challenge the teacher directly. It is often easier to discuss values and personal concerns in writing than orally, since inadvertent or ambiguous nonverbal signals are not so dominant. As the number of commuting part-time students and adult learners increases, technologies provide opportunities for interaction not possible when students come to class and leave soon afterward to meet work or family responsibilities.

The biggest success story in this realm has been that of time-delayed (asynchronous) communication. Traditionally, time-delayed communication took place in education through the exchange of homework, either in class or by mail (for more distant learners). Such time-delayed exchange was often a rather impoverished form of conversation, typically limited to three conversational turns:

1. The instructor poses a question (a task).
2. The student responds (with homework).
3. The instructor responds some time later with comments and a grade.

The conversation often ends there; by the time the grade or comment is received, the course and student are off on new topics.

Now, however, electronic mail, computer conferencing, and the World Wide Web increase opportunities for students and faculty to converse and exchange work much more speedily than before, and more thoughtfully and "safely" than when confronting each other in a classroom or faculty office. Total communication increases and, for many students, the result seems more intimate, protected, and convenient than the more intimidating demands of face-to-face communication with faculty.

Professor Norman Coombs reports that, after 12 years of teaching Black history at the Rochester Institute of Technology, the first time he used e-mail was the first time a student asked what he, a White man, was doing teaching Black history. The literature is full of stories of students from different cultures opening up in and out of class when e-mail became available. Communication also is eased when student or instructor (or both) is not a native speaker of English; each party can take a bit more time to interpret what has been said and compose a response. With the new media, participation and contribution from diverse students become more equitable and widespread.

2. Good Practice Develops Reciprocity and Cooperation Among Students

[For many] learning is enhanced when it is more like a team effort than a solo race. . . . Working with others often increases involvement in learning. Sharing one's ideas and responding to others' [especially for the collaborative learner] improves thinking and deepens understanding.

The increased opportunities for interaction with faculty noted above apply equally to communication with fellow students. Study groups, collaborative learning, group problem solving, and discussion of assignments can all be dramatically strengthened through communication tools that facilitate such activity.

The extent to which computer-based tools encourage spontaneous student collaboration was one of the earliest surprises about computers. A clear advantage of e-mail for today's busy commuting students is that it opens up communication among classmates even when they are not physically together. For example: One of us, attempting to learn to navigate the Web, took a course taught entirely by a combination of televised class sessions (seen live or taped) and by work on a course web page. The hundred students in the course included persons in Germany and the Washington, DC, area.

Learning teams helped themselves "learn the plumbing" and solve problems. These team members never met face-to-face. But they completed and exchanged Myers-Briggs Type Inventories, surveys of their prior experience and level of computer expertise, and brief personal introductions. This material helped teammates size one another up initially; team interactions then built working relationships and encouraged acquaintanceship. This kind of "collaborative learning" would be all but impossible without the presence of the media we were learning about and with.

3. Good Practice Uses Active Learning Techniques

Learning is not a spectator sport. [Most] students do not learn much just sitting in classes listening to teachers, memorizing prepackaged assignments, and spitting out answers. They must talk about what they are learning, write reflectively about it, relate it to past experiences, and apply it to their daily lives. They must make what they learn part of themselves.

The range of technologies that encourage active learning is staggering. Many fall into one of three categories: tools and resources for learning by doing, time-delayed exchange, and real-time conversation. Today, all three usually can be supported with "worldware," i.e., software . . . originally developed for other purposes but now used for instruction, too.

. . . Apprentice-like learning has been supported by many traditional technologies: research libraries, laboratories, art and architectural studios, athletic fields. Newer technologies now can enrich and expand these opportunities. For example:

• Supporting apprentice-like activities in fields that themselves require the use of technology as a tool

such as statistical research and computer-based music, or use of the Internet to gather information not available in the local library.

• Simulating techniques that do not themselves require computers, such as helping chemistry students develop and practice research skills in "dry" simulated laboratories before they use the riskier, more expensive real equipment.

• Helping students develop insight. For example, students can be asked to design a radio antenna. Simulation software displays not only their design but the ordinarily invisible electromagnetic waves the antenna would emit. Students change their designs and instantly see resulting changes in the waves. The aim of this exercise is not to design antennae but to build deeper understanding of electromagnetism.

4. Good Practice Gives Prompt Feedback

Knowing what you know and don't know focuses your learning. In getting started, students need help in assessing their existing knowledge competence. Then, in classes, students need frequent opportunities to perform and receive feedback on their performance. At various points during college, and at its end, students need chances to reflect on what they have learned, what they still need to know, and how they might assess themselves.

The ways in which new technologies can provide feedback are many—sometimes obvious, sometimes more subtle. . . . Computers . . . have a growing role in recording and analyzing personal and professional performances. Teachers can use technology to provide critical observations for an apprentice; for example, video to help a novice teacher, actor, or athlete critique his or her own performance. Faculty (or other students) can react to a writer's draft using the "hidden text" option available in word processors: turned on, the "hidden" comments spring up; turned off, the comments recede and the writer's prized work is again free of "red ink."

As we move toward portfolio evaluation strategies, computers can provide rich storage and easy access to student products and performances. Computers can keep track of early efforts, so instructors and students can see the extent to which later efforts demonstrate gains in knowledge, competence, or other valued outcomes. Performances that are time-consuming and expensive to record and evaluate—such as leadership skills, group process management, or multicultural interactions—can be elicited and stored, not only for ongoing critique but also as a record of growing capacity.

5. Good Practice Emphasizes Time on Task

Time plus energy equals learning. Learning to use one's time well is critical for students and professionals alike. Allocating realistic amounts of time means effective learning for students and effective teaching for faculty.

New technologies can dramatically improve time on task for students and faculty members. . . . as well as increase[ing] time on task by making studying more efficient. Teaching strategies that help students learn at home or work can save hours otherwise spent commuting to and from campus, finding parking places, and so on. Time efficiency also increases when interactions between teacher and students, and among students, fit busy work and home schedules. And students and faculty alike make better use of time when they can get access to important resources for learning without trudging to the library, flipping through card files, scanning microfilm and micro-fiche, and scrounging the reference room.

For faculty members interested in classroom re-search, computers can record student participation and interaction and help document student time on task, especially as related to student performances.

6. Good Practice Communicates High Expectations

Expect more and you will get it. High expectations are important for everyone—for the poorly prepared, for those unwilling to exert themselves, and for the bright and well motivated. Expecting students to perform well becomes a self-fulfilling prophecy.

New technologies can communicate high expectations explicitly and efficiently. Significant real-life problems, conflicting perspectives, or paradoxical data sets can set powerful learning challenges that drive students to not only acquire information but sharpen their cognitive skills of analysis, synthesis, application, and evaluation. . . .

With technology, criteria for evaluating products and performances can be more clearly articulated by the teacher, or generated collaboratively with students. General criteria can be illustrated with samples of excellent, average, mediocre, and faulty performance. These samples can be shared and modified easily. They provide a basis for peer evaluation, so learning teams can help everyone succeed.

7. Good Practice Respects Diverse Talents and Ways of Learning

Many roads lead to learning. Different students bring different talents and styles to college. Brilliant students in a seminar might be all thumbs in a lab or studio; students rich in hands-on experience may not do so well with theory. Students need opportunities to show their talents and learn in ways that work for them. Then they can be pushed to learn in new ways that do not come so easily.

Technological resources can ask for different methods of learning through powerful visuals and well-organized print; through direct, vicarious, and virtual experiences; and through tasks requiring analysis, synthesis, and evaluation, with applications to real-life situations. They can encourage self-reflection and self-evaluation. They can drive collaboration and group problem solving. Technologies can help students learn in ways they find most effective and broaden their repertoires for learning. They can supply structure for students who need it and leave assignments more open-ended for students who don't. Fast, bright students can move quickly through materials they master easily and go on to more difficult tasks; slower students can take time and get more feedback and direct help from teachers and fellow students. Aided by technologies, students with similar motives and talents can work in cohort study groups without constraints of time and place.

TECHNOLOGY IS NOT ENOUGH

The Seven Principles cannot be implemented by technophiles alone or even by faculty alone. Students need to become familiar with the principles and be more assertive with respect to their own learning. When confronted with teaching strategies and course requirements that use technologies in ways contrary to the principles, students should, if possible, move to alternatives that serve them better. If teaching focuses simply on memorizing and regurgitating pre-packaged information, whether delivered by a faculty lecture or computer, students should reach for a different course, search out additional resources or complementary experiences, establish their own study groups, or go to the professor for more substantial activities and feedback.

Faculty members who already work with students in ways consistent with the principles need to be tough-minded about the software- and technology-assisted interactions they create and buy into. They need to eschew materials that are simply didactic, and search instead for those that are interactive, problem-oriented, and relevant to real-world issues, and that evoke student motivation.

Institutional policies concerning learning resources and technology support need to give high priority to user-friendly hardware, software, and communication vehicles that help faculty and students use technologies efficiently and effectively. Investments in professional development for faculty members, plus training and computer lab assistance for students, will be necessary if learning potentials are to be realized.

Regardless of whether one chooses to use locally developed instruments or those from a source such as Flashlight to assess courses, instruction, and learning, it is important to all involved that assessment and evaluation occur on a regular basis. The quality of instruction and learning must be defined, measured, and improved upon. Student feedback is important to institutions regarding both, and improvement in instruction and learning depends on it. Faculty also have a responsibility to use student feedback and other indicators of quality for self-assessment, and to always strive toward excellence in teaching.

CHAPTER 12

Standards, Accreditation, and How Policy Makers View Distance Learning

STANDARDS

The word *standards* is used to denote an acceptable quality of the entity being measured. Often it is used interchangeably with words like *guidelines*, *credentials*, and *best practices*. A standard is a level against which something is measured. Standards are set in industry; in the assessment of water and air quality; in the approval of medications; in food preparation, handling, and transportation; in professional licensure; and in education. Usually referring to average but acceptable quality, standards are set using a judgmental process. Setting a standard is a process where appropriate parties answer the question, "How good is good enough?" Standards might apply to the amount of emissions from a manufacturing plant that is acceptable or safe, or the level of performance a person needs in order to be promoted to a higher job level in a company. It may refer to meeting the requirements for obtaining a license to practice law or to drive a car. Using the driver's license as a simple example, we know that in order to obtain one, there are standards one must meet related to age, knowledge of rules of the road, and driving ability. Once these standards have been met, the individual is granted a driver's license.

Establishing standards in education has been an ongoing process since formal education began. It is a fluid process, meaning that as education changes, standards also must change. That is, standards, once set, do not remain appropriate forever and must be revisited and revised from time to time to match educational changes. Individuals with a stake in the outcome, such as faculty, administra-

tors, students, community members, and organizations, must be involved in defining and designing standards.

Distance education has become a prevalent means of delivering higher education over the past decade. Until now, the standards that were used in traditional education have been applied to this new entity; however, in the past 5 years, several educational organizations have developed new, more appropriate standards/guidelines for distance education. The organizations have developed these standards/guidelines for institutions that are embarking on new distance education endeavors or for those that already have distance education in place and want to assess its quality or make changes to its structure. By understanding and implementing these guidelines and standards, institutions may ensure that their distance education system is sound and the education delivered of acceptable quality. Based on research and professional expertise, these documents are offered as "works in progress" and are subject to scrutiny, revision, and change as distance education matures.

Four documents that focus on standards, guidelines, and principles of good practice have been developed by professional organizations: the American Council on Education (ACE), the American Federation of Teachers (AFT), the National Education Association (NEA) and Blackboard, and the Western Cooperative for Educational Telecommunications (WCET). While each document has a unique focus, there are many common themes. The documents, are briefly summarized below and found in their entirety in Appendices U, V, W, and X, respectively.

1. **Guiding Principles for Distance Learning in a Learning Society** (http://www.acenet.edu) was first developed in 1996 by ACE and adopted by the Distance Education and Training Council, a national accrediting organization that is approved by the U.S. Department of Education (see Appendix U). This document suggests guiding principles for meeting changing educational and training processes. Areas covered include learning design, learner support, organizational commitment, learning outcomes, and technology.

2. **Distance Education: Guidelines for Good Practice** was developed and prepared by AFT's Higher Education Program and Policy Council in May 2000 (see Appendix V). This document focuses more on faculty rights and responsibilities, student needs, course considerations (e.g., class size, materials, evaluation), and institutional accreditation.

3. **24 Measures of Quality in Internet-Based Distance Learning** (from the report, "Quality on the Line") is based on a study by NEA and Blackboard, Inc. in April 2000. This document suggests benchmarks for seven different areas of curriculum and instruction (see Appendix W).

4. **Best Practices for Electronically Offered Degree and Certificate Programs**, initially drafted in 1996 by the WCET (www.wiche.edu/telecom), and adopted in 2001 by the eight regional accrediting commissions, outlines best practices for electronically offered degrees and programs. The regional accrediting commissions that have adopted the document include:

- Commission on Higher Education, Middle States Association of Colleges and Schools
- Commission on Institutions of Higher Education, New England Association of Schools and Colleges
- Commission on Technical and Career Institutions, New England Association of Schools and Colleges
- Commission on Institutions of Higher Education, North Central Association of Colleges and Schools
- Commission on Colleges, Northwest Association of Schools and Colleges
- Commission on Colleges, Southern Association of Colleges and Schools
- Accrediting Commission for Community and Junior Colleges, Western Association of Schools and Colleges
- Accrediting Commission for Senior Colleges and Universities, Western Association of Schools and Colleges (see Appendix X).

While the documents are not put forth as "standards" documents, they all demonstrate a move toward standards and, taken as a whole, demonstrate a move well on its way.

The four documents were produced by four separate organizations and make many similar points. There is overlap from document to document but the focus of each is distinct. The guidelines and standards suggested by these organizations are all-encompassing and offer valuable guidance for distance education providers everywhere. The move toward standards for distance education is structured, purposeful, and critical to the quality of the enterprise.

ACCREDITATION

According to a report commissioned by the Council for Higher Education Accreditation, the accreditation system increasingly will have to accommodate the growing number of distance education courses. Although the report states that the system will be able to function for distance education programs, "it raises concerns about how new technologies will affect the quality of instruction" (McCollum, 1998, p. A34).

The accreditation report states that "accrediting bodies must take into account the effect that distance education has on student life and the roles of professors when evaluating the quality of education in the courses" (McCollum, 1998, p. A34). The report further states that contact with professors is essential, as is professors' work on faculty committees to ensure quality in education.

The report offers the following recommendations:

- Institutions should set guidelines for measuring student performance in distance-education courses;
- When judging institutions, accreditors should consider contact between students and professors, and the use of distance-teaching techniques that have proven effective;
- Institutions should make distance education a consideration when hiring and training faculty

members, to assure that professors are prepared to use the new teaching technologies; and

- Institutions should keep up to date with technology to assure that students don't have difficulty "attending" classes. (McCullom, 1998, p. A34)

The report, one of the council's initial efforts to investigate issues relative to distance education and accreditation, maintains that adherence to high standards is already part of most distance education programs (McCullom, 1998).

Accreditation standards should be the same for both face-to-face and distance learning. However, the criteria for accreditation should be re-examined in light of the differences between face-to-face and distance learning. That is, accreditation decisions often are based on input variables (e.g., number of library books, number of faculty with terminal degrees, financial resources, and others) rather than on student outcomes. Is this an appropriate model for distance education? Will accreditation be mandatory? On what criteria will policies pertaining to distance learning be made? These questions will be subject to debate in years to come.

POLICY MAKERS' VIEWS OF DISTANCE EDUCATION

Many state legislatures have begun including distance education in their education funding. Attitudes held by state policy makers with regard to the manner in which technology has been integrated into the teaching and learning process was the subject of a 1998 study. Interviews were conducted with 21 state legislators considered to be "leading 'technology activists' in their states" (Ruppert, 1998, p. 41). Some concerns were expressed by the legislators about the use of technology on university campuses.

The cost of distance education was one concern. In addition to colleges and universities investing much in technology, most often without the support of faculty, institutions are reallocating funds, originating new technology fees, and seeking funding through grants and businesses in order to acquire and employ technology. Some policy makers questioned technology's appropriateness as well as its impact on teaching and learning. Furthermore, they questioned

whether their previous investments were being used appropriately and to their full capacity. Legislators recognized that along with a need for greater planning, the goals and expectations of the use of technology in higher education must be clarified.

While many state legislators believe that technology "should be a part of every student's education, they did not believe that every student can be educated best through technological means" (Ruppert, 1998, p. 43). State legislators agree that students need to be prepared for the workforce by being afforded technology-based skills, but they caution that technology as an instructional tool has limitations.

The following opinions reflect the legislators' views, both of consensus and those that were mixed, regarding the uses of technology as their states' goals or objectives:

- legislators placed a high priority on the need to focus technology efforts first and foremost on enhancing the quality of student learning both inside and outside the classroom;
- a high priority was placed on the use of technology to expand access to post-secondary education;
- where population is geographically dispersed, legislators viewed technology as an alternative to building new campuses;
- many felt technology was critical for removing barriers to access for non-traditional students;
- most legislators agreed that the profile of students attending college is changing rapidly;
- they emphasized the importance of keeping costs down, but most did not think technology was going to help achieve this goal;
- some legislators expressed concern about faculty workload issues;
- most agreed that faculty are not in a position to make the most of what technology can offer;
- a majority believed that technology has a critical role to play in increasing an institution's administrative efficiency; and
- some legislators agree that distance learning is only one way to greater programmatic and instructional efficiencies (Ruppert, 1998, pp. 44–45)

Legislators believe that in addition to developing a plan for technology that is appropriate to the institution's mission, campuses need to coordinate their technology efforts with each other and decide how to capitalize on the technology resources currently available to them. Also important to legislators is the need for campuses to remain focused on the students who will be using technology and to allocate money for training and provide adequate technical support.

An overriding theme stemming from the legislators' interviews was the "essential and critical need for state policymakers and colleges and universities to plan wisely and invest strategically in the educational technology of the future" (Ruppert, 1998, p. 48).

CHAPTER 13

Summary, Lessons Learned, and the Future

Distance learning is no longer an idea, it is a well-established entity seen more and more around the world. The technologies of the last decade of the 20th century have become the foundation for a new way of offering and delivering education. Distance education has developed quickly since the 1980s, has spread across the United States and around the world, and continues to accelerate. Technologies are becoming more sophisticated and inexpensive, and providers of education are becoming savvy in their knowledge of and ability to use them. Higher education is a dynamic, diverse, and changing reality, with technology as one of its mainstays.

Over the years since distance learning began in earnest, many have argued that it would be a substandard way of providing educational opportunities for people. Some argued that distance education was an experiment that specialized in job-related skills training (Biemiller, 1998). These skeptics further argued that spontaneous debate, poetry readings, and discussions could happen effectively only in the face-to-face classroom. Hands-on laboratory experiences have been cited as another activity not suited for distance learning. Others questioned how instructors would be assured of the authenticity of the learner. Often these sentiments were and still are expressed by individuals who have not experienced teaching and learning with technologies firsthand. Many of these individuals have softened their views and, after trying this new way of teaching, have become converts. From the early years, there were skeptics and there were believers. Believers have recounted experiences of their own that provide examples of successful courses delivered via distance in the arts and sciences as well as in the professional schools. For example, a lab course such as cellular biology allows students to gain new insights by watching living cells

in time-lapsed movies that have been produced by attaching a video camera to the microscope (Olsen, 2000). An online history course permits students to view streaming videos of famous historical figures like early presidents or literary figures delivering famous speeches. Students in technology-enhanced music courses have the advantage of accessing a full range of musical scores, hearing them performed, seeing the sheet music, and learning about their composers over the World Wide Web (Sircar, 2000). Foreign language courses use streaming audio to provide students with correct pronunciation of words. And, business students access up-to-the-minute stock market reports anytime, anywhere with a click of the mouse. One might argue that these same kinds of activities can occur in the face-to-face classroom as well. And that is so, but a look inside traditional classrooms reveals that it is the exception rather than the rule. Embedded in the culture of the "classroom" of distance education courses is technology. Tools of technology are used exclusively. The pedagogical tools are rich and provide students with exciting new opportunities for learning. Technology is *the* way of teaching and learning at a distance.

Once considered an "alternative" form of education, distance learning is now part of the mainstream. The Internet/Web is responsible for "changing the way information is provided and people interact" (Kearsley, 1998, p. 22). Faculty teaching distance education courses must know how to use the technology; they must develop appropriate teaching strategies, presentation skills, and competence in the delivery system. It is anticipated that within the next decade, many new faculty entering academe will have earned their degrees via distance learning and will have that experience upon which to build (Kearsley, 1998).

Although distance learning is now part of the mainstream of higher education, this does not mean that traditional institutions as we have known them for the past century will disappear. They will have their place in the world of education. Each, however, will cater to very different populations. There will always be students who want the campus experience, such as kids fresh out of high school who want to go away to college and enjoy all that a residential experience affords them. But there will be many students who will willingly forego the residential experience in favor of convenience, choice, and flexibility. For the working professional, for example, distance learning is an attractive way to access education while continuing a career.

One important factor driving the mainstreaming of distance education is that "it is what the customer wants—the customer being the students (and their parents) who want learning to be convenient and flexible" (Kearsley, 1998, p. 26).

Institutions that engage in distance education will need to make changes in the way they provide courses and services to students. Investments in new technologies will be required, as will training and professional development for faculty. The many aspects of distance education are presented throughout this book and will not be recounted here, but attention must be paid to the elements that make distance education a success. These elements include:

1. knowledge and skills about effective pedagogy, and when and how to use them (Chapter 6),
2. knowledge of how to design and develop effective courses and programs, including how to create a clear syllabus and course web site, how to encourage interaction and community building, how to provide effective feedback, and how to track student progress (Chapter 9),
3. provision of critical student services, including administrative, course-related, and special services for all students (Chapter 10), and
4. knowledge of how to evaluate the quality of the product being delivered (Chapter 11).

LESSONS LEARNED

We have learned many lessons that have helped us to promote increased access, enriched learning experiences, more flexibility and convenience, and students who are prepared to meet the challenges of today's world. As exemplified many times throughout this book, distance education has developed and expanded very quickly over the past 2 to 3 decades. Many of the lessons learned have been through trial and error. What was once acceptable has now fallen by the wayside. What was once "state of the art" is now passé. The passage of time has changed the face of distance learning, and it is expected that many more changes will be witnessed over the next decade and beyond. Some of the important lessons that have been elaborated upon in earlier chapters bear repeating.

Lesson 1

The format and pedagogy used in face-to-face courses are not appropriate for courses delivered via distance. For example, early ITV and online courses often were taught in the same way as traditional face-to-face courses. The only difference was that they were delivered using technology. It quickly became obvious that this new medium demanded new pedagogy, and changes were made that capitalized on the technologies that were available. These changes resulted in improved courses.

Lesson 2

Faculty and students must have opportunities to learn about the technology used in online and ITV courses. This enables them to be effective users of the technologies. With this new way of teaching and learning come demands for faculty to develop new teaching techniques. Rather than standing in front of a room full of students and lecturing, faculty now have an assortment of options and tools with which to present materials to students. The technologies of today have opened the door to a world of choices, enhancements, and ways of conveying information never seen before. Along with these choices have come increased responsibilities and focus. Distance education has forced faculty to become more organized and prepared, and, some may say, more active in their role in the teaching and learning experience. It also has put students in charge of their own learning and involvement.

Lesson 3

Support services for faculty and students are a must for effective distance learning. We also have learned that for those involved in distance education to be successful, support services for students and faculty must not only be in place, but must be assessed and updated frequently to stay in step with the changes in technology, and it is most desirable that they be available 24/7.

Lesson 4

Institutional administration must be invested in the distance education enterprise at their institution for it to be successful. Without the backing and support of the administration, distance education courses and programs will, at best, function as marginal entities.

THE FUTURE OF DISTANCE LEARNING

Technology and distance education have come a long way since their beginning. Looking at the big picture, distance education is still in its infancy but is maturing quickly. Over the past century, institutions of higher education have changed from an agrarian model to one in which the needs of the Industrial Age were met. Now we are in a new age—the Age of Information and Technology. The world is different, the students are different, and institutions must change to meet new demands.

The changes in technology, especially over the past decade, have occurred at lightning speed. Higher education institutions around the world are using technology to enhance traditional campus-based courses and to deliver programs and courses using ITV, online, or in some combination of these and other technologies. Technology has taken center stage in the teaching and learning process. Following the model of the private business sector, educational institutions have adopted the Internet as a powerful means for instantaneous access to the most up-to-date information. Institutions have claimed first ITV and now the World Wide Web as their choices for providing access to learners everywhere.

How do we predict what higher education will be like in the future with the increasing use of tech-

nologies in instruction, with anytime, anywhere learning, and with the changing demographics of the university and college "student body"? Many researchers have tried to imagine higher education in the 21st century. With the evolution of the digital age, communication technology is a cause for concern as well as for celebration (Brown & Duguid, 1996).

A Cause for Concern

The traditional college educational experience with on-campus, face-to-face classes, hands-on libraries, student organizations, and student support services may be a reality in the future for fewer students who can afford this privilege financially and with respect to time. Also of concern is the perceived value of an online degree and whether it will merit the same respect as a degree earned from a conventional campus. Some voice concern that students learning at a distance forfeit much of what is experienced by students who attend classes on campus. For example, on-campus students

> leave college knowing not just things, but knowing people, and knowing not just academic facts, but knowing social strategies for dealing with the world. Reliable friendships and complex social strategies can't be delivered and aren't picked up through lectures, but they give an education much of its value." (Brown & Duguid, 1996, p. 13)

Distance-based knowledge delivery, some say, not only is indicative of the misunderstanding about how people learn, but minimizes the value of the experience of face-to-face interaction and the socialization process that college campuses afford their students. Some feel that the learning process within communities involves being physically present with others in a community setting. They say the degree itself represents not only the quality of the education received, but how accessible the institution has made that educational experience (Brown and Duguid, 1996).

On the other hand, the experiences of graduate students differ from those of undergraduates in that graduate students experience a more practical approach, "like apprentices being led into a craft by masters of the practice" (Brown & Duguid, 1996, p. 14), while undergraduates endure a more delivery-like approach to education. Undergraduates, however, tend to develop a sense of the multitude of communities on campus and participate in the meaningful socialization process with which they take their places in the real world. There is a growing demand for universities to find new ways of reaching people beyond the campus as well as beyond graduation. The Internet is providing a dynamic, interactive educational experience, more so than the early broadcast-type courses.

Looking beyond the traditional paradigm of distance education, Brown and Duguid (1996) present their view of distance learning.

> First, distance teaching was developed with broadcast technology in mind. In the hands of institutions like the Open University (OU) in England, broadcast media have successfully allowed teachers to reach people who had little or no access to conventional schools. Questioning the privilege of the classroom more than the practice, however, such developments have only minimally altered the underlying delivery structure of pedagogy.
>
> Second, when distance learning shifts education on-line and off campus, it can restrict the essential access to the authentic communities. . . . Students in dislocated, virtual campuses are unable either to engage fully with a range of communities, as undergraduates should, or to participate in particular ones, as graduates must.
>
> Third, the focus on distance and delivery overlooks not only the needs of students, but all too often the strengths of new technologies, which are distinctive because they are interactive. . . . The explosion of interactive and midcast (as opposed to broadcast or narrowcast distribution) technologies for the Internet argues that in the 21st century mediated communications will expand the possibility for rich, distal interactions—urging consideration of more than distance in distal education. (pp. 15–16)

Open learning seeks to empower students by minimizing boundaries imposed upon them by traditional institutions and provides them with unlimited access to learning. However, while open learning challenges the institution's "conventional role as gate-keeper to academic information, it simultaneously underestimates the importance of institutions representing educational achievement" (Brown & Duguid, 1996, p. 17).

With respect to the future, Brown and Duguid issue a caution as we move toward an "Electronic Worldwide University." They posit that it may pro-

vide students only with an illusion of interaction, resulting in "a placeless university for isolated individuals" (Brown & Duguid, 1996, p. 17).

There is a need for people to rethink their way of looking at distance education and think in the direction of open learning as an alternative. This new approach "steers a path between the academy's centralizing tendencies and the optimistic faith that technologically mediated open learning offers" (Brown & Duguid, 1996, p. 18). This approach is not without its limitations, but Brown and Duguid offer open learning as a useful discussion piece.

As they imagine the future university, Brown and Duguid suggest that in addition to access to authentic communities and having resources in both local and distal communities with faculty drawn from communities of practice, there would be universally accepted standards of work, and the future institutions would be essentially administrative bodies. There would be a variety of fees depending on what types of courses were offered. Students might be required to spend some time on a campus engaging in group activities; however, there would be great flexibility with opportunities for practical experience for students and mentoring programs. The ultimate goal would be to produce graduates who are capable of changing in a world that is always changing.

A Cause for Celebration

While Brown and Duguid tend to be cautious in their view of the future of distance learning in higher education, others have adopted a more liberal perspective. John Sperling, Ph.D., founder and chairman of Apollo Group, Incorporated, sees the universities of the future as very diverse in their structure, but continuing to provide their students with an affective as well as a cognitive education. He predicts, however, that institutions will emerge as for-profit organizations, traded publicly in global markets. He sees universities, worldwide, as having evolved toward a common model under the power of four forces. By 2025, there will be "more rapid transformation of information and communications technologies, internationalization of economic processes and practices, the adoption of English as a universal language, and the technology-driven demand for higher education" (Sperling, 1999, pp. 4–5). Sperling feels that the rapid growth in communication technologies will result in the most significant changes, and it will be difficult to predict the consequences of these changes. The quality of anytime, anywhere education has been questioned in the past and continues to be questioned today. Students of the future will be more demanding of high quality than today's students, who are more interested in the convenience and flexibility of their education.

> The successful university will be a communications hub responsible for carrying out its traditional task of organizing and packaging information for distribution to students; however, instead of one or two channels, distribution will be through a variety of mediums, many, if not most, not yet invented or imagined. This will necessitate the unbundling of faculty roles [i.e., separating teaching from content, development, and assessment] and the emergence of a variety of new specialties; similar to those found in the production studios of broadcasting companies and advertising agencies. Instead of individual faculty members or faculty committees preparing curriculum, there will now be course designers, curriculum writers and editors—for multi-media productions there will also be producers and directors. (Sperling, 1999, p. 5)

Sperling cites both Singapore and the United States as two nations whose higher education institutions have been most influenced by rapidly changing technologies, the increasing demand for technology in higher education, English as the predominant language, and the internalization of economic practices. In Singapore, every school, business, and home is connected to the national network, Singapore One. According to Sperling, that network provides a model for advanced communication that could link all nations that choose to participate in a global communication system. Singapore One provides every citizen of that country access to higher education.

In the United States, government and businesses have adopted information and communications technologies to a greater extent than in any other large nation in the world. Many corporations that have their own educational training programs have assumed the title "university," such as McDonald's Hamburger U., which trains students in how to operate a franchise. These "corporate universities" number some 4,000 in the United States. With the advanced technologies used by these entities, public and nonprofit institutions are

likely to consolidate with these corporate structures over the next 25 years.

Society has expectations of higher education institutions that should guide what these institutions aim for. In a survey of state governors conducted in 1998,

> the top four items in terms of perceived importance were [to]: (1) encourage lifelong learning, (2) provide education any time and any place, (3) require collaboration with business and industry in curriculum and program development, and (4) integrate on-the-job experience with academic programs. In sharp contrast, the bottom four items in descending order of perceived importance were: [to] (1) maintain faculty authority for curriculum content, quality, and degree requirements, (2) maintain present balance of faculty research, teaching, and community service, (3) insure a campus based experience for a majority of students, and (4) maintain traditional faculty roles and tenure. (Sperling, 1999, p. 6)

Lifelong learning, which is of greatest importance, puts huge demands on higher education. "In 1970, less than 20% of the U.S. population was over 25 years of age; today that percentage has more than doubled to 45%" (Sperling, 1999, p. 6). Specifically, more than 6 million students in this country are older than 25 years, and 80% of them are full-time workers. Today, working adults need access to higher education that is convenient, flexible, and efficient. Furthermore, they want educational opportunities that will help them improve their professional positions. The shrinking traditional-age student body will have access to the most prestigious institutions, and many mediocre institutions will either shut down or be forced to adjust their size to cater to young students. Faculty roles will change as well. Faculty researchers will be concentrated in large research institutions and the rest will find teaching their main responsibility.

> The university of 2025 will cast a curious shadow on the university of 2000. Many will be very large (some mega). Others will be wired into the fabric of symbiotic institutions. All will be wired into the global information/intelligence/knowledge system. Current U.S. systems of control and regulations will be replaced with mechanisms that are responsive to the market. Students will drive service definition and will be located wherever there is a digital connection and a demand. (Sperling, 1999, p. 17)

A Cause for Action

Sir John S. Daniel of Britain holds still another view. He posits that higher education today has three issues that need to be addressed so that future generations will not be denied "intellectual liberation of the academic mode of thinking" (Daniel, 1997, p. 11). The issues are cost, flexibility, and access. A new configuration for higher education, the mega-university (Figure 13.1), already found in Asia, Africa, Great Britain, and Europe, will be significant in addressing these issues.

Additionally, intelligent use of technology will provide a means for university systems to become learning-centered rather than teaching-centered. That is, university-wide networks must provide access for students both on and off campus. They also must create a commonality of computing conference software for students using different computer environments. Daniel purports that when faculty use technology in their teaching, they are giving better value to their students. Technologies allow for individual learning to take place as opposed to what occurs in remote-group teaching (Daniel, 1997). The technology should be interactive, user-friendly, cost-effective, and fast, and provide easy access. Because the United States has the strongest university system in the world, Daniel says, the rest of the world

Figure 13.1. The Mega-Universities: Basic Data

Country	Name of Institution	Founded	Students (as of 1995*)	Academic Staff (1996)	
				Part-time	*Full-time*
China	China TV University System	1979	530,000 (in 1994)	13,000	18,000
France	Centre National d'Enseignement à Distance	1939	184,614 (in 1994)	3,000	1,800
India	Indira Gandhi National Open University	1985	242,000	13,420	232
Indonesia	Universitas Terbuka	1984	353,000	5,000	791
Iran	Payame Noor University	1987	117,000 (in 1996)	3,165	499
Korea	Korea National Open University	1982 [1]	210,578	2,670	176
South Africa	University of South Africa	1873 [2]	130,000	1,964	1,348
Spain	Universidad Nacional de Educación a Distancia	1972	110,000	3,600	1,000
Thailand	Sukhothai Thammathirat Open University	1978	216,800	3,108	429
Turkey	Anadolu University	1982	577,804	680	579
United Kingdom	The Open University	1969	157,450	7,376	815

* except as noted

[1] As the Korea Air and Correspondence University

[2] As the University of the Cape of Good Hope

[Taken from Daniel, J. S. (1997, July/August). Why Universities Need Technology Strategies. *Change*, p. 14. Reprinted with permission.]

watches the United States to see what happens in higher education. This will be their model.

> The traditional classroom of the campus university has had a long run as the preferred means for achieving the ultimate goals of the university. But the classroom model is approaching its "sell-by" date. It is not the means that are important, but the ends to which the university aspires. They are the appeal to reason and evidence, the link between conversation and community, the synergy between research and learning—in short, the academic mode of thinking and working. A good technology strategy can give . . . the means to continue to achieve those timeless purposes in a new millennium. (Daniel, 1997, p. 17)

University of Phoenix (UOP) President Jorge Klor de Alva also predicts what the future may hold for higher education vis à vis distance learning. He states that most learners will need to be retrained several times throughout their working lives in order to stay competitive with other workers. Thus, access to lifelong learning opportunities will be critical to their success. He further implies that since most workers will have to acquire their educational updates while on the job, technology, with its anytime, anyplace capacity, certainly will be the medium of choice. He cites the results of the survey of U.S. state governors (see Sperling, 1999) and those of another poll of university presidents, faculty, and administrators conducted by the North Central Association of Colleges and Schools. In the latter, respondents felt that the trends likely to have the most impact were: "increasing demands for accountability [80%], expanding use of distance education [78%], increasing attention to teaching and learning [72%], and expanding use of the Internet [71%]" (Klor de Alva, 1999–2000, p. 53). President Klor de Alva argues that in today's economy no higher education institution can afford to resist the changes that are inevitable. He feels that the needs of tomorrow's students will demand something quite different from the traditionally delivered college education. "Web-based education, an inherently location-less medium, is likely to push to the margins of history a substantial number of those institutions and regulatory bodies that seek to remain geographically centered" (Klor de Alva, 1999–2000, p. 55). The nature of the new "student body" requires institutions to provide individuals with an education while they are working full-time, a workplace-

relevant faculty and curriculum, a convenient, time-efficient and cost-effective education with superb customer service (Klor de Alva, 1999–2000).

> If . . . any university . . . wants to survive [in the new millennium, it must be] primarily in the business of education rather than of brick and mortar classrooms and self-created curriculum. . . . [I]ts transformation in the future should be . . . dictated primarily by what learners need, not by what it has traditionally done. (Klor de Alva, 1999–2000, p. 57)

Klor de Alva proposes that the UOP and other colleges that expect to prosper should be in the business of producing content and having a wide-based distribution network with some campus-based delivery. He sees education as becoming a process of skills certification and feels that effective marketing, quality assurance, and effective use of new technologies to communicate new knowledge, will mark the difference between colleges that succeed and those that do not. At highest risk for failure are nonelite, private campus-based institutions. In conclusion, Klor de Alva (1999–2000) observes:

> Societies everywhere expect from higher education the provision of an education that can permit them to flourish in the changing global economic landscape. Institutions that can continually change to keep up with the needs of the transforming economy they serve will survive. Those that cannot or will not change will become irrelevant, will condemn misled masses to second-class economic status or poverty, and will ultimately die, probably at the hands of those they chose to delude by serving up an education for a non-existent world. (p. 58)

Dr. Farhad Saba, CEO of *Distance-Educator.com* (an online publication), has a view that is close to that of Dr. Klor de Alva, but that has a new twist, which is closely in tune with the sentiments of Dr. George Connick (see Foreword). Dr. Saba feels that unless universities totally restructure to fully embrace communication technologies, they are destined to fail. He states that

> distance education is going to be another opportunity missed for advancing and meeting the needs of the students as long as it is used in the confines of an out-of-date organizational structure that has not changed much for well over a century. (Saba, 2001, p. 2)

Since technology offers an instructor opportunities to do so much more than teaching in a traditional technology-less classroom, the approach must be new. For example, faculty must have the support of instructional designers, programmers, course producers, and media specialists to optimize the instruction they deliver to their students. The instruction will be student-centered rather than faculty-centered. It will be individualized for each student rather than for the group of students. Saba likens this phenomenon to that of the physician who is supported by other paramedical professionals, nurses, and hospital personnel in their individualized care of patients. Teaching with technology is not about replicating the traditional classroom experience. It is about individualized and personalized instruction. It is about better teaching, better education, and a better experience for students.

In an interview with Young (2001), Dr. Saba compared the adoption of technology in education with that in business and industry.

> In the 1990s, when business and industry decided to adopt postmodern technologies, what we now call information technologies, to bring down their cost of operation and increase their productivity, they were also talking about massive organizational restructuring. The term that was used in business and industry was re-engineering the corporation. Re-engineering the corporation meant that their entire management system needed to be changed. We haven't seen anything of the sort in universities.

Using distance education to deliver courses within the structure of brick-and-mortar institutions is begging the question. To make optimal use of the adoption of technology in education, there need to be new structures outside of the physical universities that have existed for centuries.

Technology is transforming the role of faculty from "the sage on the stage" to "the guide on the side," with faculty "serving more as learning coaches, advisors, and role models than as data delivery devices" (Daviss, 2000, p. 8).

> That new role for faculty in a wired world also will transform the function and meaning of a university. . . . To begin to discover that new meaning,

schools need only to follow one piece of advice by a faculty member [who said], "Just do it. The technology is now cheap enough and simple enough. You'll never solve all the problems and answer all your questions in advance. If you try, you'll go crazy. Find a few people who want to blaze the trail in distance learning, give them plenty of incentives and support, and others will follow." (Daviss, 2000, p. 8)

It is not a question of distance replacing a traditional campus-based education. Both campus-based and distance education have important roles to play. "This is about individualized education to an extent we can't imagine today" (Daviss, 2000, pp. 8–9). Some universities have been created as distance and online institutions. Most of these deliver all courses and programs at a distance using technology (see Appendix Y).

A CLOSING NOTE

The speed at which technology has been improved to date gives us but a glimpse of what will happen over the next several decades. This is just the beginning of a higher education system in which there will be a significant presence of distance delivery. Students will be able to access education offered around the world from nearly any institution, while remaining in the comfort of their own homes or at their workplaces. Many of the technologies that will be used by students in the future have not even been imagined yet (Sperling, 1999). Inventions and new technologies will mushroom as the future unfolds.

We have seen much growth in the use of technology in institutions, including a significant increase in the number of courses and programs that employ web pages, online content, Internet resources, e-mail, and synchronous and asynchronous components. We have seen an increase in programs that are delivered entirely online. More than two-thirds of higher education institutions in the United States offer distance learning courses and programs (Johnstone, 2001). We have seen major changes in student support services for those choosing technology-based courses and programs. Even in the context of the traditional institution, use of electronic application, registration, and library services are among a few of the administrative functions that have become the norm.

In today's world students not only can get an education without being geographically near a college or university, but can select courses and programs they desire from institutions around the world. There is no limit to the possibilities. Some say that the United States, through distance education, will attract a new market of international students. Distance education will be instrumental in providing these learners an American higher education degree (Oblinger, Barone, & Hawkins, 2001).

Today, more that ever before, institutions must provide opportunities for lifelong learning. We have the technological resources, the market, and the means. It is imperative that we move into the future, implementing this new way of learning for the 21st century. It was predicted at the end of the 20th century that by the year 2007 nearly half of adults taking university courses will be doing so through distance learning (White, 1999). While that predic-tion was surely appropriate in 1999, with the rapid change that has taken place in just 3 years, this author predicts that by the year 2005, more than half of *all* students participating in higher education will be involved in some form of distance education. As the future becomes the present, it is hoped that people everywhere will have opportunities for learning.

It has been established that distance learning has taken the world by storm. The technology is here and the time is right. We have moved into the 21st century with a 21st-century model for higher education. What began as a "trickle in the early 1990s became a flood by the close of the decade" (Ely, 2000, p. 26). Our future will be enriched and made limitless by all the choices made possible by distance education. We must move forward with confidence and advance into this new land of educational opportunity. The future is here!

Course Evaluation for ITV Courses

Please complete the following questionnaire and return it to your site coordinator. YOUR RESPONSES ARE CONFIDENTIAL. Your feedback is very important and will be used together with other student responses to improve [your university's] programming. Thank you.

1. Social Security Number _____ – _____ – _____

2. Sex: Male _____ Female _____

3. Age: _____

4. Course name: _____

5. At what location are you taking this course?
   _____

6. What is the highest level of education you have completed? (Please check only one response.)

   _____ some high school

   _____ high school diploma

   _____ GED

   _____ some college

   _____ associates degree

   _____ bachelors degree

   _____ masters degree

   _____ other (specify)

7. What is your present occupation?
   _____

8. Have you ever taken a course in this mode before this one? _____yes _____no

9. How did you hear about this course?

   _____ newspaper

   _____ from a friend

   _____ brochure

   _____ other (specify) _____

10. How far did you have to commute *one way* to get to this class? _____ miles

11. How far is it from your home to the nearest University of Maine campus (*one way*)? _____miles

12. Using the response key below, please indicate your level of agreement with the following statements by circling the appropriate number.

    1 = strongly disagree

    2 = disagree

    3 = somewhat disagree

    4 = somewhat agree

    5 = agree

    6 = strongly agree

a. I was satisfied with the registration process.

   1   2   3   4   5   6

b. I was satisfied with the pace at which the instructor taught the course content.

   1   2   3   4   5   6

c. I was satisfied with the instructor's organization of the class sessions.

   1   2   3   4   5   6

d. I was satisfied with the instructor's explanation of concepts.

   1   2   3   4   5   6

e. I was satisfied with the graphics the instructor used to clarify course content.

   1   2   3   4   5   6

f. I was satisfied with the quality of the audio.

   1   2   3   4   5   6

g. I was satisfied with the quality of the video.

   1   2   3   4   5   6

h. Overall, the delivery quality was adequate to allow me to learn the content.

   1   2   3   4   5   6

i. The course syllabus was clear.

      1   2   3   4   5   6

j. The information I received during registration about this course was *accurate*.

      1   2   3   4   5   6

k. The information I received during registration about this course was *helpful*.

      1   2   3   4   5   6

l. I was satisfied with the timeliness of interaction with the instructor (i.e., the instructor was there when I needed assistance).

      1   2   3   4   5   6

m. The instructor made me feel like my questions and comments were important.

      1   2   3   4   5   6

n. The instructor's responses to my questions and concerns were helpful.

      1   2   3   4   5   6

o. I felt "connected" to other students taking the course.

      1   2   3   4   5   6

p. I was able to obtain course materials and books in a timely manner.

      1   2   3   4   5   6

q. Corrected tests and assignments were returned in a timely manner.

      1   2   3   4   5   6

r. I wish I could have taken the videotapes home to review.

      1   2   3   4   5   6

s. I felt the workload for this course was comparable to that in other courses I have taken at this level.

      1   2   3   4   5   6

t. I would take another course if it was offered in this mode.

      1   2   3   4   5   6

u. I would recommend this course to another student.

      1   2   3   4   5   6

v. Overall, I was satisfied with this course.

      1   2   3   4   5   6

Please respond to the following statements by circling the response which best reflects your feelings. Choose one.

13. Feeling that I am a part of a class is:

   a. not particularly important to me.

   b. somewhat important to me.

   c. very important to me

14. Classroom discussions are:

   a. rarely helpful to me.

   b. sometimes helpful to me.

   c. almost always helpful to me.

15. When an instructor hands out directions for an assignment, I prefer:

   a. figuring out the instructions on my own.

   b. trying to follow the directions on my own, then asking for help as needed.

   c. having the instructions explained orally first.

16. I need faculty comments on my assignments:

   a. within a few weeks.

   b. within a few days.

   c. right away.

17. As a reader I would classify myself as:

   a. good—I usually understand the text without help.

   b. average—I sometimes need help to understand the text.

   c. slower than average—I usually need help to understand the text.

18. If I have to go to a site or center to take exams:

   a. I can go anytime.

   b. I may miss some assignments or exam deadlines if sites or centers are not open evenings and weekends.

   c. I will have difficulty getting to sites or centers even in the evenings or on weekends.

19. People sign up for courses for different reasons. Below are some of the reasons. *Please indicate how important each of these reasons was in your decision to enroll in this course.* For example, if the course is required for your program and this was a very important reason for your decision, then you would circle 5 for the first item below.

    1 = Not Important — to — 5 = Very Important

    a. The course is required in my degree program.
       1   2   3   4   5

    b. The course content is of interest.
       1   2   3   4   5

    c. The course is important to my future career goals.
       1   2   3   4   5

    d. I thought taking a college course would be fun.
       1   2   3   4   5

    e. My employer wanted me to take the course.
       1   2   3   4   5

    f. My employer paid for the course.
       1   2   3   4   5

    g. I wanted to take a college course rather than learn on my own.
       1   2   3   4   5

    h. I wanted to start earning a college degree.
       1   2   3   4   5

    i. This course will help me acquire some of the skills and knowledge I need to get a job.
       1   2   3   4   5

20. If this course had *not* been offered in a location near where you live, would you have traveled to a university campus to take a course?

    _____yes _____no _____not sure

    If *no*, please explain. _____

21. If this course had *not* been offered in this *mode*, would you have traveled to a university campus to take a course?

    _____yes _____no _____not sure

    If *no*, please explain. _____

22. On how many occasions did you view class videotapes for review purposes?

    _____ once

    _____ two times

    _____ three times

    _____ four times

    _____ five times

    _____ six or more times

23. How much extra would you be willing to pay for course materials that would allow you the convenience of taking this course entirely from your home (with the exception of taking examinations at a site or center)? $_____

24. In the space below, please feel free to write additional comments you may have about this course. Your valuable input is greatly appreciated.

Thank you for your assistance.

Course Evaluation for Asynchronous Courses

Please complete the following questionnaire and return it in the enclosed postage paid return envelope. YOUR RESPONSES ARE CONFIDENTIAL. Your feedback is very important and will be used together with other student responses to improve [your university's] programming. Thank you.

1. Social Security Number (optional) ___–__–___

2. Sex: Male _____ Female _____

3. Age: _____

4. Course name: _____

5. Where are you taking this course?

   _____ at home

   _____ at a site

   _____ at a center

6. What is the highest level of education you have completed? (Please check only one response.)

   _____ some high school

   _____ high school diploma

   _____ GED

   _____ associates degree

   _____ bachelors degree

   _____ some graduate work

   _____ masters degree

   _____ other (specify) _____

7. What is your present occupation? _____

8. Have you ever taken a course in this mode before this one? _____ yes _____ no

   If *yes*, how many times? _____

9. How did you hear about this course?

   _____ newspaper

   _____ from a friend

   _____ brochure

   _____ other (specify) _____

10. Did you receive a post card referring you to the online Asynchronous Guide?

    _____ yes _____ no _____ not sure

11. Why did you choose to take this course in this format?

12. Now that you have completed this course, how comfortable are you using this technology?

    _____ not comfortable

    _____ somewhat comfortable

    _____ very comfortable

13. How would you rate the pace of this course?

    _____ too slow _____ about right _____ too fast

14. In what location did you complete your computer work for the course? (If you used multiple sites, please specify the percent of work completed at each site.)

    _____ at a site

    _____ at a center

    _____ at home

    _____ other (specify) _____

15. If you used a site or center, how far (in miles) was it from your home? _____ miles

16. How many hours per week did you spend completing work for this course? _____ hours

17. If you ran into a problem using a computer, were you able to get assistance?

    _____ yes _____ no _____ n/a

    If *yes*, who provided assistance? _____

    If *yes*, was the problem solved? ___ yes ___ no

    Were instructions for using the computer available to you? _____ yes _____ no

18. How much prior computer experience did you have before taking this course?

    _____ I had used e-mail.

    _____ I had used computer conferencing.

    _____ I had used the World Wide Web.

    _____ I had used MAC or Windows.

    _____ other (specify) _____

19. Using the response key below, please indicate your level of agreement with the following statements by circling the appropriate number.

    1 = strongly disagree

    2 = disagree

    3 = somewhat disagree

    4 = somewhat agree

    5 = agree

    6 = strongly agree

    7 = not applicable

    a. The information in the Asynchronous Guide which I viewed during registration was helpful.

       1   2   3   4   5   6   7

    b. I was satisfied with the instructor's organization of the course online.

       1   2   3   4   5   6   7

    c. I was satisfied with the instructor's explanation of concepts.

       1   2   3   4   5   6   7

    d. The technical introduction was useful to me.

       1   2   3   4   5   6   7

    e. I followed the suggested procedures given in the technical introduction.

       1   2   3   4   5   6   7

    f. The quality of the videotaped lecture materials was good.

       1   2   3   4   5   6   7

    g. The information I received about logons and passwords was clear.

       1   2   3   4   5   6   7

    h. The quality of the examples given to demonstrate concepts was good.

       1   2   3   4   5   6   7

    i. The *technical support* services were helpful.

       1   2   3   4   5   6   7

    j. The *content support* I received was helpful.

       1   2   3   4   5   6   7

    k. The *moral support* I received was helpful.

       1   2   3   4   5   6   7

    l. The instructor made me feel like my questions and comments were important.

       1   2   3   4   5   6   7

    m. The instructor's responses to my questions and concerns were helpful.

       1   2   3   4   5   6   7

    n. I felt "connected" to other students taking the course

       1   2   3   4   5   6   7

    o. I was able to obtain course materials and books in a timely manner.

       1   2   3   4   5   6   7

    p. I received feedback on tests and assignments in a timely manner.

       1   2   3   4   5   6   7

    q. I was satisfied with the timeliness of interaction with the instructor.

       1   2   3   4   5   6   7

    r. I felt the workload for this course was comparable to that in other courses I have taken at this level.

       1   2   3   4   5   6   7

    s. I received adequate directions for using the computer technologies in the course (World Wide Web, e-mail, computer conferencing, etc.) productively.

       1   2   3   4   5   6   7

    t. I would take another course if it was offered in this mode.

       1   2   3   4   5   6   7

u. I would recommend this course to another
student.

  1   2   3   4   5   6   7

v. Overall, I was satisfied with this course.

  1   2   3   4   5   6   7

Comments:

20. Please indicate your level of agreement with the
following statements by circling the appropriate
number according to the response key below.

  1 = strongly disagree

  2 = disagree

  3 = somewhat disagree

  4 = somewhat agree

  5 = agree

  6 = strongly agree

  7 = not applicable

a. I found other students' comments online in
this course helpful.

  1   2   3   4   5   6   7

b. The amount of information delivered was
manageable.

  1   2   3   4   5   6   7

c. Online course discussions were productive
and easy to follow.

  1   2   3   4   5   6   7

d. The instructor's online comments were clear
and easy to follow.

  1   2   3   4   5   6   7

e. The time spent on coursework for this course
was about the same as other college courses I
have taken.

  1   2   3   4   5   6   7

f. I was able to structure my study habits to
meet the demands of this course.

  1   2   3   4   5   6   7

g. I found course activities to be useful and
relevant to content.

  1   2   3   4   5   6   7

h. The instructor explained how my performance in the course would be evaluated.

  1   2   3   4   5   6   7

i. I found the instructor's assessment of my
performance meaningful.

  1   2   3   4   5   6   7

j. I was kept informed of my progress in the
course.

  1   2   3   4   5   6   7

k. I felt the expectations for a course offered in
this format were realistic.

  1   2   3   4   5   6   7

l. I found the self-assessment activities in this
course useful.

  1   2   3   4   5   6   7

21. If this course had *not* been offered in this *mode*,
would you have traveled to a university campus
to take a course?

  ____ yes   ____ no   ____ not sure

22. Approximately what percentage of the course
materials did you read:

  _____ on the computer?   _____ on paper?

23. Approximately what percentage of your
discussion with your instructor was:

  _____ by e-mail?   _____ by telephone?

  _____ by computer conferencing?

24. If you did *not* complete the course, please explain
why.

Thank you for your valuable feedback!

BEX Interview Protocol

- Was the information received prior to the course enough to enable you to use the course package/materials effectively?

- Did you know the objectives of the course; were they clearly written/stated in understandable language?

- Were the printed materials clear?

- How would you rate the feedback on your activities in the course?

- How convenient were the course materials to access/use?

- How did you find the pace of the course? (too fast, about right, too slow)

- Did the materials make you feel like their creators/producers knew what they were doing? Were the materials user-friendly? Appealing?

- How essential was the information you got on the Internet to reaching the objectives of the course, assignments, work?

- Were you instructed how to approach this "new" learning environment and how to use it for your own learning?

- Were the technical skills you learned necessary to carry out the objectives and assignments of the course?

- How relevant are the courses to your day-to-day practice?

- Did you find the courses intellectually challenging?

- Were the courses in the BEX program worth the time you spent on them?

- How did these courses compare with face-to-face courses you have taken?

- Was the estimated study time for each module correct?

- Do you feel you benefited from the courses? How?

- Did you cover all the modules? If no, why?

- Did you have difficulty contacting the professor if you needed to? How would you rate the teaching approach?

- How would you rate the workload in studying the subject and completing the assignment requirements? Reasonable or unreasonable?

- Did you have any problems operating the computer programs to access materials?

- How confident were you about using the "mouse"?

- Overall, how would you rate the program thus far? (1 = poor; 5 = excellent)

- Overall, how would you rate the technology thus far? (1 = poor; 5 = excellent)

- Overall, how would you rate the instructional materials thus far? (1 = poor; 5 = excellent)

APPENDIX D

Oregon Colleges Online: Student Guidelines

Who Should Take Distance Learning Courses?

A person taking distance learning courses needs to be a self-motivated, independent learner. If a student needs to have an immediate instructor/classmate response, probably a distance education class would not be a good choice. Anyone who has difficulty getting to campus due to work and family responsibilities or travel restrictions will find distance education courses very convenient.

How Do I Get Started?

If you are pursuing a degree or certificate, the first step is to apply for admission to the community college of your choice. The college you choose to "attend" does not have to be the college within your local area. You may enroll in any college within the state. Contact the Admissions Office of that college for the application form; complete it; and return it to the college. If you wish to enroll for an occasional course, it is not necessary to apply for admission to the college. Just contact the college and register for the course.

How Do I Register for Classes?

Methods of registration vary from college to college so be sure to check with the Registration Office of the college where you have applied or that is offering the course in which you are interested.

How Much Do Distance Learning Courses Cost?

Tuition is individually set by each college and will vary between $30–$40 per credit hour, plus any additional fees that may apply. You will be informed of the exact cost when you register for classes.

How Do I Purchase Textbooks and Other Supplies?

Almost all distance learning courses require textbooks. Books can be ordered from the college bookstores using a major credit card. Call the book-store of the campus you are "attending" for more information.

What Other Services Are Available to Me?

All student services that are available to on-campus students are also accessible to distance learning students. It is advisable to contact a distance learning advisor to make sure the classes you have registered for will apply to your selected program of study. Or, if you haven't decided what area of study is for you, they will help you choose courses that will apply to any general education requirements. Most distance learning courses qualify for financial aid and veterans' benefits. Contact the college's Financial Aid Office for more information.

Can I Obtain a Degree Through Distance Learning?

The associate of arts Oregon transfer (AAOT) degree is available through distance learning. Four of the community colleges (Central Oregon, Lane, Portland, and Chemeketa) have the degree available totally through their college. The other colleges work together to provide the courses necessary to complete the program. Course requirements for the AAOT vary from college to college so be sure to check with the college where you are registered. Chemeketa Community College also offers associate of applied science and associate of general studies degrees by distance learning.

How Do I Begin a Distance Learning Course?

Many distance learning courses begin with an orientation. This is an opportunity for the instructor to discuss the course objective and requirements, and to distribute and discuss the course syllabus. The syllabus will provide all the information necessary for successfully completing the course. If you can't attend the orientation, call the instructor and make arrangements for obtaining this information.

Each student will want to establish a home institution. This will be your primary contact for financial aid, counseling, course information, as well as the granting of your AAOT degree.

(Reprinted with permission from Oregon Department of Community Colleges and Workforce Development. Web site: *http://occdl.chemeketa.edu*)

Oregon Colleges Online: Are Distance Learning Courses for Me?

How well would distance learning courses fit your circumstances and lifestyle? To find out, complete this survey. Pick one answer for each question. When finished, click the *Send Survey* button at the bottom of the page and the results will be automatically evaluated.

The 13 questions in the survey reflect some of the realities about taking distance learning courses.

1. My need to take this course now is:
   - High—I need it immediately for degree, job, or another important reason.
   - Moderate—I could take it on campus later or substitute another course.
   - Low—It's a personal interest that could be postponed.

2. My favorite type of class would have me . . .
   - Watching a performance.
   - Doing the activity myself.
   - Hearing a lecture.

3. I would classify myself as someone who:
   - Often gets things done ahead of time.
   - Needs reminding to get things done on time.
   - Puts things off until the last minute.

4. When I'm in a face-to-face class of about 20 people,
   - I always participate in classroom discussion.
   - I may participate in classroom discussion once in a while.
   - I try to avoid participating in classroom discussion.

5. When an instructor hands out directions for an assignment, I prefer:
   - Figuring out the instructions myself.
   - Trying to follow the directions on my own, then asking for help as needed.
   - Having the instructions explained to me.

6. I need faculty comments on my assignments:
   - Within a few weeks, so I can review what I did.
   - Within a few days, or I forget what I did.
   - Right away, or I get very frustrated.

7. Considering my professional and personal schedule, the amount of time I have to work on distance education courses is:
   - More than enough for a campus class or distance education course.
   - About the same as for a class on campus.
   - Less than for a class on campus.

8. When I am asked to use VCRs, computers, voice mail, or other technologies new to me:
   - I immediately try out the new tool.
   - I try to read all the instructions before I start working with the new tool.
   - I prefer to have someone right there with me when I actually use the new tool.

9. As a reader, I would classify myself as:
   - A very strong reader with an extensive vocabulary. I usually understand text without help.
   - A good reader, but occasionally I have questions after I read something.
   - Actually, I'd rather not do much reading. I sometimes need help to understand the text.

10. How do you prefer to spend class time?
    - Working independently on my own projects.
    - Listening to lecture and taking notes.
    - Working in small groups of two or three other students.

11. How do you like to learn about new ideas? Check the best response.
    - On my own, reflecting on the information previously given.
    - In a small group, where we can share ideas together in discussions.
    - Working on a hands-on activity in a face-to-face class to apply ideas immediately.

12. Going to campus to take exams or complete work:
    - Is easy for me.
    - Can be difficult at times.
    - Is very difficult.

(Reprinted with permission from Oregon Department of Community Colleges and Workforce Development. Web site: http://occdl.chemeketa.edu)

Oregon Colleges Online: Effective Course Elements

ELEMENTS OF EFFECTIVE DISTANCE LEARNING COURSES

A number of elements have been proven to be effective in distance learning courses. While individual implementations will vary, the following elements are expected to be incorporated into proposed distance learning courses.

Orientation

Orientation information should contain the following items as a minimum:

- Assessment methods
- Class participation requirements (attendance at on-campus sessions, if any; interaction with students/faculty; written assignments, examinations, grading criteria, etc.)
- Technical requirements (i.e., Internet access, VCR, computer capabilities, etc.)
- Required texts/readings
- Sources of course/research materials (i.e., library access, instructor notes, etc.)
- Assignments, methods for submission, and due dates
- Examination methods and timelines
- Information on how to contact the instructor (e-mail, fax, telephone, etc.)

Interactivity

Interaction among students and between students and faculty should be embedded in the course structure. Interactivity can be accomplished in one or more of the following ways:

- Online discussion, recorded lecture, and/or distributed orientation sessions

- Chat room (an online discussion activity)—which can be asynchronous (students join and leave a continuous discussion) or synchronous (students are required to join and participate together at a fixed time)
- Threaded discussion—a discussion is started around a topic and the participants respond to the topic and to comments made by others
- Listserv, through which questions or notices are posted by any participant and automatically sent to all participants' mail boxes
- E-mail—an important component for private communications among students and between students and faculty and for discussions, delivery of written assignments, critiques, and tests

Presentation Strategies

A variety of methods should be embedded in the design of distance learning courses.

- Alternative experiences. Activities such as lab packs, site visitations, or on-campus labs are all activities that address direct and indirect learning.
- Video recorded and audio recorded elements of a course that might be delivered online or distributed separately. Copyright restrictions must be observed and followed.
- Interactive elements. Activities that involve computer-assisted instructional elements or multimedia presentations can be included; however, delivery and development are two elements that should be considered. Simple graphic images, maps, etc., may be delivered via the Internet. Because of the time necessary for downloading, courses that make intensive use of complex graphic images may need to have supplemental graphic materials furnished on computer disc or CD-ROM.
- Textbooks and study guides. Texts with a unifying study guide, either electronic or printed, can be a core part of any distance learning course. Electronic publishing or text information is an alternative to hardcopy distribution. Copyright restrictions must be observed and followed.

Active Learning

Planned learning strategies that engage students in the learning process should be embedded in distance learning course designs. These strategies should focus on students' knowledge and ability to demonstrate identified learning outcomes. Depending on the desired outcomes, active learning strategies might emphasize ways to enable students to:

- Make accurate observations and formulate questions
- Understand the differences between quantitative and qualitative information
- Identify, locate, access, and apply information for a specified purpose
- Analyze and evaluate information on the basis of origin, viewpoint, currency, relevance, and completeness
- Evaluate solutions/interpretations for validity and appropriateness and make necessary adjustments
- Gather, use, and document information
- Organize information to develop/support ideas
- Clearly and logically articulate the student's own position on an issue
- Effectively communicate with a variety of audiences
- Synthesize and communicate messages in written, visual, verbal, and nonverbal modes
- Work cooperatively as well as independently
- Make connections and apply knowledge among various disciplines
- Recognize influence of culturally grounded assumptions on perception and behavior
- Demonstrate understanding of and openness toward varying cultural customs and values
- Draw justifiable inferences about other cultures without stereotyping or being biased
- Articulate an understanding of local and global concerns
- Analyze global economic, social, political, and environmental issues from multiple perspectives

Research

Students must be involved in activities that include accessing, interpreting, and applying information. Depending on identified outcomes, these activities might include:

Information literacy (the access, interpretation, and application of information for research, general information gathering, or problem solving) needs to involve activities that develop the following skills:

- Use of the Internet to locate and access information
- Interpreting information to assess its accuracy and appropriateness
- Structuring and applying basic research principles
- Applying information to solve a problem

Outcomes Assessment

Distance learning courses should use assessment tools and practices to measure student progress toward outcomes on a regular and recurring basis. They should assure:

- Outcomes and assessment methods are defined in achievable and measurable terms.
- Learning design is consistent with intended learning outcomes.
- Delivery structure and course design facilitate achievement of learning outcomes.
- Assessment is relevant to content and learner's resources.
- Assessment is timely, appropriate, and responsive to needs of learning.
- Learning outcomes are reviewed with changes in content or updating of materials.
- Learning outcomes are relevant and appropriate.

(Reprinted with permission from Oregon Department of Community Colleges and Workforce Development. Web site: http://occdl.chemeketa.edu)

APPENDIX G

Oregon Colleges Online: Distance Learning Course Design Considerations

Learning activities are designed to fit teaching/learning requirements.

- All distance learning activities include clearly defined learning outcomes.
- Students understand expectations of learner activities.
- Distance learning efforts provide flexible opportunities for interaction.
- Assessment methods used are appropriate to the course and learning methods employed.
- Course content, instructional methods, technologies, and context complement each other.
- Selection and application of technologies are appropriate for the intended outcomes, subject matter, and characteristics and circumstances of the learner, and are cost effective.
- Learning activities and modes of assessment are responsive to the needs of individual learners.
- The learning experience is designed and organized to increase the learner's control over the time, place, and pace of instruction.
- Outcomes address content mastery and increased learning skills.
- Students with skills in subject matter, instructional methods, and technologies work collaboratively to create learning opportunities.
- Instructional offerings are evaluated on a regular basis for effectiveness; evaluation results are utilized for improvement.

Distance learning opportunities are available to learners through a variety of fully accessible modes of delivery and resources.

- A learner support system to assist the learner in using the resources is provided. This system includes technology and technical support, site facilitation, library and information resources, advising, counseling, and problem-solving assistance.
- Course development models and support services consider the needs of the learner in relation to the learning mode(s) used and make provision for delivery of appropriate resources based on the design of the learning activities, the technology involved, and the needs of the learner.
- Access to support services, such as scheduling, registration, and library resources, is convenient, efficient, and responsive to learner needs, as well as consistent with the aim of providing learning at a distance.
- Distance learning activities provide the learner with all information pertinent to the learning opportunity, such as course prerequisites, modes of study, evaluation criteria, and technical needs.
- Support systems are reviewed regularly to ensure their currency and effectiveness.

Distance learning programs organize learning around demonstrable learning outcomes, assist the learner to achieve those outcomes, and assess learner progress by reference to those outcomes.

- Course design enables individual learners to help shape learning outcomes and how they are achieved. Learning outcomes are described in observable, measurable, and achievable terms.
- Instructional design is consistent with and shaped to achieve the intended learning outcomes. Distance learning technologies and delivery systems are used in ways that facilitate the achievement of intended learning outcomes.
- Learning outcomes are assessed in a way that is relevant to the content, the learner's situation, and the distance learning systems employed.
- Assessment of learning is timely, appropriate, and responsive to the needs of the learner.
- Learning outcomes are reviewed regularly to assure their clarity, utility, and appropriateness for the learners.

(Reprinted with permission from Oregon Department of Community Colleges and Workforce Development. Web site: http://occdl.chemeketa.edu)

Guide to the WGU Web Site

For assistance with using the WGU web site, call WGU (toll free for callers within the United States) at 877–HELP–WGU (877–435–7048), or e-mail your questions to helpme@wgu.edu.

OVERVIEW

The WGU web site is an extensive site that contains the information typically found in a university catalog, brochure, and class schedule. The site can be divided into seven main sections. These are represented by the links found at the top of every page: About WGU, Academics, Catalog, Admission, Library, Bookstore, and Union. Sections may be "entered" by clicking on the name of the section. The following list indicates what can be found in each of those sections:

About WGU: This section is designed to serve as a primer about WGU—its mission, structure, the people and institutions involved, the way WGU provides students with courses and programs, answers to frequently asked questions (FAQs), our privacy policy, and even an introduction to WGU's unique terminology.

Academics: This section contains WGU's Student Handbook—a complete guide to WGU policies and procedures—along with an in-depth explanation of WGU's competency-based approach to higher education, a faculty list, and info on WGU's accreditation status.

Catalog: This section is comparable to a traditional institution's print-based catalog. It contains the "meat" of what WGU offers—its courses, class sections, and degrees/certificates. It is through this section's search and browse functions that visitors and students can find courses and programs.

Admission: Through this section of the site, visitors can find directions for applying for admission to WGU and the online application for admission form.

This section also contains information about tuition and instructions on how to drop a class.

Library: Through this link, WGU students may enter the WGU Central Library. This library, operated by the University of New Mexico, will provide WGU's distant students with access to library services. As the WGU site evolves, this section also will contain information and links to the libraries of WGU-affiliated education providers, where appropriate.

Bookstore: Similar to the Library link, the Bookstore link serves as the entrance to the WGU Online Bookstore. The Online Bookstore can provide materials that are required for courses and allow students to order those materials online.

Union: The Union section serves as the gateway to several student services. This is where students (and potential students) can learn about financial aid, transfer/articulation, and career advising services. Links to some of WGU's forms (transcript request form, tuition payment form, and others) also can be found here.

In addition to the navigation links provided at the top of every page of the site, there are some additional navigational tools at the bottom of every page. Those tools include:

Guide: This link allows visitors to the site to return to this Guide to the site from any page.

Students: This link takes visitors directly to information pertinent to potential students.

Educators: This link takes visitors directly to information pertinent to potential education providers.

Corporate: This link takes visitors directly to information of interest to potential corporate partners.

Site Map: This is a text-based map of the WGU site's main sections and each of the topics that fall under those sections.

Contact: Through this link, visitors to the WGU site can find out how to contact WGU.

(Reprinted with permission from Western Governors University. Web site: www.wgu.edu)

Compressed Video: Tips for Managing Your Conference

Before the conference begins:

1. The compressed video unit in your room should be on when you arrive. If your unit has not been turned on, please ask your local support staff for assistance, if necessary.

2. Assign one person in each classroom to be the "camera person" to take over the touch panel controls. Check the camera presets after everyone has taken their seats. Reset them if necessary.

3. Turn on and preview the document camera before you begin, if you intend to use it.

4. Connect and load the computer program you intend to use. Check the image from the computer screen on the local monitor to be sure the connections have been properly made.

Once the conference begins:

1. It is helpful if one person facilitates the videoconference.

2. At the beginning of each conference or class, the instructor/facilitator should establish the protocols for interaction. Consider the following:

   - At the beginning of each conference, check in with each participating site so that students actually see the system in action and get a sense of how it switches from site to site.

   - Have the facilitator move the conference from location to location on a regular basis by asking for feedback and/or questions. Remember the system is voice-activated and will switch to a new location only when someone speaks.

   - Interruptions can be an effective, if awkward, way of making a program interactive. Keep in mind that a raised hand will not be seen when an individual wants to make a comment. The system is voice activated. Also, remember that the system switches in response to "dominant and consistent" audio. Ask people to speak up and use a complete sentence when they want to be seen on the system. For example, a comment such as, "This is Jane Doe from USM. I have a comment to make," would cause the camera to switch to the USM location.

3. Check the audio and video from every location. Ask one person at each site, one at a time, if they can see and hear one another across the system. If you ask a blanket question, "Can everyone hear and see me?" everyone will answer at the same time and the system will get very confused and not switch from site to site.

4. If you are having difficulty hearing the audio from any site, check for proper microphone placement, and if you are still having difficulty hearing, ask the site to realign the audio in the room. Do not adjust the audio level on the remote monitor.

5. Remind everyone of the beep tone at the end of the program, which signals 5 minutes before the end of the conference or class.

6. Take time for introductions. You may want to go from site to site and have everyone introduce him- or herself. Use participants' names as often as possible.

7. Ask participants to place the Location Name in a visible place so that people will know the site names when the conference switches location.

The first class session:

1. At the beginning of the first class, take time to discuss the technology. Point out the items in the room and explain how to use the microphone. If you wish, compressed video support staff will be available to talk to the class about the technology and explain the functions of the equipment in the classroom.

2. If the class is not full, ask students at all locations to move to the seats at the far end of the table. This yields better visibility for students and will give the instructor a better view of the students.

3. Encourage students to let you know if they cannot hear or see something during the class.

4. Be sure students know what to do in case of technical problems. They may call a technical support person (give phone number here) or ask their local support staff for assistance. They also can use the telephone in the room to call the broadcast classroom and talk with the instructor by phone. Classroom numbers should be listed within each classroom.

5. Review procedures for tests and assignments and the nature of support students will receive through support staff. A student fact sheet (available to all) will summarize what support is available and how to contact appropriate personnel.

6. Make sure students receive a class syllabus by the first class. If they have not, let them know when and how they will receive it.

7. If the instructor is using computer conferencing and e-mail, he or she should check to be sure all students have received a user name and password. Consider asking each student to e-mail the instructor to confirm that they have access and that their computer is configured accurately.

8. Faculty also should post a schedule of office hours and be available before and after class to respond to individual questions. Students also should be told how to reach the instructor in other ways.

9. If students will be asked to use overhead cameras at remote locations, they should be given an opportunity to practice. Students should be asked to write their names on a piece of paper and to use the overhead camera to send the list to all participants. Students should be asked to introduce themselves and switch from the overhead to the table camera as each person speaks. This will help students become comfortable using the equipment before they present their material more formally.

(Reprinted with permission from the University of Maine System and Mary Lampson, author.)

WebCT Tools and the Principles of Good Practice They Support

Seven Principles of Good Practice per Chickering and Gamson (1987)

1. Encourage faculty to student interaction
2. Encourage student to student interaction
3. Promote active learning
4. Communicate high expectations
5. Facilitate time on task
6. Provide rich, rapid feedback
7. Respect diverse learning

WebCT Tool	Examples of How Tool Is Being Used	Principles of Good Practice the Tool Facilitates	Learning Styles
COURSE CONTENT AND RELATED TOOLS			
Content Module	Compilation of chapter outlines Presentation of detailed content for each "chapter" or "learning module"	• Diverse learning • Communicates high expectations	• Linear learners • Learner to content interactivity • Facilitates directed instruction through constructivism • Provides global picture • Advanced organizer
Syllabus	Presentation of course instructor information	• Faculty–student interaction • Rich, rapid feedback • Time on task	
Compile Pages	Students can compile pages from path and create their own customized study guides.	• Time on task	

WebCT Tool	Examples of How Tool Is Being Used	Principles of Good Practice the Tool Facilitates	Learning Styles
Glossary	Use the glossary to define terms but also provide media, such as images, audio, etc., that will explain terms more completely. For instance, if this is a foreign language course, include an audio clip which pronounces the term correctly.	• Time on task. Students can access definitions in course without stopping to thumb through notes and texts • Rich, rapid feedback	
Search	Insert the search tool on all path pages so students can easily locate topics in the course.	• Time on task	
Index	Build an index to cross-reference key terms and concepts to the detail content within the course.	• Time on task • Active learning	• Global view of contents
CD-ROM	In literature course, tie in reading of Walt Whitman (or other writers) with discussion questions and projects where resources are available on either CD-ROM or the Web. For instance, the Dickinson archives at Harvard are in the process of being digitized.	• Time on task	
Movie	Run clips of writers—poets, novelists, and dramatists—reading and discussing their own work. Run film clips—for film studies and drama studies—to illustrate staging, directing variations, etc.	• Diverse learning	• Visual learners • Demonstration of techniques
MyNotes	Use the Notes (Annotations) function to have students create their own annotations of various text or image documents posted within path pages in the course; then have the students compile their notes and share them with the whole class. Opens a whole world of discussion regarding interpretation, how one approaches text and image, etc.	• Active learning	• Detailed oriented
Resume Session	The resume session link at the top of the home page is built in to WebCT 3x so students can pick up at the last place they were in the course path pages.	• Time on task	• Sequential learners
Audio	Use sound clips of musicians, artists, poets, and writers playing, reading, and discussing their own work.	• Diverse learning • Rich, rapid feedback	• Auditory learners

WebCT Tool	Examples of How Tool Is Being Used	Principles of Good Practice the Tool Facilitates	Learning Styles
Images	Use the images database to house images that the instructor has created, or where copyright is not a problem. Perfect for history classes (maps, images of current landscapes, diagrams of battle-fields, architectural drawings, etc.), art and art history, and cultural studies (advertising, etc.).	• Faculty–student interaction • Student–student interaction • Active learning	• Visual learners
Bookmarks	Provide the bookmark tool on path pages so students can create their own customized shortcuts to key pages.	• Time on task	• Sequential learners • Self-paced learners
Link	Use the link feature to mix media on path pages. For instance, in an art class, include the image of Van Gogh's "Starry Night," an audio clip of the song, and a web link to the Van Gogh museum in Amsterdam.	• Time on task (helps students reach needed materials quickly) • Active learning	• Links to other resources that may promote different learning styles • Facilitates guided learning
References	Provide students with appropriate references that tap several types of media, e.g. journals, textbooks, websites, etc.	• Diverse learning • Active learning • Communicates high expectations	
Targets	List learning objectives for each path or even each path page. Tie this tool to self-test questions, which evaluate these learning objectives.	• Communicates high expectations • Faculty–student interaction • Time on task	
COMMUNICATION TOOLS			
Discussions	"I have an attendance forum where the online students are required to post a brief 'attendance' message each week. I have a public forum for each major topic we cover in the course, and I require the students to post a certain number of messages and/or replies to these forums. For example, I might have a forum called 'Societal Issues and the Internet' where students can post their thoughts on legal and ethical issues, or post information about articles they have read that are related to the topic."	• Faculty–student interaction • Student–student interaction • Rich, rapid feedback • Active learning • Diverse learning	• Verbal learners • Social learners • Textual learners
Mail	". . . the mail tool provides the necessary private mail between students and faculty in the course. Also, having private mail inside WebCT helps to organize and store mail specific to the course instead of getting mixed up in all the other e-mail that flows into a faculty's system."	• Faculty–student interaction • Student–student interaction	

WebCT Tool	Examples of How Tool Is Being Used	Principles of Good Practice the Tool Facilitates	Learning Styles
Chat	"The feedback that we had from the students was that the chat room was a very useful feature to keep in touch with the professor, answer questions, or plainly 'feeling like being in class'." "What I like most about WebCT this week, by the way, is my office hours. I used to try having office hours with webchat, and I had to keep hitting the chat button every minute or so, or I would miss someone. All I have to do is enter the chat room, turn on the sounds, hang out my 'sign' on the main page, and then I just putter around and do other things."	• Faculty–student interaction • Student–student interaction • Diverse learning • Rich, rapid feedback • Active learning	• Verbal learners • Social learners
Whiteboard	". . . that is, the important thing here is not the option to make pictures, but the possibility of SHARING them with other people. For example, an instructor could be handling a class using the chat tool, and showing slides pasting them in the whiteboard tool, and even drawing it in a 'real-time' way. Students could participate in the class, making exercises and showing real presentations using the whiteboard, and asking questions using the chat tool."	• Faculty–student interaction • Student–student interaction • Active learning • Diverse learning	• Collaborative • Visual learners
Calendar	Some use the calendar as the "grand central station" of their course, outlining each day the activities a student should be completing and directing students to course resources and external URLs.	• Time on task	• Concrete, sequential • Advanced organizer
EVALUATION TOOLS			
Quiz	Practice quizzes Mini "pop" quizzes Surveys Include graphics, charts, tables, links to other web sites, streaming media, video, audio, etc.	• Rich, rapid feedback • Communicate high expectations • Time on task • Faculty–student interaction • Active learning	• Can direct student learning through selective release
Self-Test	Practice questions Test knowledge questions At the end of the chapter or learning module, have several self-test questions which directly test the learning objectives for that module.	• Rich, rapid feedback • Communicates high expectations • Diverse learning	• Can direct student learning • Allows for self-evaluation • Self-paced learners

WebCT Tool	Examples of How Tool Is Being Used	Principles of Good Practice the Tool Facilitates	Learning Styles
Assignments	Describe written assignments, such as papers, essays, and formal lab reports in detail. The grading criteria can be given and any external materials (example of assignment, files, or URLs) can be suggested.	• Rich, rapid feedback. Provides a forum for extended and meaningful feedback that the student cannot lose and can access any time • Faculty–student interaction • Time on task	
My Grades	Release grades to students as well as other types of information such as the group they might be assigned to, general remarks on participation, etc.	• Rich, rapid feedback	• Concrete, sequential • Achievement oriented
STUDY TOOLS			
Presentations	Use the student presentation tool to let students share their own animation, audio, video—or archival information—if they have been able to find the materials, for instance, in hard copy form.	• Faculty–student interaction • Student–student interaction • Active learning • Diverse learning • Rich, rapid feedback	• Collaborative • Constructivist—provides for application of knowledge construction • Visual
My Progress	Provide this tool to students so they can quickly evaluate their participation in class.	• Rich, rapid feedback • Diverse learning • Faculty–student interaction • Time on task	• In a constructivist environment, this tool can help students track themselves
Student Homepage	Use the student home pages as an introductory "ice-breaker" activity so students can get to know each other. Have students list web sites in their home page that are related to the course. Students can write a brief description of the site. This is a web adaptation of an annotated bibliography.	• Student–student interaction • Diverse learning	
Navigation	Navigation and user orientation	• Time on task	

(Modified and reprinted with permission from WebCT.)

APPENDIX K

Course Synthesis Matrix

Name(s) _____

Directions: Below is a blank matrix with the course synthesis reflection questions down the left column. Across the top, list which two courses you are reflecting on for this form. In the column on the right indicate the course for which you are reflecting. You have the option of working alone or with a partner.

Reflection Areas	Course 1: Course 2:
Area 1: Reflect on the ideas, concepts, and theories learned and write a one- to two-sentence purpose statement for why the subject is important to the field of professional school-age care. This reflection area will assist you in writing sections 3 and 4 of the portfolio.	
Area 2: Reflect on the course objectives and analyze how the course objectives helped you reach your overall goals for professionalizing your goals as a provider.	
Area 3: Reflect on the feedback you've received from peers and the professors. In what directions will you go, what are your strengths and your challenges? Share what you have learned from other members of the cohort via bulletin board interactions and assignments. This reflection will assist you in writing sections 1, 2, and 3 of the portfolio.	
Area 4: Reflect on the course assignments. Rate how the assignments have helped you reach your goals. Were you able to integrate the material into other areas of your professional life, and if so, how? This reflection area will assist you in writing section 4 of the portfolio.	
Area 5: Reflect on how the course helped expand your understanding of the role of adults in and out of school programs. This could include how to work effectively with children, staff, parents, and the community. Share tips, tools, language in any or all areas. (During a course you may or may not have addressed all of these. Often a principle can be adapted to fit more than one area.) This reflection area will assist you in writing sections 3 and 4 of the portfolio.	

| Reflection Areas | Course 1: |
	Course 2:
Area 6: How has this course helped you further develop your skills and understanding of the tasks of being an observer, programmer, teacher, nurturer, discipliner, community networker, and administrator? This reflection area will assist you in writing sections 3 and 4 of the portfolio.	
Area 7: Reflect on and track these areas: vocabulary, research, resources, and generation issues that you might want to refer to in SAC495. This reflection area will assist you in writing sections 3 and 4 of the portfolio, and will help with section 5 (resources and research), too.	

(Reprinted with permission from Laurie Ollhoff, Concordia University.)

Performance Assessment

*School-Age Care
Professional Portfolio SAC495*

*Faculty Evaluation of
Professional Portfolio*

Student's Name _____

Name of Faculty _____

PART ONE: PORTFOLIO EVALUATION— SECTION-BY-SECTION

Directions: This part is worth 50% of total grade. Rate each section based on the Primary Trait Score Scale created for that section.

Section One:

- Professional Resume
- Official University Transcript (this is required even though your transcript won't include the last term)

    5 = The resume is effectively organized and well written, with concise information about the learner's qualifications. The information presented utilizes professional language and is presented in a professional manner. Transcript is submitted. (There is no excuse for not submitting a transcript; learners were given this requirement 3 months in advance.)

    4 = As above, but phrasing in the resume is vague.

    3 = The phrasing is unclear, grammar is poor, fails to demonstrate professional stature, no transcript.

    2 = Phrasing and language in resume do not demonstrate application of educational knowledge in School-Age Care.

    1 = As above, but is also poorly organized.

Additional Comments:

Section Two:

- Two letters from professionals in the field of School-Age Care who evaluate job performance and who can attest to learner's growth and learning
- Two letters of reference from an instructor in the program
- Any documents, honors, etc., earned

    5 = The section contains letters from employers that effectively document the learner's academic journey. The strengths of the learner are clearly defined *and* represent growth in SAC knowledge. Honors shared relate to learner being a professional in the field.

    4 = As above, but letters are unclear, strengths are present, but not necessarily related to learner's growth.

    3 = The presentation of the section is disorganized, letters are vague, nonspecific, (e.g., learner demonstrates potential).

    2 = The letters don't provide evidence to demonstrate the educational journey.

    1 = As above and items are missing.

Additional Comments:

Section Three:

- Summary of personal education autobiography
- Philosophy of the Purpose of School-Age Care
- Philosophy of the Role of Adult–Child Interactions
- Philosophy of the role of SAC as a partnership with Families, Schools, and Communities
- Philosophy of Social Preparation

5 = The section contains effectively organized, well-written, concise documentation of the learner's academic journey. The information presented is coherent, properly cited, and effective. Language utilized demonstrates knowledge, skills, and attitudes of a professional educated in Generation Three School-Age Care.

   Each paper should demonstrate the criteria below, either in part or in full. Evaluate the section as a whole rather than on each individual paper.

   → *Articulates purpose of School-Age Care*: facilitates the positive development of children and youth. Learner must state *how and why* SAC professionals see this as their role.

   → *Role of adults*: adult–child interaction versus supervising, or explanation of functional tasks; observer, programmer, teacher, nurturer, discipliner, community networker, administrator, or explanation of how adults can use the five founda-tions—empowerment, play, community building, maturity, and self-discipline—to facilitate the positive development.

   → *Effective nurture*: learner defines nurture as more than hugs and Band-Aids. E.g., effective nurture is knowing when a child needs hugs or encouragement to try.

   → *Effective discipline*: learner defines effective discipline as discipline that is educative in nature versus stopping misbehavior

→ *Identifies need for teaching social skills*: learner states how and why professionals in SAC teach social skills.

4 = As above; however, philosophies and ideas stated in the thesis statements are not fully developed by supporting paragraphs. Evidence is vague or lacking.

3 = As in item four; additionally the presentation of the section is disorganized, fails to demonstrate a pattern of learning, sequential information is missing.

2 = As in item three; additionally there is no evidence to demonstrate the educational journey and the self-directedness of the learner. The learner lacks the ability to connect learning to the practice.

1 = As above, but is also poorly organized, poorly written.

Additional Comments:

Section Four:

- Contribution to the field of school-age care.

5 = This section is effectively organized, well written, and contains clear explanation of SAC theory and application of theory to field.

   → *Identify the audience*: The people in the field of school-age care have varying roles. Learner *must* identify the audience (e.g., program managers, site leaders, front line workers, or technical assistance providers).

   → Learner *must* state why he or she thinks this paper or project will benefit the field.

   → Learner was instructed and counseled with, to include explanation and use of the following:

*   *Generation Three perspective of child care*—positive development and social preparation.

*   *Articulate the purpose of School-Age Care*: learner clearly articulates a purpose of SAC that is more than providing children a safe place, or a place to keep children and youth busy.

*   *Identify the role of adults in School-Age Care*: learner clearly demonstrates that the adult role is more than that of a babysitter or supervisor.

*   *The qualities of the adult–child inter-actions*: learner identifies and explains the importance of interactions (some papers might include adult–parent interactions, or School-Age Care to school personnel).

*   *The benefits to children*: how children will benefit from this contribution to the field.

*   *Identify the principles of effectiveness*: identify and explain one or more principles that connect to the topic of the paper.

→   References included at the end of the paper.

4 = Clearly identified audience and mentioned all SAC theories (listed above); however, the explanations included were vague.

3 = The presentation of the section is disorganized, some of SAC theories are mentioned, but may not be defined, and fails to demonstrate application of SAC theory.

2 = The learner fails to connect learning, to demonstrate understanding of the assignment, and SAC theories are presented in vague language.

1 = Section is poorly organized, poorly written, and lacks evidence of learning.

Additional Comments:

Section Five: Resource Section

•   Web Sites

•   Further Reading

•   Community Resources, Agencies for Collaboration

•   Human Resources

5 = The section contains effectively organized, concise, and accurate documentation of resources. The information presented includes web sites, resources for further reading, resources particular to their program, and human resources.

4 = Only has three of the main sections.

3 = Only has two of the main sections.

2 = Has three or fewer resource sections, but information is vague.

1 = Has two or fewer resource sections, but information is not deemed reliable.

Totals by Section

Section One   _____

Section Two   _____

Section Three   _____
(double the points, so if the learner scored 4, write in 8)

Section Four   _____
(triple the points, so if the learner scored 4, write in 12)

Section Five   _____

Total   _____   divided by 25 = _____%

Grade According to this Scale

22.5 to 25 = A 90–100%

20 to 22   = B 80–89%

17.5 to 19 = C 70–79%

15 to 17   = D 60–69%

Part Two: Program Objectives

This portion of the evaluation tool uses the program objectives to determine the performance of the learner's work. Each objective is numbered, followed by three subobjectives that reflect what the learner should know, be able to do, and demonstrate a disposition for.

Directions: This portion of the portfolio assessment will be 50% of the learner's grade. For each objective and subobjective, reviewer should state in which section evidence is found.

Rate the evidence on the following scale:

1 = evidence does not meet criteria: from no evidence found to vague nondescriptive evidence

2 = meets criteria: evidence is found in at least one section of the portfolio and it clearly meets stated objective

3 = evidence exceeds criteria: evidence is found in more than one section of the portfolio and evidence clearly meets stated objective

Objectives/Knowledge/Skill/ Disposition	Portfolio Evidence (State section in which evidence is found.)	Does Not Meet 1	Meets 2	Exceeds 3	Notes
1. Articulate the role of adults who work in out-of-school time settings, and the importance of the unique adult–child interactions in facilitating the positive development of children and youth.	(see sections 2–4)				
a. *Knowledge*: clear definition of School-Age Care, functional tasks, generations of care language, strand theory, and circle of influence; articulates the societal trends/changes and the need for School-Age Care; language used demonstrates knowledge that adult role is to facilitate; knows why the role adults play in SAC is unique; learner uses words beyond supervise and role model.					
b. *Skill*: able to identify the functional roles and apply them correctly; able to identify characteristics of various generations of care and articulate the differences; able to apply adult role appropriately to various situations.					
c. *Disposition*: demonstrates the disposition of someone who facilitates, willing to look for solutions, willing to guide and not direct.					

Objectives/Knowledge/Skill/ Disposition	Portfolio Evidence *(State section in which evidence is found.)*	Does Not Meet 1	Meets 2	Exceeds 3	Notes
2. Understand and be able to implement the principles of resiliency and the characteristics of quality in a school-age child care setting.	(see sections 2–4)				
a. *Knowledge*: factors that support resiliency, 40 assets, brain development, role of adult, ERE, 16 principles, five foundations.					
b. *Skill*: able to design intentional programming and plan interactions to support each child's growth and learning.	(see section 2)				
c. *Disposition*: employers noticed a change in student; professional approach to the tasks.					
3. Articulate and demonstrate effective use of the theories for facilitating positive development in out-school-settings.	(see sections 3–4)				
a. *Knowledge*: the Ollhoff Theories; articulates this knowledge throughout the portfolio.					
b. *Skill*: able to analyze situations and apply theory appropriately; able synthesize theories into tools or products for the field.					
c. *Disposition*: student demonstrates the attitude of problem solver and uses the theories to make a positive difference in the life of *each* child.					
4. Describe and demonstrate effective techniques of nurture, and the short- and long-term effects of healthy nurture.	(see sections 2–4)				
a. *Knowledge*: defines range of interactions that nurture positive growth and development; knows the difference between effective nurture and too high or low nurture.					

Objectives/Knowledge/Skill/ Disposition	Portfolio Evidence (State section in which evidence is found.)	Does Not Meet 1	Meets 2	Exceeds 3	Notes
b. *Skill*: adult is able to analyze his or her own actions and the needs of a child; able to match interactions of nurture to positively effect a child's under-standing of self and capabilities; able to identify social and cultural needs of a child.					
c. *Disposition*: demonstrates a caring, supportive nature for children; demonstrates an understanding for appropriate professional boundaries; desire to work supportively with families and schools, for the best interests of the child.					
5. Describe and demonstrate effective techniques of discipline and how they affect a growing sense of self-discipline.					
a. *Knowledge*: demonstrates knowledge that social skill development is critical for gaining self-discipline; understands the importance of community building and how to enhance a child's sense of belonging and significance.					
b. *Skill*: able to identify social skill abilities of children, guides the development of needed skills, sets appropriate boundaries so child gains skills of self-discipline.					
c. *Disposition*: demonstrates the desire to apply learning in child care setting; willingness to work with a child to ensure skills are integrated appropriately into social settings.					
6. Identify characteristics and attitudes that are markers for at-risk behavior.	(see sections 3–4)				
a. *Knowledge*: identify the signs and patterns that could lead to long-term problems, identify resources for support.					

Objectives/Knowledge/Skill/ Disposition	Portfolio Evidence (State section in which evidence is found.)	Does Not Meet 1	Meets 2	Exceeds 3	Notes
b. *Skill*: demonstrates knowledge of steps to take when concerned about a child, able to make an action plan, and work with the children, families, and schools.					
c. *Disposition*: displays the desire					
7. Identify the variety of social skills and demonstrate how to teach them.	(see sections 2–4)				
a. *Knowledge*: articulate SAC's role in the socialization process.					
b. *Skill*: demonstrates a working knowledge of identifying social skill deficits and how to teach skills.					
c. *Disposition*: Demonstrates the desire to help children gain life and social skills so that they can thrive in today's society.					
Total					

Total points for each column, then add all the columns together. Divide the total by 108.

Point Total _____   Percentage Total _____

Principles for Teaching Excellence in the School of Human Services at Concordia University, St. Paul, Minnesota

By Jim and Laurie Ollhoff

The School of Human Services has adopted these seven principles to guide the development and direction of the adult education programs. Each principle is expanded, with implications and ideas for teaching practice.

1. Excellent teachers help adult students to be comfortable.

Many adult students have insecurities and fears when it comes to continuing their education. They feel underprepared. They feel like they have been out of school too long. They feel old, too far behind, and too out-of-practice. They think, "What am I doing here?" They have an imposter syndrome, "What if they find me out?" Many of the adult learners have had a bad experience in the educational system, which is why they dropped out long ago. They are intimidated by instructors, by the institution, and by other students. Instructors who don't understand those concerns will face extremely tentative and superficial learning. Instructors don't have to name the fears, but they do need a plan to help the adult learners feel comfortable. For the adult student, the relationship with the teacher becomes very important. The instructor should help the students realize that helping them succeed is our number one goal.

Ideas for implementing principle one:
- Explain your communication plan in the syllabus. When will you be responding to e-mails? When will you do bulletin boards?
- Explain your grading standards, and the degree with which you will be flexible on assignments.
- Write to the students, asking them for input on preparing your module.
- Make a video, introducing yourself and explaining the syllabus.
- Give a lot of feedback.
- Call the students.
- Make conference calls.
- Participate vigorously on the bulletin board.
- Do e-mail reflections at the end of each week— ask students where were they most inspired by learning this week? Where were they most disconnected or bored with learning this week? What have they learned this week that they will put into practice?

2. Excellent teachers have a variety of methods and processes to help students learn.

It is important to meet the variety of learning styles and personalities as you plan your curriculum. No one style of dispensing information or processing that information will work for everyone.

Ideas for implementing principle two:
- Be creative with other forms of assignments, besides written papers.
- Give students a choice for how to present their work to you.
- Allow students to use PowerPoint, audiotapes, videos.
- In a chat room, do a role reversal: the students are the author of the text, and you are the learner.

3. Excellent instructors care more about learning than about teaching.

Instructors must work to help the learners become responsible for their own learning. The students not only should be involved in their learning, but should be involved in the content of the course.

Ideas for implementing principle three:

- Set measurable objectives for learning.

- Before the class starts, ask the students to send you their goals for the class.

- At the end of the class, ask the students to evaluate whether the course objectives, as stated in the syllabus, were met.

- Help them to know how to succeed in understanding your discipline.

- Remember that your primary role is not to dispense information; it is to provide guidance and mentoring as they learn the topic.

- At the end of the class, ask them if their goals were met.

4. Excellent instructors are facilitators of learning, rather than dispensers of information.

Information is everywhere. In the universities of the Middle Ages, there were no bookstores or libraries, so professors had to dispense information. Today, anything an instructor says in the classroom can be found on the Internet in less than a minute. The critical role for instructors today is to help learners through the reflective process of analysis, synthesis, and evaluation of the information. Finding information—reliable information—is one of the keys in today's educational system. New information and new theory need to be connected to the experiences of the field professional.

Instructors should help students know how to continue their learning after the class is over. What are the World Wide Web sites that must be regularly accessed? What are the Internet discussion groups in which students should regularly participate? What are the professional organizations that students should join? What are the organizations, businesses, colleges, or networks that are doing the most cutting-edge work? What are the conferences or symposia that students should regularly attend? Who are the researchers, theorists, and problem solvers that could be accessed easily via the Internet?

Ideas for implementing principle four:

- Make heavy use of bulletin boards. This is where new information can be synthesized, analyzed, and wrestled with.

- Share with students the structure of the discipline you teach. How is it organized?

- Make your interactions with students about processing the information, not dispensing information.

- Keep in mind that this is a practitioner-oriented program. What kinds of application should they make to the field?

- Consider how many different ways you can give feedback.

- Require that they discover web sites.

- Consider how they will combine new information with what they already know.

- Lead learners to new resources.

5. Excellent teachers plan copiously and teach passionately.

The degrees in the School of Human Services are practitioner-oriented adult programs, where we ask that students demonstrate a high level of autonomy. The danger in this kind of program is that the instructors will surrender their role as leader. The instructor still is the teacher—but the definition of teacher is different than it used to be. Instructors dare not leave their teaching to chance. They dare not allow the learning to happen "by chance." Instructors must plan—and plan copiously—for the acts of getting students to be comfortable with the topic; for processing, analyzing, and synthesizing information; and for developing new applications to their profession.

Ideas for implementing principle five:

- Plan out each chat.

- Develop teaching and learning objectives for each week.

- Use the chat room as a compass to ensure that the learners are developing in the desired direction.

- Sit down with the department chair and talk through your course, to see if it makes sense.

- Explain to the learners how you became excited about your discipline, and why you teach it.

6. Excellent teachers help students reflect on their practice.

All the students in our programs are field professionals. They have the opportunity to learn a new theory and immediately put it into practice. Learners, however, often need mentoring in the process of reflecting on whether the new concept worked. Humans tend to be good at learning when the feedback is immediate and clear. However, when feedback is delayed and ambiguous (as in almost all social situations), then learning becomes more difficult. We desire graduates who can reflect on their practice effectively, making decisions about future practice.

Ideas for implementing principle six:

- Respect and use their prior learning and the events that have shaped their understanding.
- Help them to critically think about their assumptions.
- Give them new lenses with which to look at their experience.
- Ask them to identify tacit beliefs.
- Ask them to identify how the new knowledge can make sense of their current experience.

7. Excellent teachers know that education is a social experience.

It is difficult to learn things when we have no emotional investment in them. But the cohort model, where 10–15 students take a long educational journey together, becomes a place of support and emotional investment. If our programs work correctly, students will learn as much or more from each other as they do from the instructors. The cohort becomes a powerful learning tool. Excellent instructors make use of this learning community.

Ideas for implementing principle seven:

- Help learners know how to work in groups more effectively.
- Let learners know why groupwork is important.
- Ask for peer editing and peer comments on assignments.
- Use simulations, role-plays, and role reversals.

(Adapted and abridged from a longer paper by Laurie Ollhoff. For a fuller treatment of adult learning theory, see Ollhoff's Adult-Learning Theories in the Concordia School of Human Services' faculty center. Reprinted with permission.)

Internet Adoption: How Much Is That Baby in the Window?

By Kelli L. Dutrow and Kathryn H. Wade

The recent case of the "Internet twins" who were simultaneously adopted by two different couples drew international attention to the issues surrounding Internet adoption services. (1) For many people, this was their first exposure to the existence of such services. The case raised serious questions about the Internet's role in adoption and the adequacy of current adoption laws. (2) Public opinion on the issues reflects a clear dichotomy. While many people are concerned that online services open the door to fraud and abuse, others view online services as an answer to their prayers for faster and easier adoptions. (3) As one commentator explained, "[i]n the emotion-charged realm of adoption, the Internet has proved a blessing and a curse . . . thousands of parents have adopted children they otherwise might never have found [but] [i]n the wrong hands . . . the Internet is a near-perfect tool for preying on vulnerable couples yearning for the child of their dreams." (4)

This paper provides an overview of adoption services and laws in the context of cyberspace. The first part of the paper describes the current status of adoption including statistics on prevalence and costs. Next, the paper reviews existing laws regulating adoption, including interstate and international transactions. Finally, discussion focuses on the risks and benefits associated with Internet adoption services. In particular, the final section of this paper addresses the adequacy of existing laws to protect the interests involved in Internet adoptions, and whether this situation demands new law.

(1) Robert Barr, *"Internet Twins" to Return to U.S.*, AP Online, Apr. 9, 2001, available at 2001 WL 17993105; J.F.O. MacAllister, Where do they belong? Twin girls become the focus of an international tussle after their birth mother places them first with one family and then another, at twice the price, 157 *Time*, Jan 29, 2001, available at http://time.com/time/magazine/article/0,9171,1101010129-96195,00.html; A tangled web of hope and fear: The Internet has eased adoption in some cases but it can also be a minefield of unscrupulous child-brokering, *L.A. Times*, Mar. 11, 2001, at E1, available at 2001 WL 2468714; Lee Hill Kavanaugh, Adoptions in cyberspace demand careful navigation, *Kansas City Star*, Feb. 2, 2001, at A1 available at 2001 WL 2591294 (quoting adoptive father Eric Keating as saying "The twins story is the kind of thing that makes people want to avoid the Internet to adopt . . ."). For a full discussion on the "Internet twins", see discussion infra Part III.

(2) See id.

(3) See generally, David Crary, Adoption and the Internet: Wondrous results but some sordid abuses, *The Canadian Press*, Tues. Jan. 23, 2001, available at 2001 WL 12572019; Byette supra note 1 (stating that because of its speed and lack of regulation, the Internet is "an ideal medium not just for making successful matches, but for unethical preying on desperate families").

(4) Crary, supra note 3.

The University of Arizona Associate Fellowship in Integrative Medicine Online Module Evaluation

In order to improve your educational experience, we request your feedback. Please complete the evaluation below and click the "submit" button to complete this module.

Please rate the usefulness of different instructional features of this module. Choose "NA" if you did not use this feature.

1 = Not useful
2 = Marginally useful
3 = Useful
4 = Very useful
5 = N/A

Practicing response to virtual patients
1   2   3   4   5

The Kojak–Columbo analogy
1   2   3   4   5

Critiquing a colleague
1   2   3   4   5

Receiving critique from colleague
1   2   3   4   5

The Spiegel Interview on support groups
1   2   3   4   5

From your bound MB readings:

The Kulik & Mahler article on spousal support and surgery
1   2   3   4   5

From your bound MB readings:

How likely are you to use the information you learned in this module?

1 = no chance
2 = maybe
3 = probably
4 = definitely

. . . in your personal life?
(*Consider: yourself, family, and friends*)
1   2   3   4

. . . in your professional life?
(*Consider: patients and interactions with colleagues*)
1   2   3   4

Would you recommend this module to a colleague who wants to learn about social support?
_____ Yes _____ No

Will you visit this module again as a reference for your clinical practice?
_____ Yes _____ No

Approximately how long did you take to do this module? _____

This module required you to write a number of responses to learn some very specific verbal responses. Did you find this step-by-step approach useful or annoying? Please explain. _____
_____
_____

Do you feel you had enough practice evaluating and prescribing social support? Too much? Please explain.
_____
_____
_____

What did you like *most* about this module? Please explain. _____
_____
_____

Thank you for your feedback! Submit your survey below and you will be finished with this module.

(Reprinted with permission from the University of Arizona Program of Integrative Medicine, Sue South and Andrew Weil.)

Student Orientation— A Guide to Online Courses: Are "Online" Courses for You?

Online courses do not require scheduled classroom attendance and usually are delivered via computer. Are these courses for you? Track your answer to each question below, then total your score.

1. Being in a classroom and/or socializing with fellow students is:
   a. Very important to me.
   b. Somewhat important to me.
   c. Not particularly important to me.

2. I usually:
   a. Put things off until the last minute.
   b. Need reminding to get things done on time.
   c. Finish things ahead of time.

3. I find classroom discussion:
   a. Usually helpful.
   b. Sometimes helpful.
   c. Rarely helpful.

4. When instructors hand out directions for assignments, I prefer:
   a. Having them explained to me.
   b. Trying to follow them on my own, then asking for help as needed.
   c. Figuring them out for myself.

5. When asked to use VCRs, computers, voice mail, e-mail, or other technologies new to me:
   a. I put it off or try to avoid it.
   b. I feel apprehensive, but try anyway.
   c. I look forward to learning new skills.

6. Considering my professional and personal schedule, the amount of time I have for an online course is:
   a. Less than for a class on campus.
   b. The same as for a class on campus.
   c. More than enough.

7. If given an address for a web site (that is, a URL), I would be able to navigate there through a browser:
   a. After some experimentation.
   b. With assistance.
   c. With no problem.

8. Faced with an assignment that required the use of an Internet search engine, I would:
   a. Seek assistance.
   b. Need time to familiarize myself with at least one search engine.
   c. Move through the assignment with confidence.

9. If required to download and install a browser plug-in, I would:
   a. Require assistance to complete the task.
   b. Look for information on the correct procedure before proceeding.
   c. Proceed with confidence.

10. I identify my comfort level with e-mail programs and Internet browsers as:
    a. Uncomfortable.
    b. Somewhat comfortable.
    c. Very comfortable.

Scoring:

Score 3 for each (a.), 2 for each (b.), 1 for each (c.). Scores range from 10 to 30. A lower score suggests online courses may be a good match for you. A higher score suggests courses with classroom meetings (e.g., ITV, compressed video, or classes with the instructor on site) may be a better match. If you scored low on questions 7 through 10, you may consider a local adult education course on using the Internet before enrolling in an online course.

A FEW FACTS:
ONLINE COURSES AND LEARNING STYLES

1. Some students prefer the independence of online courses; others find it uncomfortable and prefer being in class meetings with others.

2. Online courses allow greater scheduling freedom, but often require more self-discipline than traditional courses.

3. Some people learn best through interaction with other students and instructors in a classroom where they get an immediate response. Online discussions take place over a period of days and offer more time to contemplate before responding.

4. Online courses often require working from written directions without face-to-face explanations by the instructor.

5. Because online courses require computers and other technologies, you should be comfortable with these technologies before taking the course.

6. While online courses may save travel time, they require at least as much time as other college courses. You should plan to schedule the same amount of time.

(Adapted from a questionnaire developed by Bob Loser, Jean Trabandit, Barbara Hathaway, and Teresa Donnell of Northern Virginia Community College's Extended Learning Institute. Taken from the University of Maine System web site. A condensed interactive version of this survey may be found at http://courseguide.unet.maine.edu/survey/survey-learning.asp.)

University College, University of Maine: System Computer Skills Survey

This short "skills survey" will help you decide if you have the skills required to take courses requiring the use of a computer. Select your answers to the questions below, then click "Submit."

1. If given an address for a web site (that is, a URL), I would be able to navigate there through a browser:

   a. After some experimentation.

   b. With assistance.

   c. With no problem.

2. Faced with an assignment that required the use of an Internet search engine, I would:

   a. Seek assistance.

   b. Need time to familiarize myself with at least one search engine.

   c. Move through the assignment with confidence.

3. If required to download and install a browser plug-in, I would:

   a. Require assistance to complete the task.

   b. Look for information on the correct procedure before proceeding.

   c. Proceed with confidence.

4. I identify my comfort level with e-mail programs and Internet browsers as:

   a. Uncomfortable.

   b. Somewhat comfortable.

   c. Very comfortable.

5. I can save files to the computer's hard drive, a floppy disk, or a network drive:

   a. Only with assistance or not at all.

   b. With some hesitation but I'm usually successful

   c. With no trouble at all.

6. When prompted to format a new floppy disk:

   a. I need assistance from someone.

   b. I have to review the steps but I manage to do it.

   c. I can do it easily.

7. When I have to retrieve a file from the computer's hard drive, a floppy disk, or a network drive:

   a. I need someone to help me.

   b. I find it a little tricky getting to the file even though I know where it is supposed to be.

   c. I can find and open it right away (assuming I know where the file is supposed to be).

8. I can use a word processing program to write research and other similar documents:

   a. Only with assistance or not at all.

   b. With little problem, as long as features such as tables, columns, and complicated formatting aren't included.

   c. With no problem at all.

(Reprinted with permission from the University of Maine System. Web site: http://courseguide.unet.maine.edu/survey/survey-internet.asp)

University College, University of Maine System: A Guide to Online Courses

Here's what faculty and students had to say about . . .

. . . Workload and self-discipline

This type of learning allows more freedom but also requires a great deal of self-discipline. As some students have noted:

> "With the demands of a family, this worked out great!"

> "I liked being able to work on the class during whatever time I chose."

> "It helps to be self-motivated."

> "Time is a critical factor in dealing with this course. As an older student with a family and other responsibilities, the course is very demanding."

. . . Prerequisites

Be sure that you have met the prerequisites. If you have not or if you are in doubt, contact the instructor and discuss your background before enrolling.

. . . Accessing the technology

Because this type of class involves interaction primarily through e-mail or computer conferences, arrange access to the level of technology required for the course in advance and take some time to get comfortable using it—particularly e-mail and the Internet. Participate in orientation exercises and workshops if they are available.

. . . Getting started and pacing yourself

At the beginning of the course, have a look at all course materials and the home page. Review the complete layout or structure of the course before completing any assignments.

. . . Submitting your work electronically

As one student noted, "I feel I learned more from this Internet course than I did from my ITV and on-site courses. I had to think and respond with my own ideas and thoughts. In the other classes I sit back and listen instead of participating." Chances are, you'll participate in class more than you ever did before, and because most of your participation will occur in writing, your instructor's comments on your assignments may take longer to receive than in traditional classes. Don't be too concerned if it takes time to get your instructor's comments back.

Make sure you clearly identify yourself and your subject in all communications. You will win the heart of your instructor! Seriously consider preparation and editing of all submissions "off line." Once you are satisfied with your effort, then it's time to post it to the computer conference or e-mail it. Use your word processor and spell checker, and proofread all your submissions. When submitting course requirements as an attachment, inquire whether your instructor can read them. It is likely most popular programs will be satisfactory.

. . . Communicating online

Since most communication among students and instructors is through e-mail and/or the Internet, good writing skills are important. In traditional learning environments, we are able to rely on facial cues and body language to understand what other people are communicating and how our communication affects them. Although you can't rely on these same cues when communicating online, you can achieve the same thing by posting messages in a courteous manner, indicating support for other classmates, replying promptly to any messages, using constructive criticism if disagreeing with another classmate, and reflecting before responding to a sensitive or controversial topic.

. . . Connecting with your instructor and classmates

And, finally, you're not alone! If you have a question about content or process, don't hesitate to ask your instructor or classmates. Be as specific as possible when seeking help. If they're available, take advantage of interaction forums, learning teams, and study groups with fellow students.

(Reprinted with permission from the University of Maine System. Web site: www.learn.maine.edu)

University College, University of Maine System: Ready for the Web? A Guide to Online Learning

ARE ONLINE COURSES A GOOD CHOICE FOR ME?

Online courses are delivered through the Internet. You'll read class materials, take quizzes, and communicate with your instructor and fellow students on the Internet. If you don't have a computer at home, you can use the computers at a <u>University College location or receive site</u>. Although you won't attend scheduled classes, a few online courses require you to go to a classroom for meetings and/or proctored exams.

Are online courses for you? To help you decide, take our brief <u>survey</u>, review the most <u>frequently asked questions</u>, and read <u>comments</u> from faculty, students, and staff.

DO I HAVE THE COMPUTER SKILLS I'LL NEED?

Many courses, whether offered online, via ITV, or by compressed video, require use of a computer. If your course requires you to use a computer, try this short <u>skills survey</u>. It may help you decide whether you'll want to sharpen your computing skills before starting.

IS MY COMPUTER MULTIMEDIA-READY?

Some courses use streaming audio and video to deliver course content, and require computers with special hardware, software plug-ins, and fast Internet connection speeds. Check the <u>course listing</u> to see whether your course requires a computer with multimedia capability. If so, you'll have to use your own computer or go to a center. (Multimedia is used in conjunction with programs such as FirstClass, WebCT, or Blackboard.)

Try this <u>test</u> to see if your home computer and Internet connection are multimedia-ready.

WHAT'S NEXT?

Scan the <u>course listing</u> to discover which software program (Blackboard, WebCT, FirstClass) is used in your course.

Note: All underlined words or phrases indicate a link. Students who click on the link will be taken immediately to the site at which the function may be completed.

(Reprinted with permission from the University of Maine System. Web site: http://www.learn.maine.edu/crs/ready.html)

The Flashlight Program Education Network of Maine—Student Evaluation

ACADEMIC GOALS:

1. Why did you decide to take this course?

_____ to fulfill a general education requirement

_____ to fulfill a requirement for my major

_____ the subject matter looked interesting

_____ the instructor has a good reputation

_____ it was offered at a convenient time

_____ it was offered at a convenient location

_____ it was offered via technology

2. What grade do you expect to receive in this course?

A _____   B _____   C _____   D _____   F _____

3. Do you plan to earn a degree from this institution?

_____ yes   no _____ (*if no, skip to question 4*)

   a. What is the highest degree you expect to earn from this institution?

   ___ Certificate ___ AA ___ AAS

   ___ BA/BS ___ MA/MS ___ PhD/EdD

   ___ other (specify) _____

   b. When do you expect to earn this degree?

   _____

4. In your lifetime, approximately how many college-level courses have you enrolled in at any institution? _____ courses

5. How far do you live from the closest University of Maine System Campus?

___ 0–5 miles   ___ 6–10 miles   ___ 11–20 miles

___ 21–50 miles   ___ 51–100 miles

___ more than 100 miles

6. Do you take this course primarily from:

___ your home   ___ your place of employment

___ the origination campus   ___ a center

___ other (specify)_____

7. How far do you live from the origination campus?

___ 0–5 miles   ___ 6–10 miles   ___ 11–20 miles

___ 21–50 miles   ___ more than 50 miles   ___ n/a

To what extent do you agree or disagree with the following statements: (write the appropriate number in the space provided at the left of the item).

   1 = strongly disagree

   2 = disagree

   3 = somewhat disagree

   4 = somewhat agree

   5 = agree

   6 = strongly agree

   7 = n/a

___ 8. The site coordinator was very helpful.

___ 9. It is easy to contact the site coordinator when I have a problem.

___ 10. The site coordinator has helped me stay in school.

___ 11. I have adequate access to library resources.

___ 12. I have adequate access to the bookstore.

___ 13. It was easy to deal with the financial aid process from a distance.

___ 14. I am satisfied with the academic advising I received.

___ 15. I have adequate access to academic tutoring services when I need them.

___ 16. I feel comfortable taking this course at this remote site.

In a typical week since this course began, approximately how much time do you spend doing each of the following for the course? Write in the number of hours in the space provided at the left of the item.

___ 17. thinking about what you are learning and discussing it with the instructor or other students.

___ 18. participating in the delivery of information to other students in the course (such as producing and/or giving a presentation, producing a study guide or discussion paper, authoring a multimedia presentation, etc.).

___ 19. studying with other students for quizzes and/or examinations.

___ 20. working on an assignment with a group of other students, where your participation is required for the course.

___ 21. working on an assignment with a group of other students, where your participation is not required.

___ 22. discussing your work on assignments completed for this course with other students.

___ 23. assisting other students who ask for help with coursework.

___ 24. reviewing detailed comments made by the instructor about an assignment or examination.

___ 25. discussing the instructor's comments on your assignments or examinations with him/her.

___ 26. communicating with the instructor outside of scheduled course times about matters of academic content.

In a typical week since this course began, approximately how much time do you spend doing each of the following for this course (include all time spent on each activity):

___ 27. communicating with the instructor outside of scheduled course times about your academic, professional, and/or personal goals.

___ 28. participating in discussions of course content with other students during class time.

Indicate how strongly you agree or disagree with each of the following statements:

1 = strongly disagree
2 = disagree
3 = somewhat disagree
4 = somewhat agree
5 = agree
6 = strongly agree
7 = n/a

___ 29. I planned specific study times this term and stuck to my schedule.

___ 30. My course schedule conflicted with my work and/or family responsibilities this term.

EXPERIENCES WITH INSTRUCTIONAL TECHNOLOGY

Compared with on-campus courses you have taken that relied primarily on face-to-face lectures, in this course, how likely are you to:

1 = much less likely
2 = somewhat less likely
3 = about the same
4 = somewhat more likely
5 = much more likely
6 = n/a

___ 31. ask for clarification when you don't understand something.

___ 32. discuss the subject matter with other students.

___ 33. work on projects with other students.

___ 34. ask other students for comments on your course work.

___ 35. discuss the subject matter with the instructor.

___ 36. provide your own comments or views.

(Note: You may add demographic questions here.)
Thank you for your valuable feedback.

Guiding Principles for Distance Learning in a Learning Society

DISTANCE LEARNING: INFORMATION AND RESOURCES

As we face a new century of learning, we also face a time of change—a time of embracing new and emerging methods of learning. Technology is one area that has made a tremendous impact on higher education. It has enabled distance learning to become a very real, very frequently employed method of instruction for educational institutions and organizations worldwide.

Two obvious key insights have emerged. The first is that the digital revolution has profoundly altered traditional limitations of time and space. In this era, when time and space have only relative existences, we lead new lives—ones in which we are no longer, as Emerson put it, "children of time or space."

The second insight is that learning permeates many sectors of society; therefore, principles of good practice must be applied not only to institutions of higher education, but to all those involved in the learning enterprise—individual learners, institutions, corporations, labor unions, associations, and government agencies. Strengthening one sector will improve the effectiveness of the other sectors and, in turn, address the learning needs of individuals and society as a whole.

Distance learning, and its various guiding principles, help learners, educators, trainers, technologists, and accreditors/state regulators to develop, deliver, and assess formal learning opportunities.

GUIDING PRINCIPLES FOR DISTANCE LEARNING IN A LEARNING SOCIETY

Developments in technology and communications have brought about dramatic change in both the learning needs and the way learning opportunities are delivered in business, labor, government, and academia. We are becoming a society in which continuous learning is central to effective participation as citizens and wage-earners. Telecommunications technologies are not only transforming our needs for education and training, they are expanding our capacity to respond to these needs. Distance learning, with a long history of serving isolated and remote learners, has now emerged as an effective, mainstream method of education and training that provides learning opportunities that are flexible and responsive to learners' needs.

Distance learning is now a key component of our new learning society, in which learners must take increased responsibility for control and direction of the learning process. Existing standards and criteria, often focusing on learning inputs, fail to acknowledge the many forms that effective learning can take; therefore, the focus needs to be on learning outcomes. The principles here are intended for learners, learning providers, and those charged with overseeing learning quality and effectiveness. These principles address central qualities that characterize all effective learning activities, regardless of setting or purpose, and are particularly relevant to distance learning.

GUIDING PRINCIPLES: OVERVIEW

These principles are not a treatise or "how-to" for institutions, organizations, or learners. Rather, they make a statement designed to address the qualities that should characterize the learning society in the years ahead. By design, the principles do not prescribe specific technologies, strategies, or methodologies, nor do they promote learning at a distance; instead the focus is on understanding and embracing the changing nature of the education and training process.

Principle: Learning Design. Distance learning activities are designed to fit the specific context for learning the nature of the subject matter, intended learning outcomes, needs and goals of the learner, the learner's environment, and the instructional technologies and methods.

Subprinciples

1. Learning opportunities include a clear statement of intended learning outcomes, learning content that

is appropriate to these outcomes, clear expectations of learner activities, flexible opportunities for interaction, and assessment methods appropriate to the activities and technologies.

2. Elements of a learning event—the learning content, instructional methods, technologies, and context—complement each other.

3. The selection and application of technologies for a specific learning opportunity are appropriate for the intended learning outcomes, subject matter content, relevant characteristics and circumstances of the learner, and cost range.

4. Learning activities and modes of assessment are responsive to the learning needs of individual learners.

5. The learning experience is organized to increase learner control over the time, place, and pace of instruction.

6. Learning outcomes address both content mastery and increased learning skills.

7. Individuals with specialized skills in content, instructional methods, or technologies work collaboratively as a design team to create learning opportunities.

8. The learning design is regularly evaluated for effectiveness, with findings used as a basis for improvement.

Principle: Learner Support. Distance learning opportunities are effectively supported for learners through fully accessible modes of delivery and resources.

Subprinciples

1. The providing organization has a learner support system to assist the learner in effectively using the resources provided. This system includes technology and technical support, site facilitation, library and information services, advising, counseling, and problem-solving assistance.

2. The provider considers the needs for learner support in relation to the distance learning mode(s) used and makes provision for delivery of appropriate resources based on the design of the learning activities, the technology involved, and the needs of the learner.

3. Access to support services—such as scheduling, registration, and record keeping—is convenient, efficient, and responsive to diverse learners as well as consistent with other elements of the delivery system.

4. Support systems are accessible to and usable by the learners and are sufficiently flexible to accommodate different learning styles.

5. The provider discloses to the learner all information pertinent to the learning opportunity—such as course prerequisites, modes of study, evaluation criteria, and technical needs—and provides some form of orientation for those desiring it.

6. Support systems for each learning opportunity are reviewed regularly to ensure their currency and effectiveness.

Principle: Organizational Commitment. Distance learning initiatives must be backed by an organizational commitment to quality and effectiveness in all aspects of the learning environment.

Subprinciples

1. Involvement in distance learning is consistent with the overall mission of the provider; policies regarding distance learning are integrated into the provider's overall policy framework.

2. The providing organization makes a financial and administrative commitment to maintain distance learning programs through completion and to support faculty and learner services needed to ensure an effective learning environment.

3. Administrative and support systems (registration, advising, assessment, etc.) are compatible with the learning delivery system to ensure a coherent learning environment.

4. The organization's curricular and administrative policies incorporate the needs of distance learning as well as traditional learning activities.

5. The provider makes a commitment to research and development of distance learning, maintaining a systematic evaluation of the content, processes, and support systems involved in its distance learning activities.

6. The provider makes a concomitant investment of resources and effort in professional development and support of both faculty and staff involved in distance learning.

7. The providing organization recognizes effective participation in distance learning through its promotion and reward system for faculty and staff and ensures that its policies regarding promotion, tenure (if applicable), and departmental/program funding reflect the integration of distance learning into the organization's mission.

8. The policies, management practices, learning design processes, and operational procedures for distance learning are regularly evaluated to ensure effectiveness and currency.

9. The provider does not distinguish between learning accomplished at a distance and learning accomplished through other means in recognizing learner achievement.

Principle: Learning Outcomes. Distance learning programs organize learning activities around demonstrable learning outcomes, assist the learner to achieve these outcomes, and assess learner progress by reference to these outcomes.

Subprinciples

1. When possible, individual learners help shape the learning outcomes and how they are achieved.

2. Intended learning outcomes are described in observable, measurable, and achievable terms.

3. The learning design is consistent with and shaped to achieve the intended learning outcomes.

4. Distance education media and delivery systems are used in a way that facilitates the achievement of intended learning outcomes.

5. Learning outcomes are assessed in a way relevant to the content, the learner's situation, and the distance education delivery system.

6. Assessment of learning is timely, appropriate, and responsive to the needs of the learner.

7. Intended learning outcomes are reviewed regularly to ensure their clarity, utility, and appropriateness for the learners.

Principle: Technology. The provider has a plan and infrastructure for using technology that supports its learning goals and activities.

Subprinciples

1. The technology plan defines the technical requirements and compatibility needed to support the learning activity.

2. The technology plan addresses system security to ensure the integrity and validity of information shared in the learning activities.

3. The technology facilitates interactivity among all elements of a learning environment and places a high value on ease of use by learners.

4. The technology selected for distance learning is fully accessible and understandable to learners and has the power necessary to support its intended use.

5. Providers communicate the purpose of the technologies used for learning and, through training, assist learners, faculty, and staff to understand its etiquette, acquire the knowledge and skills to manipulate and interact with it, and understand the objectives and outcomes that the technologies are intended to support.

6. The technology infrastructure meets the needs of both learners and learning facilitators for presenting information, interacting within the learning community, and gaining access to learning resources.

(Reprinted with permission from the American Council on Education. Web site: http://www.acenet.edu)

APPENDIX V

Distance Education: Guidelines for Good Practice

The American Federation of Teachers (AFT), Higher Education Department, maintains that educational quality, not financial gain, should guide where, when, and how distance education is employed. Drawing from the findings of a survey of 200 members of AFT, on scholarship on distance education, and on the advice of AFT's higher education program and policy council in the 1999–2000 academic year, these Guidelines for Good Practice in Distance Education were developed.

THE STANDARDS

1. Faculty must retain academic control.

- To receive college credit, distance learning courses offered by the institution should be reviewed and approved in advance by the faculty. Review is necessary even when changing a course from a classroom mode to a distance learning mode. Faculty do not always make perfect decisions, but their choices are much likelier to be based primarily on educational concerns aimed at student learning rather than market incentives that elevate convenience, attractiveness, and digestibility above all else.

- Decisions about particular courses should be made at the departmental or interdepartmental level, including the decision to award credit for distance courses generated by transfer from another institution or provider.

- Distance education courses for credit should be taught by faculty appointed and evaluated through traditional processes involving the faculty and the department.

- Teaching and research faculty, not just "curriculum specialists," must be involved in developing the curriculum. A number of studies (see, among others, *Classroom Research*, K. P. Cross & M. H. Steadman, 1996) have demonstrated the importance to student learning of establishing a feedback loop between classroom teaching, curriculum development, and scholarly research. That loop becomes inoperative when teaching faculty operate from workbooks based on a prefabricated curriculum that the faculty member had little role in developing, a curriculum that was not shaped directly by the practitioner's experience in teaching these classes or conducting research on these subjects. Students deserve teachers who know all the nuances of what they are teaching and who can exercise professional judgment and academic freedom in doing so.

2. Faculty must be prepared to meet the special requirements of teaching at a distance.

Background. Faculty teaching distance education courses must become proficient in the communication technology employed in their distance education courses. They must be prepared—either on their own or working in teams with other specialists—to design courses that take full advantage of the potential of the medium in which they are operating. Faculty teaching web-based courses must possess strategies and skills to communicate with their students electronically in the absence of visual and oral cues. Faculty members teaching web-based courses must prepare, in advance, highly structured written materials and graphics covering every detail of the course. Faculty must be prepared to be available to students on an extended basis electronically. They must answer questions right away, grade papers very quickly, and follow up with students within a week or two if they are not participating in class. To handle these responsibilities effectively:

- Faculty must be provided adequate training and technical support—in terms of hardware, software, and troubleshooting. Support should include special assistance in instructional design. Upon request, the institution must enable faculty

201

members to work with knowledgeable instruct-
tional and technical design specialists in designing courses, as long as the faculty member has
the final say about presentation.

- Additional compensation should be provided to
faculty to meet the extensive time commitments
of distance education. Compensation can be
provided in the form of credit toward lead
assignment, which means that the additional
time counts toward the faculty member's
required workload for the term. The need for
extra time is most pressing the first year, but that
may not be the end of it. The report of the 1999
University of Illinois Distance Education Seminar
indicates that the second iteration of an online
course may require as much time and effort in
making improvements as the first required in
changing format. "It is not until the third
iteration that the preparation effort begins to
diminish," according to the Seminar report.

- Institutional reward systems for faculty—
including policies regarding promotion, tenure,
and special funding for faculty projects—should
accord positive recognition for the creative work
of formulating distance programs.

- Because distance education calls on a specialized
set of skills, teaching distance education courses
should be a matter of faculty choice.

3. Course design should be shaped to the potentials of the medium.

Background. As we all know, live theater is a special
experience that delivers a unique brand of emotional
impact. In most cases, however, live theater looks
claustrophobic and strangely inert when it is filmed
"straight on" without the camera moving among
different locations, doing close-ups, and engaging in
its own special tricks. This tells us that you can't "do"
film the same way you do a live performance. Each
medium has its own strengths and weaknesses and
can deliver different kinds of dramatic experiences.

The literature on distance education suggests a
similar relationship between same-time same-place
instruction and distance education. It may not always
be effective to simply transfer a live lecture and
accompanying course materials into an electronic
course on the same subject. Similarly, faculty members
who try to literally "match" traditional classroom
interaction with the kind of interaction available in a
distance education course may well be frustrated and
disappointed. . . . [Thus,] faculty members developing
distance education courses should approach course
design—curriculum planning, class projects, visual
aids, library materials, and student interaction—not in
terms of replicating the traditional classroom, but in
terms of maximizing the potential of the medium that
will be employed . . . .

4. Students must fully understand course requirements and be prepared to succeed.

Every institution, as a matter of good practice, should
have procedures in place to ensure, to the extent
possible, that new distance education students have
the wherewithal to perform successfully.

- All first-time distance education students should
be given a clear statement of course requirements
in advance. This should include: (1) all course
requirements, (2) the weekly time commitment
and specific computer skills required by the
course, and (3) a presentation of the practical
difficulties of working at a distance and what is
needed to manage those challenges successfully.
This information must be provided either in
written form or through a same-time same-place
video or Internet-based orientation program.

- Students should be required to submit a written
statement to the institution delivered
electronically. As little as a paragraph or two
explaining the student's aim, the statement
would be designed to demonstrate (1) that the
student possesses the proper equipment and
knows how to make it work, (2) that the student
has the skills needed to perform effectively in a
writing-based medium, and (3) that the student
has motivation and realistic expectations.

- If potential problems surface in the student's
response, training in advance of the course must
be provided to those who have the appropriate
equipment but do not know how to use it
properly, and advice should be offered to
students who appear to have problems with
written communication skills or motivation.

- Students require reliable, extended-time technical support throughout the course. In all course materials, institutions should specify the nature and extent of technical support to be provided. A telephone contact for technical support is essential, with as many hours of availability as is feasible.

- Since distance education will not suit every student, states and localities are obligated to ensure that no one is offered distance education as his or her only option for obtaining a college education.

5. Close personal interaction must be maintained.

- To maximize communication electronically, distance learning courses should, to the greatest extent possible, incorporate both real-time electronic interchange through devices such as chat rooms and discussion groups, and asynchronous forms of communication such as e-mail and computer bulletin boards.

- Wherever it is feasible, opportunities for same-time same-place interchange between the teacher and student, or among students, should be built into credit courses taught at a distance . . . . Access anytime/anywhere is a great advantage, but a campus visit helps each student to understand that he or she is part of a learning enterprise greater than this one course. On-campus students are surrounded with those reminders each day, motivators that enrich them as they make their way through an academic program.

6. Class size should be set through normal faculty channels.

- Class size should be established through normal faculty channels to ensure that education rather than bureaucratic or financial considerations drive the process.

- Class size should encourage a high degree of interactivity. Given the time commitment involved in teaching through distance education, smaller class size should be considered, particularly at the inception of a new course.

7. Courses should cover all material.

- The amount of material covered in a distance education course, and the depth with which it is covered, should equal that of a classroom-based course.

8. Experimentation with a broad variety of subjects should be encouraged.

Background. Some faculty members have more difficulty teaching certain subjects at a distance than others do. There is not sufficient evidence to believe that distance education can be ruled out, a priori, for any particular kind of credit course. If a faculty member is having a problem with a particular course, another professor in another location may be fixing that problem right now; there is no reason to declare most problems unsolvable under the right conditions. Similarly, the weight of the evidence is that higher order thinking skills, as opposed to rote training, can be acquired in distance education.

Thus, experimentation in offering a variety of subjects through distance education should be encouraged. Some faculty members report success in supervising real or virtual laboratory activities, and even practica, at a distance. However, "hands-on" activities . . . should be reviewed very carefully by the department faculty prior to approval.

- Institutions should not continue to offer courses that have been unsuccessful. If attrition rates are high or test scores low, or if the teacher reports disappointing results, the faculty should declare a "time out" during which a careful evaluation is conducted, along with an exploration of successful learning techniques employed elsewhere. If the faculty determines that problems have been overcome, the course can be re-instituted.

9. Equivalent research opportunities must be provided.

Background. To a varying extent, all college degree programs—whether 2-year, 4-year, or graduate—must provide numerous and varied opportunities for students to conduct independent research. Students need to have access to a broad spectrum of research materials in all formats and to learn how to evaluate such material critically. This requires a partnership between faculty and librarians, working together, to develop in students information literacy—competencies that allow individuals to recognize when information is needed and to locate and use effectively the needed information. As has often been reported, the ability to critically evaluate material is especially important in light of the mass of seemingly authoritative, but sometimes bogus, material seen on the Internet.

- Opportunities for distance education students to conduct independent course-related research must be substantially the same as opportunities provided to other students.

- Distance education students should be given access to all possible electronic research material. Students must be shown how to connect with online articles, books, and catalogs at the college library or cooperating libraries. Students should be given the names, e-mail addresses, and phone numbers of librarians trained to handle electronic requests for material.

- For any course requiring independent research, as long as it is feasible, distance education students should be expected to visit a campus or public library at least once to confer with professional librarians and employ the variety of informational materials and professional resources available there.

- If there is no accessible location where a student can obtain needed hardcopy research, and there is no online source, the college should arrange, as some have, to get books and materials to students through overnight mail, either for sale or loan. This is known as document delivery, although in many locations a quick turnover cannot be expected.

10. Student assessment should be comparable.

- The level of achievement expected of students, and tested for in a distance education environment, should be as challenging as that in a classroom-based course . . . . Differences in electronic and classroom educational techniques may dictate different forms of assessment or different emphases in assessment. But the overall standard of student achievement should be equivalent.

- As a matter of prudence, steps should be taken to limit the possibility of fraud and abuse in a distance education environment. Whenever possible it is preferable to bring students to one or more public places and utilize a proctor in administering exams. Colleges should follow the development of new electronic security technologies aimed at curbing fraud and utilize those that are effective and cost efficient.

11. Equivalent advisement opportunities must be offered.

- Care must be taken to offer distance education students pursuing college degrees repeated opportunities for individualized advisement by academic professionals. Same-time same-place advisement should be made available particularly at key junctures in the student's academic career, but telephone contact is an acceptable alternative when that is not practicable.

12. Faculty should retain creative control over use and reuse of materials.

Background. Until now, faculty members have developed courses and course materials largely on their own. Since the faculty member taught any further iterations of the course, he or she effectively maintained control over subsequent changes in course materials and the overall quality of the presentation. Courses developed for distance education may differ from this model in a variety of ways:

- The faculty member may have worked in collaboration with other institutional employees, such as design and technical support personnel, in assembling the course,

- The institution's technical facilities may have been used to mount the course for video or the Web,

- The course and course materials may be in an easily reproducible form.

As a result of these differences, the institution may claim ownership of the course and all materials related to it. If it assumes ownership, the institution may seek to reproduce the course year after year, utilizing different faculty to teach the same material or make changes in the course over time without involving the faculty member who created it. There is not enough space here, nor is this the right venue, to explore the range of legal and negotiation issues surrounding the ownership of intellectual property in distance education. The use and reuse of course materials, however, raise an issue of quality and educational good practice.

- The faculty member(s) developing a course should maintain creative control over the use and reuse of the course in subsequent years. In the absence of such control, students have no guarantee that the course they take is of the same quality as in previous years and has been updated to reflect changes in the subject area.

13. Full undergraduate degree programs should include same-time same-place coursework.

Background. The fact that distance education may be a good option for teaching a particular course, or set of courses, does not automatically mean that it is acceptable to offer an entire undergraduate degree program, 2-year or 4-year, without providing students in-class experience. Four years ago, AFT's higher education division wrote, "Our experience as educators tells us that teaching and learning in the shared human spaces of a campus are essential to the undergraduate experience and cannot be compromised too greatly without rendering the education unacceptable." This view was reaffirmed in the report of the 1999 University of Illinois Seminar on Distance Education, as well as AFT's survey of distance education instructors.

- The faculty at each institution should assume responsibility for carefully considering how much coursework is appropriate to be obtained through distance education. Deliberation should take place at the campus, department, and interdepartment levels, allowing for differences among disciplines and an appropriate amount of experimentation. [AFT believes that] faculty, as a general rule, should consider permitting up to 50% of a full undergraduate course of study to be offered at a distance.

- Procedures should be established to ensure, on a case-by-case basis, that a full undergraduate distance education program is available to those students truly unable to participate in classroom

education at any time after considering all other options.

- A full program taught at a distance may be acceptable at the graduate level and for some certificate programs, as determined by the faculty.

14. Evaluation of distance coursework should be undertaken at all levels.

- All institutions offering distance education coursework should become laboratories of program evaluation. Areas for evaluation should include the characteristics of successful and unsuccessful distance education students; variations among academic disciplines; faculty–student interaction; student performance; and the efficacy of offering large parts or all of an academic program by distance learning.

- Evaluation of distance education should become a priority concern of the federal government. The federal government should take two steps immediately:

  → Create a national information clearinghouse to share data about successful and unsuccessful practices; and

  → Initiate a priority program of targeted research in distance education in the areas outlined above.

- Regional and specialized accreditation agencies should establish high standards for distance education programs and ensure that distance education programs are always included in the evaluation of the institutions that offer them.

CONCLUSION

Clearly, every faculty union should become deeply involved in technology decision making. Faculty should negotiate with management on a variety of technology-related subjects, such as workload (including e-mail and prep time), compensation, training, jurisdiction, staffing levels, class size, acceptance of credits from other institutions, travel to other sites, and grading responsibilities. Unions also must attempt to negotiate protection of intellectual property rights in cyberspace for their members. Materials and technical assistance for local unions attempting to fulfill these responsibilities are available from the American Federation of Teachers.

The potential benefits of distance education, coupled with its successful application in many forums, clearly warrant a continuing effort to develop quality programs. Plenty of room should be left for experimentation, and we should not be defeatist when we encounter problems. But as we move forward, we must insist on the high standards outlined here— standards that, we believe, are not impossible to meet and are worth sticking to, point by point. When problems arise, we must make every effort to surmount obstacles, but we also must be prepared to say about distance education, "not us, not now" when the required level of quality cannot be achieved.

Some believe that distance education erects too many impediments to faculty–student interaction and therefore should be abandoned or severely restricted. Others say that the "market" will demand conven- ience and a flashy presentation style above all other values and that higher education had better adapt or lose out to competitors. It is indisputable that colleges and universities should develop courses that are as attractive as possible and no more onerous than necessary. But credit-bearing coursework must produce education that lasts, and to achieve that, we must develop and stick to high standards of good practice. We hope this report makes a positive contribution to reaching that goal.

(Modified and reprinted with permission from the Higher Education Program and Policy Council of the American Federation of Teachers.)

Benchmarks for Success in Internet-Based Distance Education

The National Education Association (NEA) and Blackboard, Inc. . . . [produced] a research-driven list of quality benchmarks for distance learning in higher education. The list of 24 quality measures is the centerpiece of "Quality on the Line"—an Institute for Higher Education Policy study commissioned by NEA and Blackboard, Inc.

With the growth worldwide of teaching and learning on the Internet, attention is being paid to the nature and quality of online higher education. Speaking before an international forum of higher education policymakers convened for the Blackboard Summit 2000, NEA President Bob Chase and Blackboard Inc. Chairman Matthew Pittinsky previewed the findings of the study and declared the 24 benchmarks essential to ensuring excellence in Internet-based learning.

"The distance from faculty to student must be measured in results achieved for our students," said Chase. "The benchmarks identified in this study are important guideposts as our nation navigates the future of online higher education."

Pittinsky said, "The quality of the education we provide for students is the driving force behind the way teaching and learning takes place. The benchmarks identified in the NEA–Blackboard study will be invaluable to colleges and universities around the world for years to come as they keep their focus on quality while working to create and improve their Internet-based teaching and learning environments."

To formulate the benchmarks, the report identified first-hand, practical strategies being used by U.S. colleges considered to be leaders in online distance education. The benchmarks distilled from this study are divided into seven categories of quality measures currently in use on campuses around the nation. Many are common sense, but the study validates their importance. The categories and benchmarks include:

INSTITUTIONAL SUPPORT BENCHMARKS

1. A documented technology plan that includes electronic security measures to ensure both quality standards and the integrity and validity of information.

2. The reliability of the technology delivery system is as failsafe as possible.

3. A centralized system provides support for building and maintaining the distance education infrastructure.

COURSE DEVELOPMENT BENCHMARKS

4. Guidelines regarding minimum standards are used for course development, design, and delivery, while learning outcomes—not the availability of existing technology—determine the technology being used to deliver course content.

5. Instructional materials are reviewed periodically to ensure they meet program standards.

6. Courses are designed to require students to engage themselves in analysis, synthesis, and evaluation as part of their course and program requirements.

TEACHING/LEARNING BENCHMARKS

7. Student interaction with faculty and other students is an essential characteristic and is facilitated through a variety of ways, including voice-mail and/or e-mail.

8. Feedback to student assignments and questions is constructive and provided in a timely manner.

9. Students are instructed in the proper methods of effective research, including assessment of the validity of resources.

COURSE STRUCTURE BENCHMARKS

10. Before starting an online program, students are advised about the program to determine if they possess the self-motivation and commitment to learn at a distance and if they have access to the

minimal technology required by the course design.

11. Students are provided with supplemental course information that includes online course objectives, concepts, and ideas, and learning outcomes for each course are summarized in a clearly written, straightforward statement.

12. Students have access to sufficient library resources that may include a "virtual library" accessible through the World Wide Web.

13. Faculty and students agree upon expectations regarding times for student assignment completion and faculty response.

STUDENT SUPPORT BENCHMARKS

14. Students receive information about programs, including admission requirements, tuition and fees, books and supplies, technical and proctoring requirements, and student support services.

15. Students are provided with hands-on training and information to aid them in securing material through electronic databases, inter-library loans, government archives, news services, and other sources.

16. Throughout the duration of the course/program, students have access to technical assistance, including detailed instructions regarding the electronic media used, practice sessions prior to the beginning of the course, and convenient access to technical support staff.

17. Questions directed to student service personnel are answered accurately and quickly, with a structured system in place to address student complaints.

FACULTY SUPPORT BENCHMARKS

18. Technical assistance in course development is available to faculty, who are encouraged to use it.

19. Faculty members are assisted in the transition from classroom teaching to online instruction and are assessed during the process.

20. Instructor training and assistance, including peer mentoring, continues through the progression of the online course.

21. Faculty members are provided with written resources to deal with issues arising from student use of electronically-accessed data.

EVALUATION AND ASSESSMENT BENCHMARKS

22. The program's educational effectiveness and teaching/learning process are assessed through an evaluation process that uses several methods and applies specific standards.

23. Data on enrollment, costs, and successful/innovative uses of technology are used to evaluate program effectiveness.

24. Intended learning outcomes are reviewed regularly to ensure clarity, utility, and appropriateness.

[Text taken from the report, "Quality on the Line—Benchmarks for Success in Internet-Based Distance Education" (http://nea.org/he/abouthe/Quality.pdf). Reprinted with permission.]

Best Practices for Electronically Offered Degree and Certificate Programs

Note: The following document is being utilized by the eight regional accrediting commissions in assessing distance education compatibility with their policies and procedures, and to promote good practices in distance education among their affiliated colleges and universities (see "Statement of Commitment by the Regional Accrediting Commissions for the Evaluation of Electronically Offered Degree Programs" found at www.wiche.edu/telecom/Accrediting%20-%20 Commitment.pdf)

INTRODUCTION

This document, *Best Practices for Electronically Offered Degree and Certificate Programs*, was developed in 1996 by the Western Cooperative for Educational Telecommunications; the second version was completed in 2001. In 2001, the *Best Practices* document was adopted by the Council of Regional Accrediting Commissions in response to the emergence of technologically mediated instruction offered at a distance as an important component of higher education. Expressing in detail what currently constitutes best practice in distance education, they seek to address concerns that regional accreditation standards are not relevant to the new distributed learning environments, especially when those environments are experienced by off-campus students. The *Best Practices*, however, are not new evaluative criteria. Rather they explicate how the well-established essentials of institutional quality found in regional accreditation standards are applicable to the emergent forms of learning; much of the detail of their content would find application in any learning environment. Taken together those essentials reflect

the values which the regional commissions foster among their affiliated colleges and universities:

- That education is best experienced within a community of learning where competent professionals are actively and cooperatively involved with creating, providing and improving the instructional program;

- That learning is dynamic and interactive, regardless of the setting in which it occurs;

- That instructional programs leading to degrees having integrity are organized around substantive and coherent curricula which define expected learning outcomes;

- That institutions accept the obligation to address student needs related to, and to provide the resources necessary for, their academic success;

- That institutions are responsible for the education provided in their name;

- That institutions undertake the assessment and improvement of their quality, giving particular emphasis to student learning;

- That institutions voluntarily subject themselves to peer review.

These *Best Practices* are meant to assist institutions in planning distance education activities and to provide a self-assessment framework for those already involved. For the regional accrediting associations they constitute a common understanding of those elements which reflect quality distance education programming. As such they are intended to inform and facilitate the evaluation policies and processes of each region.

Developed to reflect current best practice in electronically offered programming, these *Best Practices* were initially drafted in 1996 and revised in 2001 by the Western Cooperative for Educational Telecommunications (www.wiche.edu/telecom), an organization recognized for its substantial expertise in this field. Given the rapid pace of change in distance education, these *Best Practices* are necessarily a work in progress. They will be subject to periodic review by the regionals, individually and collectively, who welcome comments and suggestions for their improvement.

OVERVIEW TO THE *BEST PRACTICES*

These *Best Practices* are divided into five separate components, each of which addresses a particular area of institutional activity relevant to distance education. They are:

1. Institutional Context and Commitment
2. Curriculum and Instruction
3. Faculty Support
4. Student Support
5. Evaluation and Assessment

Each component begins with a general statement followed by individual numbered paragraphs addressing specific matters describing those elements essential to quality distance education programming. In the original document these are . . . followed by protocols in the form of questions designed to assist in determining the existence of those elements when reviewing either internally or externally distance education activities. The protocols are not reprinted here; however, institutions and readers are invited to view the entire document, including the protocols, at www.wiche.edu/telecom.

THE BEST PRACTICES

1. Institutional Context and Commitment

Electronically offered programs both support and extend the roles of educational institutions. Increasingly they are integral to academic organization, with growing implications for institutional infrastructure.

1a. In its content, purposes, organization, and enrollment history if applicable, the program is consistent with the institution's role and mission.

1b. It is recognized that a healthy institution's purposes change over time. The institution is aware of accreditation requirements and complies with them. Each accrediting commission has established definitions of what activities constitute a substantive change that will trigger prior review and approval processes. The appropriate accreditation commission should be notified and consulted [as to] whether an electronically offered program represents a major change. The offering of distributed programs can affect the institution's educational goals, intended student population, curriculum, modes or venue of instruction, and can thus have an impact on both the institution and its accreditation status.

1c. The institution's budgets and policy statements reflect its commitment to the students for whom its electronically offered programs are designed.

1d. The institution assures adequacy of technical and physical plant facilities, including appropriate staffing and technical assistance, to support its electronically offered programs.

1e. The internal organization structure which enables the development, coordination, support, and oversight of electronically offered programs will vary from institution to institution. Ordinarily, however, this will include the capacity to:

- Facilitate the associated instructional and technical support relationships.

- Provide (or draw upon) the required information technologies and related support services.

- Develop and implement a marketing plan that takes into account the target student population, the technologies available, and the factors required to meet institutional goals.

- Provide training and support to participating instructors and students.

- Assure compliance with copyright law.

- Contract for products and outsourced services.

- Assess and assign priorities to potential future projects.

- Assure that electronically offered programs and courses meet institution-wide standards, both to provide consistent quality and to provide a coherent framework for students who may enroll in both electronically offered and traditional on-campus courses.

- Maintain appropriate academic oversight.

- Maintain consistency with the institution's academic planning and oversight functions, to assure congruence with the institution's mission and allocation of required resources.

- Assure the integrity of student work and faculty instruction.

1f. In its articulation and transfer policies the institution judges courses and programs on their learning outcomes, and the resources brought to bear for their achievement, not on modes on delivery.

1g. The institution strives to assure a consistent and coherent technical framework for students and faculty. When a change in technologies is necessary, it is introduced in a way that minimizes the impact on students and faculty.

1h. The institution provides students with reasonable technical support for each educational technology hardware, software, and delivery system required in a program.

1i. The selection of technologies is based on appropriateness for the students and the curriculum. It is recognized that availability, cost, and other issues are often involved, but program documentation should include specific consideration of the match between technology and program.

1j. The institution seeks to understand the legal and regulatory requirements of the jurisdictions in which it operates, e.g., requirements for service to those with disabilities, copyright law, state and national requirements for institutions offering educational programs, international restrictions such as export of sensitive information or technologies, etc.

2. Curriculum and Instruction

Methods change but standards of quality endure. The important issues are not technical but curriculum-driven and pedagogical. Decisions about such matters are made by qualified professionals and focus on learning outcomes for an increasingly diverse student population.

2a. As with all curriculum development and review, the institution assures that each program of study results in collegiate level learning outcomes appropriate to the rigor and breadth of the degree or certificate awarded by the institution, that the electronically offered degree or certificate program is coherent and complete, and that

such programs leading to undergraduate degrees include general education requirements.

2b. Academically qualified persons participate fully in the decisions concerning program curricula and program oversight. It is recognized that traditional faculty roles may be unbundled and/or supplemented as electronically offered programs are developed and presented, but the substance of the program, including its presentation, management, and assessment, are the responsibility of people with appropriate academic qualifications.

2c. In designing an electronically offered degree or certificate program, the institution provides a coherent plan for the student to access all courses necessary to complete the program, or clearly notifies students of requirements not included in the electronic offering. Hybrid programs or courses, mixing electronic and on-campus elements, are designed to assure that all students have access to appropriate services.

2d. Although important elements of a program may be supplied by consortial partners or outsourced to other organizations, including contractors who may not be accredited, the responsibility for performance remains with the institution awarding the degree or certificate. It is the institution in which the student is enrolled, not its suppliers or partners, that has a contract with the student. Therefore, the criteria for selecting consortial partners and contractors, and the means to monitor and evaluate their work, are important aspects of the program plan. In considering consortial agreements, attention is given to issues such as assuring that enhancing service to students is a primary consideration and that incentives do not compromise the integrity of the institution or of the educational program. Consideration is also given to the effect of administrative arrangements and cost-sharing on an institution's decision-making regarding curriculum. Current examples of consortial and contractual relationships include:

- Faculty qualifications and support.
- Course material:
  a. Courses or course elements acquired or licensed from other institutions.

b. Courses or course elements provided by partner institutions in a consortium.

c. Curricular elements from recognized industry sources, e.g., Microsoft or Novell certification programs.

d. Commercially produced course materials ranging from textbooks to packaged courses or course elements.

- Course management and delivery:
  a. WebCT, Blackboard, College, etc.

- Library related services:
  a. Remote access to library services, resources, and policies.
  b. Provision of library resources and services, e.g., online reference services, document delivery, print resources, etc.

- Bookstore services.

- Services providing information to students concerning the institution and its programs and courses.

- Technical services:
  a. Server capacity.
  b. Technical support services, including help desk services for students and faculty.

- Administrative services:
  a. Registration, student records, etc.

- Services related to orientation, advising, counseling, or tutoring.

- Online payment arrangements.

- Student privacy considerations.

2e. The importance of appropriate interaction (synchronous or asynchronous) between instructor and students and among students is reflected in the design of the program and its courses, and in the technical facilities and services provided.

3. Faculty Support

As indicated above, faculty roles are becoming increasingly diverse and reorganized. For example, the same person may not perform both the tasks of course development and direct instruction to students.

Regardless of who performs which of the tasks, important issues are involved.

3a. In the development of an electronically offered program, the institution and its participating faculty have considered issues of workload, compensation, ownership of intellectual property resulting from the program, and the implications of program participation for the faculty member's professional evaluation processes. This mutual understanding is based on policies and agreements adopted by the parties.

3b. The institution provides an ongoing program of appropriate technical, design, and production support for participating faculty members.

3c. The institution provides to those responsible for program development the orientation and training to help them become proficient in the uses of the program's technologies, including potential changes in course design and management.

3d. The institution provides to those responsible for working directly with students the orientations and training to help them become proficient in the uses of the technologies for these purposes, including strategies for effective interaction.

4. Student Support

Colleges and universities have learned that the twenty-first century student is different, both demographically and geographically, from students of previous generations. These differences affect everything from admissions policy to library services. Reaching these students, and serving them appropriately, are major challenges to today's institutions.

4a. The institution has a commitment—administrative, financial, and technical—to continuation of the program for a period sufficient to enable all admitted students to complete a degree or certificate in a publicized timeframe.

4b. Prior to admitting a student to the program, the institution:

- Ascertains by a review of pertinent records and/or personal review that the student is qualified by prior education or equivalent experience to be admitted to that program, including in the case of international students, English language skills.

- Informs the prospective student concerning required access to technologies used in the program.
- Informs the prospective student concerning technical competence required of students in the program.
- Informs the prospective student concerning estimated or average program costs (including costs of information access) and associated payment and refund policies.
- Informs the prospective student concerning curriculum design and the timeframe in which courses are offered, and assists the student in understanding the nature of the learning objectives.
- Informs the prospective student of library and other learning services available to support learning and the skills necessary to access them.
- Informs the prospective student concerning the full array of other support services available from the institution.
- Informs the prospective student about arrangements for interaction with the faculty and fellow students.
- Assists the prospective student in understanding independent learning expectations as well as the nature and potential challenges of learning in the program's technology-based environment.
- Informs the prospective student about the estimated time for program completion.

4c. The institution recognizes that appropriate services must be available for students of electronically offered programs, using the working assumption that these students will not be physically present on campus. With variations for specific situations and programs, these services, which are possibly coordinated, may include:

- Accurate and timely information about the institution, its programs, courses, costs, and related policies and requirements.
- Pre-registration advising.
- Application for admission.
- Placement testing.

- Enrollment/registration in programs and courses.
- Financial aid, including information about policies and limitations, information about available scholarships, processing of applications, and administration of financial aid and scholarship awards.
- Secure payment arrangements.
- Academic advising.
- Timely intervention regarding student progress.
- Tutoring.
- Career counseling and placement.
- Academic progress information, such as degree completion audits.
- Library resources appropriate to the program, including, reference and research assistance; remote access to data bases, online journals and full-text resources; document delivery services; library user and information literacy instruction; reserve materials; and institutional agreements with local libraries.
- Training in information literacy including research techniques.
- Bookstore services: ordering, secure payment, prompt delivery of books, course packs, course-related supplies and materials, and institutional memorabilia.
- Ongoing technical support, preferably offered during evenings and weekends as well as normal institutional working hours.
- Referrals for student learning differences, physical challenges, and personal counseling.
- Access to grievance procedures.

4d. The institution recognizes that a sense of community is important to the success of many students, and that an ongoing, long-term relationship is beneficial to both student and institution. The design and administration of the program takes this factor into account as appropriate, through such actions as encouraging study groups, providing student directories (with the permission of those listed), including off-campus students in institutional publications and events, including these students in definitions of the academic community through such mechanisms as student government representation, invitations to campus events including graduation ceremonies, and similar strategies of inclusion.

5. Evaluation and Assessment

Both the assessment of student achievement and evaluation of the overall program take on added importance as new techniques evolve. For example, in asynchronous programs the element of seat time is essentially removed from the equation. For these reasons, the institution conducts sustained, evidence-based and participatory inquiry as to whether distance learning programs are achieving objectives. The results of such inquiry are used to guide curriculum design and delivery, pedagogy, and educational processes, and may affect future policy and budgets and perhaps have implications for the institution's roles and mission.

5a. As a component of the institution's overall assessment activities, documented assessment of student achievement is conducted in each course and at the completion of the program, by comparing student performance to the intended learning outcomes.

5b. When examinations are employed (paper, online, demonstrations of competency, etc.), they take place in circumstances that include firm student identification. The institution otherwise seeks to assure the integrity of student work.

5c. Documented procedures assure that security of personal information is protected in the conduct of assessments and evaluations and in the dissemination of results.

5d. Overall program effectiveness is determined by such measures as:

- The extent to which student learning matches intended outcomes, including for degree programs both the goals of general education and the objectives of the major.
- The extent to which student intent is met.
- Student retention rates, including variations over time.
- Student satisfaction, as measured by regular surveys.

- Faculty satisfaction, as measured by regular surveys and by formal and informal peer review processes.
- The extent to which access is provided to students not previously served.
- Measures of the extent to which library and learning resources are used appropriately by the program's students.
- Measures of student competence in fundamental skills such as communication, comprehension, and analysis.
- Cost effectiveness of the program to its students, as compared to campus-based alternatives.

5e. The institution conducts a program of continual self-evaluation directed toward program improvement, targeting more effective uses of technology to improve pedagogy, advances in student achievement of intended outcomes, improved retention rates, effective use of resources, and demonstrated improvements in the institution's service to its internal and external constituencies. The program and its results are reflected in the institution's ongoing self-evaluation process and are used to inform the further plans of the institution and those responsible for its academic programs.

5f. Institutional evaluation of electronically offered programs takes place in the context of the regular evaluation of all academic programs.

(Text taken from www.wiche.edu/telecom/Article1.htm Reprinted with permission.)

Online Institutions: Anytime, Anywhere Learning

CAPELLA UNIVERSITY

www.capellauniversity.edu

Founded

- 1993
- Accredited in 1999 by the Commission on Institutions of Higher Education of the North Central Association of Colleges and Schools

Enrollment

- 3,700 students in 40 countries

Certificates/ Degrees

- BS in Business, MBA
- Information Technology
- Certificates, masters, and doctoral programs in Education, Business, Psychology, Human Services

Partners

- University of Pennsylvania
- Thunderbird Graduate School of International Management
- Carnegie Mellon University
- London School of Economics and Political Science

CARDEAN UNIVERSITY

www.cardean.edu

Founded

- 1999 by Unext.com, a high-profile, well-financed online venture
- Accredited by the Accrediting Commission of Distance Education and Training Council
- First institution to receive degree authorization from the Illinois Board of Higher Education

Certificates/Degrees

- Continuing professional education
- Degree programs
- MBA
- Courses in: Accounting, Business, Communication, E-Commerce, Finance, Management and Organizational Behavior Marketing, Pre-MBA, Quantitative Methods

Partners

- Carnegie Mellon University
- London School of Economics and Political Science
- Stanford University
- Columbia Business School

JONES INTERNATIONAL UNIVERSITY

www.jonesinternational.edu

Founded

- 1995
- Accredited by Commission on Institutions of Higher Education of the North Central Association of Colleges and Schools

Certificates and Degrees

- Bachelor of Arts Degree Completion Program in Business Communication
- Master of Arts in Business Communication
- Master of Education in E-Learning
- Courses in business

Partners

- University of Pennsylvania
- Thunderbird Graduate School of International Management
- London School of Economics and Political Science
- Stanford University
- Columbia University
- Michigan State University
- Rutgers University
- Corporations

THE OPEN UNIVERSITY

www.open.ac.uk

Founded

- 1971

Enrollment

- 200,000 students

Certificates/Degrees

- Bachelors degrees
- Certificates in Management Accounting
- MBA

PENN STATE WORLD CAMPUS

www.worldcampus.psu.edu

Founded

- 1998

Enrollment

- 2,700 students in 50 states and 20 countries

Certificates/Degrees

- 200 courses, 26 certificate and degree programs
- Masters degrees in Adult Education (M. Ed.)
- Intercollegiate Masters of Business Administration (MBA)
- Baccalaureate degree in Letters, Arts, and Sciences
- Associates degrees in a variety of areas

Partner

- Penn State University

UNIVERSITY COLLEGE (UC) OF THE UNIVERSITY OF MAINE SYSTEM

www.learn.maine.edu

Founded

- 1989
- Accreditation: UC is a service that delivers programs accredited through UMS campuses

Enrollment

- 11,000 students

Certificates/Degrees

- Associates degrees in Applied Science in Education, Business Administration, Financial Services, Liberal Arts, Liberal Studies, Library and Information Technology
- Bachelors degrees in Behavioral Sciences, Business Administration, Nurse Completion, University Studies, Mental Health and Human Services, and Library and Information Technology
- Masters degrees in Adult Education (self-designed), Computer Engineering, Counseling, Electrical Engineering, Health Policy, Management, Liberal Studies
- Graduate certificates in Human Services, Information Systems, Public Policy
- Undergraduate Certificates in Human Services, Classical Studies, Liberal Arts, Education, and Environment

Partners

- Seven University of Maine System Campuses

UNIVERSITY OF MARYLAND UNIVERSITY COLLEGE

www.umuc.edu

Founded

- 1996
- Accredited by the Commission on Institutions of Higher Education of the Middle States Association of Colleges and Schools

Certificates/ Degrees

- Incomplete degree programs online
- Undergraduate degrees: Accounting, Business Administration, Communication, Computer and Information Science, Computer Studies, Environment Management, Fire Science, Human Resource Management, Humanities, Information Systems Management, Legal Studies, Psychology, Social Science

- Graduate degrees
  - → Doctor of Management
  - → MBA: Regular MBA, Executive MBA, Dual MBA
  - → Masters of Science in Accounting, Biotechnology Studies, Computer Systems Management, Electronic Commerce, Health Care Administration, Information Technology, Management, Technology Management, Telecommunications
  - → Education and Teaching
  - → Masters of International Management
  - → Masters of Software Engineering
  - → Executive Masters Programs

Partner

- University of Maryland

UNIVERSITY OF PHOENIX ONLINE

www.uofponline.com

Founded

- 1989

Enrollment

- 29,000 students

Certificates/Degrees

- Undergraduate, graduate, and doctoral degrees in: Business, Management, Technology, Education, Nursing.

Partner

- University of Phoenix

WALDEN UNIVERSITY

www.waldenu.edu

Founded

- 1970
- Accredited by the Commission on Institutions of Higher Education of the North Central Association of Colleges and Schools

Certificates/Degrees

- Masters degrees in Education, Professional Psychology, Public Health
- Doctoral degrees in Applied Management and Decision Sciences, Education, Health Services, Human Services, Professional Psychology
- Psychology certificate

Partners

- Indiana University
- Howard University
- Walter Reed Army Medical Center
- Fort Dix Education Office

WESTERN GOVERNORS UNIVERSITY

www.wgu.edu

Founded

- 1997
- Accredited in June 2001 by the Accrediting Commission of the Distance Education and Training Council

Certificates/Degrees

- Competency-based
- Associate of Arts in Business or Information Technology
- Bachelors degree in Business Information Technology
- Masters degree in Learning and Technology
- Graduate certificates in Technology Proficiency, Instructional Design
- Undergraduate Certificates in Information Technology–Network Administration

Partners

- 45 education providers in 18 states (Alaska, Arizona, Colorado, Hawaii, Idaho, Indiana, Montana, Nebraska, Nevada, New Mexico, North Dakota, Oklahoma, Oregon, South Dakota, Texas, Utah, Washington, and Wyoming), Guam, and Canada
- Articulation agreements with eight educational institutions

References

Alexander, S., Villaneuva, L., & Werner, M. (2001). *Is there a future for Napster?* GSU students' paper for P. Wiseman's law and the internet summer course.

Armstrong, L. (2000, November/December). Distance learning: An academic leader's perspective on a disruptive product. *Change*, pp. 20–27.

Baird, J. S., Jr. (1987). Perceived learning in relation to student evaluation of university instruction. *Journal of Educational Psychology*, 79(1), 90–91.

Baker, R. (1997). *Strategic plan for the Oregon Community Colleges for distance learning*. Salem: Oregon Community Colleges.

Bay, J. W., Johnson, J. L., & Silvernail, D. L. (1988, September). *The impact on faculty of teaching on instructional television*. Paper presented at the Interactive Technology and Telecommunications Conference, Augusta, ME.

Biemiller, L. (1998, October 9). U. of Utah president issues a pointed warning about virtual universities. *The Chronicle of Higher Education*, p. A32.

Bleed, R. (2000, October 11). The internet, computing, and academe: Future directions. *The Chronicle of Higher Education*. Retrieved on December 7, 2000, from http://chronicle.com/colloquylive/transcripts/2000/10/20001011educause.htm.

Blumenstyk, G. (1996, May 31). Maine's large distance education network gets mixed reviews. *The Chronicle of Higher Education*, p. A15.

Blumenstyk, G. (1998, February 6). Western Governor's University takes shape as a new model for higher education. *The Chronicle of Higher Education*, pp. A21, A24.

Boettcher, J. C. (1998). How much does it cost to develop a distance learning course? It all depends. *Syllabus*, 11(9), 56–58.

Brenden, D. R. (1977). Face-to-face and telelecture interaction session: Presenting a course by telelecture. *Journal of Industrial Teacher Education*, 14(2), 53–59.

Brown, J. S., & Duguid, P. (1996, July–August). Universities in the digital age. *Change*, pp. 11–19.

Campbell, C. S., Lum, J. F., & Singh, N. (2000). SMIL: You're really learning now. *Syllabus*, 14(1), 24, 26, 61.

Canfield, A. A. (1980). *Canfield instructional styles inventory manual*. (Available from Humanities Media, Box 188, Rochester, MI 48063).

Carnevale, D. (1999, December 12). Instructor cuts dropout rate by giving extra attention to online students. *The Chronicle of Higher Education*. Retrieved on December 20, 2000, from http://www.chronicle.com/free/99/1299121601u.htm.

Carnevale, D. (2000a, January 7). Survey finds 72% rise in number of distance education programs. *The Chronicle of Higher Education*, p. A57.

Carnevale, D. (2000b, March 3). From a distance students learn the subleties of jazz. *The Chronicle of Higher Education*. Retrieved on March 3, 2000, from, http://www.chronicle.com/free/2000/03/200000901u.htm.

Carnevale, D. (2000c, March 23). Coastline Community College tests online video counseling for distance learners. *The Chronicle of Higher Education*. Retrieved on January 23, 2002 from http://www.chronicle.com/free/2000/03/2000032301u.htm.

Carnevale, D. (2000d, August 11). Accrediting bodies consider new standards for distance-education programs. *The Chronicle of Higher Education*. Retrieved on August 14, 2000, from http://www.chronicle.com/free/2000/08/2000081101u.htm.

Carnevale, D. (2000e, November 28). Accrediting committee grants candidate status to Western Governor's University. *The Chronicle of Higher Education*. Retrieved on November 28, 2000, from http://www.chronicle.com/free/2000/11/2000112801u.htm.

Carnevale, D. (2000f, April 26). San Diego State's senate created detailed policy for distance courses. *The Chronicle of Higher Education*. Retrieved on May 3,

2000 from http://www.chronicle.com/free/2000/04/2000042601u.htm.

Carr, S. (2000a, March 7). 2 professors find that online chats are unpopular. *The Chronicle of Higher Education*. Retrieved on April 8, 2000, from http://www.chronicle.com/free/2000/04/20000040701u.htm.

Carr, S. (2000b, April 14). Science instructors ask: Can you teach students at a distance how to use microscopes? *The Chronicle of Higher Education*, p. A62.

Carver, J., & Mackay, R. C. (1986). Interactive television brings university classes to the home and workplace. *Canadian Journal of University Continuing Education*, *15*(1), 19–28.

Cathcart, H. R. (1989). Cited in M. Eraut (Ed.), *The international encyclopedia of educational technology* (p. 529). New York: Pergamon.

Chaffee, E. (2001). Keeping our eyes on the target: The "other" use of technology in education. *Technology Source*. Retrieved from http://horizon.unc.edu/TS/commentary/2001-01b.asp.

Chickering, A. W., & Ehrmann, S. C. (1996). Implementing the seven principles: Technology as lever. *A.A.H.E. Bulletin*, *49*(2), 3–6.

Chickering, A. W., & Gamson, Z. (1987, June). Seven principles for good practice in undergraduate education. *The Wingspread Journal*, 9, p. 2.

Chu, G. C., & Schramm, W. (1967). *Learning from television: What the research says*. Stanford: Institute for Communication Research.

Cini, M. A., & Vilic, B. (1999). Online teaching: Moving from risk to challenge. *Syllabus*, *12*(10), 38–40.

Community College of Maine Annual Report: Year One (1989–1990). (1990, June 25). Augusta: University of Maine at Augusta, Office of Distance Education.

Community College of Maine Annual Report: Year Two (1990–1991). (1991, June 30). Augusta: University of Maine at Augusta, Office of Distance Education.

Conway, K. (1996). Putting technology in its place: Evolution of the IAT. *Syllabus*, *10*(2), 26–29.

Coombs, N. (2000). Transcending distances and differences. *A.A.H.E. Bulletin*, *53*(2), 3–5.

Cox, G. M. (2000, November/December). Why I left a university Internet company. *Change*, pp. 12–18.

Creswell, K. (1986). Does instructional TV make the grade? *Journal of Educational Television*, *12*(1), 19–27.

Cross, K. P., & Steadman, M. H. (1996). *Classroom research: Implementing the scholarship of teaching*. San Francisco: Jossey-Bass.

Daniel, J. S. (1997, July/August). Why universities need technology strategies. *Change*, pp. 11–17.

Daniel, J. S. (1998, April 26–28). *Distance learning: The vision and distance learning: The reality—What works, what travels?* Retrieved on April 18, 2001, from http://www.open.ac.uk/vcs-speeches/wguslc.html.

Daniel, J. S. (2000, June 19). *Open learning for a new century*. Retrieved on April 18, 2001, from http://www.open.ac.uk/vcs-speeches/Taiwan.html.

Daviss, B. (2000, December 18). Teaching in a wired world. *National Crosstalk: A Publication of the National Center for Public Policy and Higher Education*, *8*(4), 1–9. Retrieved on December 18, 2000, from http://www.highereducation.org/crosstalk/ct1000/news1000–wired.shtml.

Denton, J. J. (1985). *An examination of instructional strategies used with two-way television*. (ERIC Document Reproduction Service No. ED 238 407)

Dutrow, K. L., & Wade, K. H. (2001). *Internet adoption: How much is that baby in the window?* GSU students' paper for P. Wiseman's law and the internet summer course.

Ehrmann, S. C. (2000). The flashlight program: Evaluating instructional uses of the web. *Syllabus*, *14*(2), 38–42.

Ellis, L., & Mathis, D. (1985). College students learning from televised versus conventional classroom lectures: A controlled experiment. *Higher Education*, *14*(2), 165–173.

Ely, D. (2000). Looking before we leap—"prior questions" for distance education planners. *Syllabus*, *13*(10), 26–28.

Epper, R. M. (1996). States use technology to enhance undergraduate education. *State Education Leader*, *14*(1), 17.

Eraut, M. (Ed.). (1989). *The international encyclopedia of educational technology*. New York: Pergamon.

Everhart, R. L. (1999). Creating virtual communities. *Syllabus*, *12*(8), 12–16.

Fraser, A. B. (1999, August 6). College should tap the pedagogical potential of the world wide web. *The Chronicle of Higher Education*, p. B8.

Gaines, C. L., Johnson, W., & King, D. T. (1996). Achieving technological equity access to the learning tools of the 21st century. *T.H.E. Journal*, *23*(11), 74–78.

Gibson, J. W., & Herrera, J. M. (1999). How to go from classroom based to online delivery in eighteen months or less: A case study in online program development. *T.H.E. Journal*, *26*(6), 57–60.

Gilmour, C. (1979). Cited in D. C. B. Teather (1989). In M. Eraut (Ed.), *The international encyclopedia of educational technology* (p. 504). New York: Pergamon.

Green, K. C. (1997, October). Think twice and businesslike about distance education. *A.A.H.E. Bulletin*, *49*(6), 3–6.

Harold, E. S. (1967). Televised lectures: Attitudes of students and faculty. *Improving College & University Teaching*, *25*(1), 43–51.

Hazari, S., & Schnorr, D. (1999). Leveraging student feedback to improve teaching in web-based courses. *T.H.E. Journal*, *26*(11), 30–38.

Hendley, V. (2000). 30 years of higher education. *A.A.H.E. Bulletin, 52*(7), 4.

Horrigan, B. (2001). Andrew Weil, M.D. on integrative medicine and the nature of reality. *Alternative Therapies in Health and Medicine, 7*(4), 96–104.

Hult, R. E., Jr. (1980). The effectiveness of university television instruction and factors influencing student attitudes. *College Student Journal, 14*(1), 5–7.

Isenberg, R. L. (2000). *Trademarks and the internet.* GSU students' paper for P. Wiseman's law and the internet fall course.

Johnson, G. R., et al. (1985). Interactive two-way television: Revisited. *Journal of Educational Technology System, 12*(3), 153–158.

Johnson, J. L. (1990a). *Evaluation report of the Community College of Maine Interactive Television System, Spring 1990.* Portland: University of Southern Maine, Testing and Assessment Center.

Johnson, J. L. (1990b). *Evaluation report of the Community College of Maine Interactive Television System, Summer, 1990.* Portland: University of Southern Maine, Testing and Assessment Center.

Johnson, J. L. (1990c). *Evaluation report of the Community College of Maine Interactive Television System, Fall 1990.* Portland: University of Southern Maine, Testing and Assessment Center.

Johnson, J. L. (1990d). *Evaluation report of the Community College of Maine Interactive Television System, Fall, 1989.* Portland: University of Southern Maine, Testing and Assessment Center.

Johnson, J. L. (1990e, July). *Report of faculty perceptions of Community College of Maine Interactive Television System, Spring 1990.* Portland: University of Southern Maine, Testing and Assessment Center.

Johnson, J. L. (1991a, March). *Report on a study of Community College of Maine Interactive Television System first time faculty, Fall 1990.* Portland: University of Southern Maine, Testing and Assessment Center.

Johnson, J. L. (1991b, March). *Report on a study of the Community College of Maine Interactive Television System returning faculty, Fall 1990.* Portland: University of Southern Maine, Testing and Assessment Center.

Johnson, J. L. (1991c, April). *A comparative study of the Community College of Maine Interactive Television System courses and live equivalent courses, Fall 1990.* Portland: University of Southern Maine, Testing and Assessment Center.

Johnson, J. L. (1991d). *Evaluation report of the Community College of Maine Interactive Television System, Spring 1991.* Portland: University of Southern Maine, Testing and Assessment Center.

Johnson, J. L. (1991e). *Evaluation report of the Community College of Maine Interactive Television System, Summer 1991.* Portland: University of Southern Maine, Testing and Assessment Center.

Johnson, J. L. (1991f). *Evaluation report of the Community College of Maine Interactive Television System, Fall 1990.* Portland: University of Southern Maine, Testing and Assessment Center

Johnson, J. L. (1992a, April). *The development and validation of the Johnson Learner Preference Scale.* Paper presented at the annual conference of the New England Educational Research Organization, Portsmouth, NH.

Johnson, J. L. (1992b). *A manual of learning styles scales for use with college students.* Portland: University of Southern Maine, Testing and Assessment Center

Johnson, J. L. (1997a). *An evaluation report: Education network of Maine courses: Flashlight student survey.* Augusta: Institutional Research and Evaluation, Education Network of Maine.

Johnson, J. L. (1997b, Summer). *A report on the interviews conducted with behavioral sciences external degree students enrolled in the BEXM 400* [Planning seminar for the individualized concentration]. Augusta: Institutional Research and Evaluation, Education Network of Maine.

Johnson, J. L. (1998, April). *Distance education and technology: An evaluation study of four delivery modes.* Paper presented at the annual meeting of the American Educational Research Association, San Diego.

Johnson, J. L. (1999a). Distance education and technology: What are the choices for higher education? *Educational Computing Research, 21*(2), 165–181.

Johnson, J. L. (1999b). *An evaluation of asynchronous courses delivered over the University of Maine System Network for Education and Technology Services, Fall 1998.* Portland: University of Southern Maine, Testing and Assessment Center.

Johnson, J. L. (2000, May). *Distance learning: How effective and who succeeds? An investigation of learning styles.* Paper presented at the annual forum of the Association for Institutional Research, Cincinnati.

Johnson, J. L., & Silvernail, D. L. (1989). College calculus for Maine high school students: An instructional television pilot project. *Journal of Maine Education, 5*(1), 41–43.

Johnson, J. L., & Silvernail, D. L. (1990, March). *Report of faculty perceptions of Community College of Maine Interactive Television System, Fall 1989.* Portland: University of Southern Maine, Testing and Assessment Center.

Johnson, J. L., & Silvernail, D. L. (1994, September/October). The impact of interactive television and distance education on student evaluation of courses: A causal model. *Community College Journal of Research and Practice, 18*(5), 431–440.

Johnstone, S. M. (2000). The evolving learning environment. *Syllabus, 14*(1), 20.

Johnstone, S. M. (2001). Electronic learning generations. *Syllabus, 15*(2), 14.

Karayan, S. S., & Crowe, J. A. (1997). Student perceptions of electronic discussion groups. *T.H.E. Journal, 24*(9), 69–71.

Kearsley, G. (1997). A guide to online education. Retrieved on August 6, 1999, from http://www.gwis.circ.gwu.edu/etl.online.html.

Kearsley, G. (1998). Trends: Distance education goes mainstream. *T.H.E. Journal, 25*(10), 22–26.

Kelly, R. (2001). An integrated approach to student services. *Distance Education Report, 5*(6), 5.

Klor de Alva, J. (1999–2000, Winter). Remaking the academy in the age of information. *Issues in Science and Technology*, pp. 52–58.

Lang, D. (2000). Critical thinking in web courses: An oxymoron? *Syllabus, 14*(2), 20–24.

Lin-Liu, J. (2002). Malaysian students turn to web cams and chat to hone foreign-language skills. Retrieved on January 30, 2002, from http://www.chronicle.com/free/2002/01/20002013001u.htm.

Lowery, B. R., & Barnes, F. M. (1996). Partnering to establish a distance learning program that is responsive to needs. *T.H.E. Journal, 23*(7), 91–95.

Lucas, C. J. (1994). *American higher education: A history*. New York: St. Martin's Griffin.

Ludwig, J. (2001, April 12). A digest of recent corporate news in distance education. *The Chronicle of Higher Education*. Retrieved on April 12, 2001, from http://www.chronicle.com/free/2001/04/2001041201u.htm.

Lyle, J. (1989). Cited in M. Eraut (Ed.), *The international encyclopedia of educational technology* (p. 516). New York: Pergamon.

Marchese, T. (2000, September/October). Learning and e-learning. *Change*, p. 4.

Martin, B., Foshee, N., Moskal, P., & Bramble, W. (1996). Lessons learned from the Florida Teletraining Project. (ERIC Document Reproduction Service No. ED 397 819)

Mayhew, L. B., Ford, P. J., & Hubbard, D. L. (1990). *The quest for quality*. San Francisco: Jossey-Bass.

McCollum, K. (1998, May 15). Accreditors urged to prepare for distance learning. *The Chronicle of Higher Education*, p. A34.

Morrison, J. L. (1997, September). Western Governor's University. *The Technology Source*. Retrieved on April 4, 2001, from http://horizon.unc.edu/TS/default.asp?show=article&id=514.

Morrison, J. L., & Mendenhall, R. W. (2001). *Renaissance at Western Governor's University: An interview with Robert W. Mendenhall*. Retrieved on May 22, 2001, from http://www.horizon.unc.edu/TS/default.asp?show=article&id=865.

Oblinger, D. G., Barone, C. A., & Hawkins, B. L. (Eds.). (2001). *Distributed education and its challenges: An overview*. Washington, DC: American Council on Education.

Ollhoff, L. (1998). *Performance assessment*. St. Paul, MN: Concordia University.

Ollhoff, L., & Ollhoff, J. (1997). *Principles for teaching excellence in the School of Human Services at Concordia University, St. Paul, Minnesota*. St. Paul, MN: Concordia University.

Olsen, F. (2000, April 7). Mount Holyoke looks at how the web can improve classroom instruction. *The Chronicle of Higher Education*, p. A47.

Olsen, F. (2001, August 16). High speed networks let a music professor in New York teach a student in Oklahoma. *The Chronicle of Higher Education*. Retrieved on August 17, 2001, from http://www.chronicle.com/free/2001/08/2001081601u.htm.

Ottenhoff, J., & Lawrence, D. (1999). Ten paradoxical truths about conference software in the classroom. *Syllabus, 13*(3), 54, 56–57.

Peterson's guide to distance learning programs. (2001). Lawrenceville, NJ: Thomson Learning.

Phipps, R. A., Wellman, J. V., & Merisotis, J. P. (1998, April 28). *Assuring quality in distance learning: A preliminary review*. Washington, DC: Council for Higher Education Accreditation.

Pierce, W. (2000). Online strategies for teaching thinking. *Syllabus, 14*(2), 21.

Porter, J. B. (1983). A closed-circuit television course in criminal law. *Improving College & University Teaching, 31*(1), 33–36.

Roget's II: The New Thesaurus (3rd ed.). (1995). Boston and New York: Houghton Mifflin.

Rosenblum, J. (2000). Design and development of online courses: Faculty working in collaboration. *Syllabus, 13*(7), 10, 12, 14.

Ruppert, S. S. (1998). Legislative views on higher education technology use. *The NEA Higher Education Journal, 14*(1), 41–48.

Saba, F. (1999a). Architecture of dynamic distance instructional and learning systems. *Distance Education Report, 3*(8), 1, 2, 5.

Saba, F. (1999b). Supporting students: Online learner services. *Distance Education Report, 3*(3), 1, 3.

Saba, F. (2001). Why distance education will fail and harm higher education. *Distance Educator.com*, pp. 1–5.

Schuell, T. J. (2000, April). *Teaching and learning in an online environment*. Paper presented at the annual meeting of the American Educational Research Association, New Orleans.

Serwatka, J. A. (1999). Internet distance learning: How do I put my course on the web? *T.H.E. Journal, 26*(10), 71–74.

Silvernail, D. L. (1985). *A comparison of the effects of live classroom and interactive television instruction on students' learning and attitudes: Preliminary findings.* Portland: University of Southern Maine, Testing and Assessment Center.

Silvernail, D. L., & Johnson, J. L. (1987). *Effects of University of Southern Maine Interactive Television System on students' achievement and attitudes.* Portland: University of Southern Maine, Testing and Assessment Center.

Silvernail, D. L., & Johnson, J. L. (1989). *A study of the relationship between learning styles, student course evaluations and perceived effectiveness of instructional television.* Portland: University of Southern Maine, Testing and Assessment Center.

Silvernail, D. L., & Johnson J. L. (1990). The impact of interactive televised instruction on college student achievement and attitudes: A controlled experiment. *International Journal of Instructional Media, 17*(1), 1–8.

Silvernail, D. L., & Johnson, J. L. (1992, June). The impact of interactive televised instruction on student evaluations of their instructors. *Educational Technology,* pp. 47–50.

Sircar, J. (2000). Laying the foundations for educational change. *Syllabus, 14*(3), 54, 56–57.

Snapshots. (2000, April 23). *USA Today,* p. 1.

Sperling, J. G. (1999). Vision of a visionary. *Assessment and Accountability Forum, 9*(1), 4–7, 17.

Sternberg, R. J. (1984). What should intelligence tests test? Implications of a triarchic theory of intelligence for intelligence testing. *Educational Researcher, 13*(1), 5–15.

Stover, H. (1986). Teaching writing by television. *Teaching English in the Two Year College, 19*(1), 19–27.

Teather, D. C. B. (1989). Cited in M. Eraut (Ed.), The international encyclopedia of educational technology (pp. 504, 506). New York: Pergamon.

Thoms, K. J. (1999). Technology via ITV: Taking instructional design to the next level. *T.H.E. Journal, 26*(9), 60–66.

Thibodeau, P. (1997, February). Design standards for visual elements and interactivity for courseware. *T.H.E. Journal, 24*(7), 84–86.

Thorman, J., & Amb, T. (1975). The video tape presentation versus the live presentation: Better, worse, or the same? *T.H.E. Journal, 1*(24), 24–27.

Truman-Davis, B., Futch, L., Thompson, K., & Yonekura, F. (2000). Support for online teaching and learning. *EDUCAUSE Quarterly, 23*(2), 44–51.

Van Dusen, G. C. (1998). Technology: Higher education's magic bullet. *The NEA Higher Education Journal, 14*(1), 59–67.

Vogt, W. P. (1993). *Dictionary of statistics and methodology.* Newbury Park, CA: Sage.

Walker, D. (2000, March 13). A distance-education pioneer plans online commencement. *The Chronicle of Higher Education.* Retrieved on March 13, 2000, from http://www.chronicle.com/free/2000/03/2000031301u.htm.

Webster's II New College Dictionary. (1999). Boston and New York: Houghton Mifflin.

Weigel, V. (2000, September/October). E-learning and the tradeoff between richness and reach in higher learning. *Change,* pp. 10–15.

Wergin, J. F., Boland, D., & Kaas, T. (1986). Televising graduate engineering courses: Results of an instructional experiment. *Engineering Education, 77*(2), 109–112.

Western Governor's University earns accreditation from the Distance Education and Training Council [Press release]. (2001, June 13). Retrieved on January 30, 2002, from http://www.wgu.edu/wgu/about/release58.html.

Western Governor's University first competency based university to achieve candidate accreditation [Press release]. (2000). Retrieved on November 27, 2000, from http://www.wgu.edu.

White, C. (2000). Learn online. *T.H.E. Journal, 27*(9), 67.

White, K. (1999). Online education—managing a rich and robust environment. *Assessment and Accountability Forum, 9*(3), 11–14.

Whittington, N. (1987). Is instructional television educationally effective? A research review. *The American Journal of Distance Education, 1*(1), 47–57.

Williams, C. (2001, January 28). When a hug is really an embrace. *Sun Journal Sunday,* p. D1.

Young, J. R. (1999, February 5). Are wireless networks the wave of the future? *The Chronicle of Higher Education,* p. A25.

Young, J. R. (2000a, April 24). The lowly telephone is central to some distance education courses. *The Chronicle of Higher Education.* Retrieved on April 24, 2000 from http://www.chronicle.com/free/2000/04/2000042401u.htm.

Young, J. R. (2000b, May 26). Distance education transforms help desks into "24-7" operations. *The Chronicle of Higher Education,* p. A49.

Young, J. R. (2000c, October 24). Instructors try out updated MOOs as online-course classrooms. Retrieved on October 24, 2000 from http://www.chronicle.com/free/2000/10/2000102401u.htm.

Young, J. R. (2001, April 10). Logging in with . . . Farhad Saba: Professor says distance education will flop unless universities revamp themselves. *The Chronicle of Higher Education.* Retrieved on April 10, 2001, from http://www.chronicle.com/free/2001/04/2001041001u.htm.

Zalatimo, S. D., & Zulick, J. M. (1979). A study of the effects of instructional television on students' learning attitude. *International Journal of Instructional Media, 6*(2), 187–195.

Index

About the Author

Judith L. Johnson is Director of the Office of Institutional Research (OIR) at the University of Southern Maine (USM), Portland. She received her Bachelor of Arts degree in psychology from the University of Maine at Farmington (1982), her Master of Science degree in counseling education from the University of Southern Maine (1985), and her Ph.D. in educational research, measurement, and evaluation from Boston College (1996). Before being appointed Director of OIR, Johnson served as Director of the USM Testing and Assessment Center for 12 years. Her research interests include university learning communities, college student retention, distance education, and student learning styles. She has conducted research and evaluation of distance education for the past 16 years and developed the Johnson Learner Preference Scale for use with college-level students.

Johnson has served the state of Maine as a member of the Maine Comprehensive Assessment Technical Advisory Committee, the Maine Educational Assessment Technical Advisory Committee, and the State of Maine Learning Results Assessment System Design Team. She was an American Association of University Women Fellow (1993–94) and has served as a visiting research consultant to the University of Central Lancashire, Preston, England, where she studied the student exchange program, technology, and student learning styles.